To Mum,
Happy
Christmas 1984
LOVE
MAID.

The Which? Guide to Buying Antiques

The Which? Guide
to Buying Antiques

PUBLISHED BY CONSUMERS' ASSOCIATION
AND HODDER & STOUGHTON

The Which? Guide to Buying Antiques
researched and written by **Rachael Feild**

Produced by Hearn Stephenson Publishing Ltd
Designed by Alan Hamp
Line drawings by Judith Hamp and John Mapp

Published in Great Britain by
Consumers' Association
14 Buckingham Street, London WC2N 6DS
and Hodder & Stoughton Limited
47 Bedford Square, London WC1B 3DP

First Edition 1982
Revised Edition 1983

ISBN 0 340 28749 7

Typesetting by Modern Word Processing, Hull
Printed and bound by Jolly and Barber, Rugby

*Frontispiece: Staffordshire 8½ inch plate in the
blue, white and rust colours of the Japanese Imari
palette, c. 1840.*

The publishers would like to thank the
many antique dealers who have
unknowingly helped in the compilation
of this *Guide*. And special thanks to
Antoine Vermoutier; Eve Weston Lewis;
the Carpet Bazaar; Phillips West 2;
Oscars Antiques, Crewkerne; William
Walter and Potterton Books for their
assistance in finding, checking and
explaining some of the material in the
more complicated sections of this book.
In addition, we would like to thank
Elizabeth White and David Benedictus
for their advice and expertise.

Contents

Prices in this Guide

The prices quoted in this *Guide* can only be an indication of what a buyer should expect to pay an established dealer for a similar piece in reasonable condition. Every price has been checked by more than one expert, but in antiques as in many other areas, if you consult two experts you are quite likely to get two different opinions. However, the items priced are neither museum pieces nor junk, and there are enough of them around to allow fairly consistent pricing. You may well pay less at auction, but buying at auction is not recommended for significant purchases without expert advice or until you have a fair working knowledge. You must always expect to pay more for a piece in exceptionally good condition, and less for one that has been poorly treated. If you are selling, you must expect to take considerably less than the resale price – at least 20%, even if the piece is perfect, and it may well be more. Prices change with inflation and other market forces such as fashion; those quoted here are valid for 1983–4.

Introduction

The moment you say 'antiques' many people imagine big money and huge profits. This book is about neither. Nor is it about junk. It is about buying antiques of reasonable quality because you like them and because they may cost no more than buying new. It is about buying things to enjoy, with the added comfort that they are likely to benefit your pocket in the long run.

There are hundreds of areas of antiques to choose from. The ones we have selected are the most practical. We all need furniture, glasses to drink out of, china to eat from, cutlery and flatware to eat with and carpets on the floor. It is possible to have antique versions of all these things. It may take time, but it can be done. It will cost money, but think of what you have to spend on these items anyway.

Two things cannot be over-emphasized. You should *only ever buy things you like* and *this is not an investment guide.* Both require some comment.

There is no point in buying antiques that are widely recognized as being in good taste if that taste is not yours. You have to live with what you buy. On the other hand, tastes change. A style that ten years ago you might have rejected as unsympathetic you may now find more congenial and possibly even quite desirable in your own mind. This is where looking at antiques and handling them is valuable, because it is the only way to arrive at an appreciation of their virtues as well as of their faults.

Investment in antiques is a professional business. It is the domain of dealers and collectors. On the other hand there is an investment aspect to buying antiques for yourself. If you follow the *Guide's* advice, you will be buying recognized antiques fairly safely (nothing is absolutely safe) in an established market in which values have, on the whole, risen steadily. If you buy new, your purchases will have second-hand value; if you buy antiques you will, after a few years, probably see your money back and you may make a profit too. Why? Partly because of rarity value – the number of genuine antiques of a given period can only decline; and partly because of the quality of workmanship and materials – both, faced with mass-market pressures, have declined drastically. This is not to say that items of the highest quality are not made now, but that the skills and sometimes the materials are both inordinately expensive.

The focus of the *Guide* then is on those items which are useful and fairly readily available in the areas of Furniture, Glass, Pottery and Porcelain, Rugs and Silver. Nothing costs over £1,500 at current prices (except canteens of silver, but they can be bought in parts), most of the items mentioned cost a great deal less, almost all are of domestic manufacture (except rugs), and dealers stock them because they are the core of the market.

How the *Guide* Works

The purpose of the *Guide* is not to tell you what to buy but to help you buy wisely the sorts of objects you like and can afford. To that end, each section gives you:

1. An introduction that describes the particular features of that area of the market and gives any essential historical background.

2. An illustrated description of the styles made, together with, where relevant: the major influences that caused changes in style – therefore an explanation of why pieces were made to look as they do; the way they were made at that time or in that place – a vital clue to authenticity; the materials used – again, evidence of whether the piece under examination is likely to be genuine as certain materials are restricted to certain periods; what sorts of object were made in a given period – another way of checking that a particular piece could be genuine.

3. Care and restoration – it is perfectly reasonable to buy certain (but by no means all) articles in a damaged state and have them repaired. This tells you when you should and when you should not, what can be done, and how to clean up objects and look after them.

4. A price guide, giving not only likely prices for a range of exemplary items but pointing out which variations are likely to raise or lower that probable price. Prices of widely available modern reproductions are sometimes quoted to put antique prices in context.

5. Illustrated definitions of the specialist terms used in this book or commonly used in the antiques trade.

6. A reading list pointing the way to more detailed knowledge.

Antique Dealers

Antique dealers are only human and they are looking to make a profit just like every other retailer. They will seek to sell their stock for whatever the market will bear. What keeps prices down is competition between dealers and the fact that private buyers can also go to salerooms and bid against the dealers.

A dealer's mark-up has to cover the following things: rent, insurance, lighting, heating, labour, restoration, transport and profit. Profit = the dealer's income; if it is large enough, some of it will be ploughed back to expand the business or to buy better quality stock.

The best dealers are considerable scholars and will be leading experts in their fields. At the top end of the market they may be called in by museums to give advice on their collections. In the middle range, which concerns us, they should still be knowledgeable and should be able to substantiate their description of a piece from reputable sources. They do not like know-alls, but they do respond to intelligent questioning and to evident appreciation of their stock. You can learn a great deal by talking to dealers, and on the whole they are happy for you to learn.

Because there is no absolute price for any antique item, prices fluctuate even in the same shop. If an item is sticking, the dealer is likely to reduce its price. If he is selling to a fellow dealer he will give a trade discount. It is for these reasons that dealers often mark their goods with codes rather than simple price tags. The codes usually refer to the stock book, in which all the expenses associated with that piece are recorded. The code may also indicate the dealer's target price for selling to the trade and his target price for selling to a private buyer. Ask if the price quoted includes VAT.

Buying from a dealer

Bargaining is often possible, but to bargain properly you need to know what you are about: no dealer is going to sell for less than he thinks is justified. Bargaining is much more likely to be successful if you are paying cash and going to carry the piece away with you. If you pretend to be trade you can lose your legal protection as a consumer. Do remember that large cheques have to be cleared and that credit card companies take a percentage of the dealer's price, which he has to allow for in his prices if you are to get the advantage of the credit card service. Dealers will usually be able to arrange transport for you if an item is large, but you will have to pay for carriage.

Any purchase of a piece should be accompanied by a receipt which states the dealer's description of the article and the price paid. If when you get your purchase home you find you have made a mistake (it's the wrong size for your room, for example), take it back, explain your reasons and ask for a refund. As long as you have bought from a reputable dealer there should be no problem.

Selling to a dealer

Whenever you sell to a dealer you have to give him room to add his mark-up. If you have bought fairly recently at full market price (salerooms excepted) it will be several years before the piece has appreciated sufficiently to cover the mark-up. An example: you buy a piece from a dealer for £60; the next month you could sell it to a dealer for, perhaps, £40 and he would sell it again for £60. If, however, you wait two years or so, you might be able to sell at £60 to a dealer who might re-sell at £85. Even at this stage you have lost money because of inflation. If you hold on to the piece for five years you might well find that you could sell it for, say, £85, at which you would be around break-even. Thereafter the chances of your getting a profit in real terms increase steadily.

Antique dealers' organizations

There are two main trade bodies that cover the good middle- and upper-range dealers. The sign of either in a dealer's window should inspire confidence, as it means that the dealer is established and respectable and you can, *in extremis,* appeal to the organization if you get into an insoluble dispute with the dealer.

The organizations are:

British Antique Dealers' Association (BADA),
20 Rutland Gate,
London SW7 1BD.

and

London and Provincial Antique Dealers' Association (LAPADA)
112 Brompton Road,
London SW3 1JJ.

To become a member a dealer must be knowledgeable, have been operating honestly for three years or more, be registered for VAT at a fixed place of business and be vouched for by established dealers who are themselves members of the organization. Both BADA and LAPADA realize, as do most dealers, that it is important to regulate their business and maintain codes of conduct that are more than merely cosmetic. BADA members prefer to trade in goods made before 1830. LAPADA members have greater flexibility.

Salerooms and Auctions

It is assumed throughout this book that you will be buying from dealers, because it is much the easiest way to buy and also the safest. However, as you acquire knowledge and confidence, auctions may well become an attractive alternative source of pieces. This is what to expect.

An auctioneer is only an agent, who is not directly responsible to the buyer except in the general terms of auction-room procedure. His sole function is to raise as much money as he can for the seller, from whom he is getting a commission. Today, many provincial sale rooms have followed the lead of the big three in London – Christie's, Sotheby's and Phillips – in charging a buyer's commission of 5% or 10% as well as the vendor's commission, but this does not apply to all salerooms.

Buying at auction

It is vitally important to discover the auctioneer's conditions of sale as they vary from one auction room to another. You will find them printed in the catalogue of every sale. Here among other things you are likely to find a disclaimer which states that the auctioneer is not responsible for the authenticity, attribution, genuineness, origin, authorship, date, age, period, condition or quality of any lot and the 'imperfections are not stated' in the description. The only general clue to poor condition is the two letters 'a.f.' at the end of a description; they mean 'as found' – in other words, significantly damaged.

You should examine the pieces you are interested in during viewing hours – usually the day before or the morning of the sale. If, after looking at a piece you would like to bid for, you have doubts, ask the advice of the auctioneers. They are usually only too willing to give you the benefit of their experience and advice. The more specialized the sale and the more up-market the auction house, the more likely it is that the auctioneer will have an expert on hand. It cannot be stressed too often, however, that experts can rarely give you guarantees; the best they çan offer is an opinion.

Before the sale check the duplicated list stating the auctioneer's estimated prices for the lots you intend bidding for. Write them beside the lot numbers in your catalogue together with your personal limits, which you should not exceed.

On the day of the sale, arrive in good time. Auctioneers can whistle through lots at an incredibly fast rate, and once bidding has started it may be difficult to find a good vantage point. Apart from that, it is a distraction to everyone if there are unnecessary interruptions to the sale.

Do not try and behave like a veteran. A nod is as good as a wink for the regular buyers, but the auctioneer has probably never seen you before and will not know that you are bidding unless you make a clear sign to attract his attention. Once you have done this however, keep your signals clear and don't fidget. The auctioneer will be looking to you for bids and may misinterpret an incidental gesture. If the bidding goes over your limit but the auctioneer looks in your direction for another bid shake your head clearly to indicate you are out of the running.

A word of warning. Do remember that in addition to the hammer price you will not only have to pay VAT on the auctioneer's commission and maybe a buyer's commission (these can put well over 10% on the hammer price) but you have to remove your purchase quickly. If you cannot remove it yourself you will have to pay for transport, and the auctioneers have the right to charge you storage until you have taken your items away. If the very worst happens and you do not arrange removal within the time stated by the auctioneer, he will have the right to sell the items

again to defray his costs. It is no wonder then that large items can sometimes be picked up relatively cheaply at country auctions.

Reserves and commission bids

It is customary for the seller to put a reserve price on each lot. This reserve is the minimum price the seller is prepared to accept, and if the bidding does not reach the reserve the auctioneer must withdraw the lot from the sale. The reserve is confidential between the vendor and the auctioneer before the sale and should not be confused with the auctioneer's estimate.

You may very well bid up to the auctioneer's estimated price only to find the lot withdrawn. This is because the reserve price is above his estimate. If this happens, all may not be lost. As long as the piece remains on his premises the auctioneer is empowered to sell it at not less than the reserve price. You may be lucky if, at the end of the sale, you go to the auctioneer and ask what the reserve was, which he is now at liberty to disclose. If the price is still within your limit you can offer to buy the lot at the reserve price by private treaty – i.e. outside the sale. The auctioneer is not obliged to accept your offer.

The auctioneer's job is to get the bidding up as high as possible, but it sometimes seems that he or she is doing this by inventing bids, appearing to pluck them out of the air when no-one is bidding. This is because he has been given instructions to bid on commission by people unable to attend the sale. Here is an example of what might happen. A lot has an estimate of £70 on the auctioneer's list. The bidding opens at £10 and goes to £40. The auctioneer stares at the ceiling and adds '£45, 50, 55, 60,' and then looks down at the bidders in the saleroom again. Someone makes a bid of £70 and the auctioneer, again staring at the ceiling, adds '£75, 80'. A bidder in the saleroom takes it up to £90. The auctioneer adds another bid of £100 and knocks the lot down to an invisible buyer. What has happened is that the auctioneer has been instructed by one absent buyer to go to £60 and by another to go to £100. All quite open and above board if you understand what is happening, but confusing and even suspicious if you do not.

A word about 'the ring'. This is a bogey that belongs largely to the past, when a group of dealers agreed among themselves that only one of them would bid for a lot so that the price would not be pushed up by their bidding against each other. After the sale the group would hold a rough-and-ready auction between themselves known as a 'knock-out'. The highest bidder would take the piece, the saleroom bidder would get his money back and the members of the group would split the margin between them. The vendor in the saleroom lost out and so did the auctioneer, who was taking his commission on a smaller price than was appropriate. There is now a law against rings: the Bidding Agreements Act exists to protect both salerooms and their clients.

Selling at auction

It remains to explain how a saleroom operates if you are the seller and not the buyer. If the piece is portable, take it to the auctioneer and ask for a valuation. If it is too big, take a photograph. If you are dissatisfied with the auctioneer's estimate get a second opinion, either from another auctioneer or from a dealer. If you decide to sell through the saleroom be realistic about your reserve, as the auctioneer will charge a fee if the piece does not sell.

Find out what the auctioneer's total charges will be for storing, handling, insuring and selling and take them into account in your reserve. Some salerooms charge a flat fee, others a percentage of the hammer price. Try and ensure that your piece goes into a specialized sale, even if it means waiting, because specialist sales attract more attention than general sales and thereby (usually) higher prices. Finally, before committing your piece, read the conditions of sale and make sure you understand them.

Reproductions

There are two kinds of reproduction – period and modern. Period reproductions mean Ed-

wardian, Victorian or earlier reproductions of previous styles. They are, if more than 100 years old, antiques in their own right. Modern reproductions are those that you can buy now, new. Anything in between is a matter of guesswork.

Certain period reproductions are just as well made as the pieces they imitate. They have the patina of age and are in every respect good pieces. They should not cost as much as the original, but as antiques of quality they still justify good prices.

A number of Victorian and Edwardian reproductions of earlier styles are not nearly as satisfactory. Machine-made of relatively inferior materials they should be viewed as secondhand when estimating their value.

Modern reproductions are, on the whole, the least satisfactory of all. Often they are even less well made than Edwardian reproductions and will not improve with use or age. Good modern reproductions are very expensive – so expensive in fact that it is probably cheaper to buy period reproductions. It is the quality of pieces that allows them to survive, become antiques and therefore valuable. If the quality is not present in a reproduction of any period it will be a poor buy in the long run.

To help assess whether something may be a reproduction – albeit a period reproduction – use the lists of characteristic products given under each period in the main chapters to see when that kind of object came into quantity production and use the notes on influences as a cross-check.

Limited Editions

Usually offered as 'the antiques of the future', limited editions are outside the purpose of this *Guide*. Limited editions are a speculators' market, to be compared more with the stock market than with the antique trade. This is not to say that some of them will not prove to be good investments, but all too often these attempts to create instant antiques are shoddy and not a little cynical. Manufactured in quantities which are so large they cannot guarantee the scarcity value implied in the promotional material, they may also suffer from poor design, inferior materials and second-rate workmanship. The best are very good indeed and will undoubtedly appreciate in value – sometimes far faster than antiques – but they are not antiques yet.

Insurance

There are some people who insure every single antique at valuation, buying peace of mind at a noticeable cost. Others under-insure and live to regret it. Which you choose depends partly on the kind of person you are but mostly on your insurance company.

Each insurance company can have different conditions and it is essential to be aware of the precise coverage of your home contents policy. Compensation for loss or theft of an individual item is usually limited either to a percentage of the total sum insured or to a fixed sum, whichever is the less. Valuables (such as pieces of silver) may have to be specified on the policy and the insurance company may demand evidence of value. Items can of course be insured individually if the general policy cover is inadequate. It is always a good idea to get and keep receipts for antiques, so that if they are lost or damaged you have not only proof of ownership but a valuation which can be scaled up as necessary.

Minimize the risk of burglary by putting things of value where they cannot readily be seen from outside. There is no point in owning beautiful things if you cannot enjoy them, but it is asking for trouble to flaunt them for any passer-by to see.

If you sell a piece, check your insurance policy and, if it was individually insured or specified, inform the insurance company.

Value Added Tax

Many dealers are registered under a special VAT scheme which means that they can charge VAT on their margin only, thus considerably reducing the cost to the customer. It is possible to sidestep this scheme and pay VAT on the entire cost, but it is worth doing only if you can claim back the VAT yourself. If an article is sold under the special scheme the dealer is not allowed to issue a VAT invoice. The invoice will state only the total price paid, but should describe the article as being over 100 years old. If you are buying at auction there is no VAT on the hammer price but it is payable on the commission.

Further Reading

The Lyle Official Antiques Review (annual)
Miller's Price Guide (annual)
British Art and Antiques Year-Book (annual)
Doreen Yarwood, *The English Home: A Thousand Years of Furniture and Decoration*, London, 1956
Bea Howe, *Antiques from the Victorian Home*, London, 1973
Official Descriptive and Illustrated Catalogue of the Great Exhibition of the Works of Industry of all Nations, London, 1851

David Benedictus, *The Antique Collector's Guide*, London, 1980
On care and restoration:
Michel Doussy, *Antiques: Professional Secrets for the Amateur*, London, 1973
Jacqueline Ridley, *The Care and Repair of Antiques*, Poole, Dorset, 1978

Furniture
Up to £1,500

Mahogany balloon back with over-stuffed serpentine seat and turned front legs, c. 1840.

Introduction

Good modern furniture can be as well designed as reasonable antique pieces. It can even be as well constructed, though this is less likely. What then are the particular advantages of antique pieces?

First, there is the nature of wood. With age, wood acquires qualities that can never be properly faked. It acquires a patina that makes it glow. Thus of two identical pieces, one made today and the other 150 years ago, the old one will look better and feel better.

Second, there is the matter of cost. Quality for quality, antiques are often actually cheaper than new. The best materials now cost a fortune and craftsmen to work them are thin on the ground, with the result that top quality modern furniture has to be very expensive.

Third, there is the matter of resale value. All our present antiques were once new pieces and they went through a long period of having secondhand value only, before they began to grow steadily in value as antiques. The same thing happens with new furniture now. Even if it is a piece that is an antique of the future, it has almost certainly got to go through a long period as a secondhand piece before it can become valuable; your grandchildren may benefit but you are unlikely to. If you buy an antique piece from a dealer you cannot of course expect to get your money back on the open market until general price levels have absorbed the dealer's margin. It might therefore be five years before you reach break-even. Thereafter, even given the vagaries of the market, you are likely to be holding the value of your possession in real terms, and you may well make a profit if ever you come to sell.

The antique furniture trade is full of stories of made-up pieces and items that owe more to restorers than to their original makers. There are also tales of pieces worth thousands lying in barns and waiting to be picked up for a few pounds. These things do happen. However the information given in this section about the kinds of furniture described should safeguard you against the worst excesses of restoration and making up, and remember that price is on your side. A dealer who is shady is not going to spend good money having a piece made up unless he can see a large margin at the other end. He or she is better off taking honest pieces and selling them at honest prices. The market prices of the pieces described here do not allow a sufficient margin for wholesale fraud. The other side of the coin is not to expect to get spectacular bargains. They are as rare as first dividends on the football pools and there are a lot of knowledgeable people out looking for them.

The real key to the secrets of antique furniture lies in its construction. Designs can be copied, but the meticulous attention to detail and the way a piece of furniture was put together provide the best proof of its age and respectability. So this summary traces the developments in carpentry, joinery and cabinet-making, for it is here that the real clues are to be found. There is a logical thread running from period to period when furniture is looked at this way. Developments and changes in design are less arbitrary than they may, at first sight, seem.

There was very little free-standing furniture made in Britain until Elizabethan days. Chests, coffers, stools, chairs, beds and simply constructed tables were built on a box-frame principle: a square skeleton, nailed or pegged together, with board panels slotted into the frame. There was not much decorative detail and little finesse, for most movable pieces of furniture were held together with glue and thick iron nails.

By the end of the 16th century the joiner had replaced the carpenter, resulting in the 'joined stool' or 'joint stool', which heralded an entirely new kind of construction. Chairs and stools were made with proper legs instead of being glorified boxes with seats and backs. The legs were strengthened with stretchers and simply decorated with reel or bobbin turning. All this was made possible by slotting one piece of the frame into another and securing it with wooden pegs or dowels: the mortise-and-tenon joint.

Oak was the most common wood used. But in Elizabethan days most of the thick timbers were requisitioned for building the 'wooden walls of England' – and in order to give furniture an air of great solidity, decoration and carving was added instead of being an integral part of the piece. The huge carved 'bulbs' on court cupboards and four-poster beds were glued to the plain turned uprights; strips of decorative carving, known as strapwork, were also added in the same way. Steel and iron hinges were nailed on with thick clout nails.

The profligate use of so much of Britain's standing forests resulted in a shortage of timber, especially of oak, at the beginning of the 17th century. Rooms were no longer panelled, cupboards and linen presses once built into the panelling were now made as free-standing pieces of furniture. Chest furniture became more sophisticated and less clumsy in construction, single drawers were built in below chests, slotting into the main frame. Legs of chairs and tables were lightened with decorative swash-turning. Except for dressers and court cupboards there was still no case furniture. In grand houses there were corner cupboards and open shelves built into panelling to display plate and silver. The coarse, heavy grain of oak was not suitable for the new fine chests on stands and for the lighter lines of chairs. Nor was oak suitable for applying the decorative inlaid panels, rich in ivory and mother-of-pearl, which began to come into the country through Holland and in ships of the newly established East India Company. Walnut and beech were favoured for their finer grain. Carving and decoration were crisper as a result.

Thus far the basic construction of furniture had hardly changed at all except in refining the joints and improving the finish. Chests were raised on stands to lighten their appearance and to accord better with the proportions of high-ceilinged rooms. Metal-working techniques had improved, particularly among locksmiths and clockmakers, and fine furniture was decorated with ornamental hinges secured with hand-made, lathe-turned screws. Gate-legged tables with hinged flaps stood against walls when not in use, and there was a more spacious air to rooms.

The Restoration of Charles II in 1660 brought a major change in fashion as he and his returning court imported the French styles to which they had grown accustomed in exile. Six years later the Great Fire destroyed much of London. When the city was rebuilt, the new houses had separate dining rooms, parlours and bedrooms, each requiring different furniture. Coupled with this great social upheaval came the art of veneering, learned from the Dutch.

Veneer, parquetry and marquetry are all variations of the same technique: thin sheets of decoratively grained or patterned woods are applied to the surfaces of furniture made from less costly woods. The surfaces must be smooth and without joins or the veneer lifts off. The old frame construction was accordingly abandoned in favour of making carcases from close-grained Baltic pine, with as many of the joints as possible on undersurfaces or inside the piece. Drawer fronts could no longer be nailed to the sides, and a crude through-dovetail joint was used. This too proved to be unsatisfactory, since the veneer lifted off the end-grain of the through joint.

By the end of the 17th century lapdovetailing, fairly chunky but effective, was in general use by cabinetmakers. Chests of drawers, chests on stands and early desk furniture were magnificently veneered with natural grains, such as oyster veneer, or richly intricate designs of fruit, flowers and birds in lighter woods which were often stained. Glass for windows was being made in quantity by the end of the 17th century, and the first pieces of case furniture were made with glass-fronted doors and thick glazing bars, in which the wealthy displayed their silver and their oriental blue-and-white porcelain.

In the 18th century market towns grew into provincial cities and expanding trade and victory in war increased the wealth of the entire nation. New customs of living and eating were adopted from the French. There were tall windows, and furniture was light, with graceful, well-proportioned lines. Walnut, imported from France and Virginia, was ideal for strong, springy legs to chairs and tables, known as cabriole legs, which did not need strengthening with stretchers. The old stool-with-back construction of chairs changed to a frame in which the back legs continued up in one piece, curving over into elegantly shaped backs. The cabinetmakers had finally rebelled against the inlaid and lacquered panels which were still being imported, and English lacquer ('japanning'), duller than the glossy oriental lacquer, was used to embellish important pieces of furniture.

Now the gentry needed bookcases and desks, display cabinets and glass-fronted cupboards to show off their collections of leather-bound books, beautifully decorated 'cabinet ware' and ornamental porcelain figures. By the mid-18th century the fashion for tea-drinking produced a whole new range of light, elegant tables, chairs and parlour furniture. Meals were now taken with all the guests sitting down on sets of matching chairs at dining tables which were still made on the gate-leg principle, but with straight or bowed legs ending, like chair legs, in crisply carved pad or ball-and-claw feet. As well as the servants' quarters and kitchen quarters there were boudoirs, morning rooms, breakfast rooms and bedrooms, all to be furnished and many of them on show.

Those who could not afford the very best scrabbled to keep up with the times. Provincial copies of fashionable furniture were made, not in subtle, springy and expensive walnut, but in elm, beech, fruitwood and even oak. As the 18th century wore on and the classical simplicity of taste and fashion came within the reach of the growing middle classes, the gentry built grander and grander houses and filled them with more and more ornate furniture. There was much ormolu and gilding, intricate swirling designs adapted from French rococo, and a fashionable passion for chinoiserie, calling for more and more delicate cabinetmaking. Bow-fronted chest and case furniture softened the simple classical lines of earlier designs as new processes of working timber were developed. But walnut was growing scarce and the fashionable designers of the day turned to an entirely new wood, coming in from England's new colonies.

Mahogany was the darling of the Georgians. Its immense strength and girth simplified construction, since it did not need supporting along its length. It needed no inlay or lacquer. It was a beautifully grained wood, ideally suited to the purity of proportion and line and to producing the plain glossy surfaces so desirable at this period. Enormous dining tables rested miraculously on central pillars with splayed tripod feet. Bookcases and display cabinets stretched the entire length of walls, their glass fronts supported by fragile-looking glazing bars in ornate geometric shapes. There were mirrors everywhere to reflect the light, and within the strict classical lines of Georgian architecture furniture took on an elegant serpentine curve.

The swirling, rococo gilt mounts on commodes and chest furniture of the earlier part of the century, so loved by William Kent and Thomas Chippendale, were at first expensively imported from France. By the 1760s Britain had caught up with and outstripped the rest of Europe in industrial progress. Ormolu, gilt metal, and brass screws, hinges, bolts, escutcheons, backplates and handles were all being made cheaply in Birmingham.

The Regency period combined all that was excellent in craftsmanship with important discoveries in engineering, both in design and construction. Newly discovered principles of load-bearing and stress were applied to furniture design, resulting in the sabre-leg and flush-sided chair, as well as a proliferation of furniture with concealed purposes, sliding tops, and ingenious construction. But if machines could be harnessed to make hinges and screws, they could also perform the most time-consuming work of the joiner and cabinetmaker. By the end of the 18th century machine-cut dovetail joints had begun to replace the slightly uneven handcut dovetails of earlier decades and thinner machine-cut veneer lay sleekly over Scandinavian pine carcases. In the first 20 years of the 19th century mass production came to the fore. After one last gigantic wave of ostentatious decadence, enshrined for ever in the Royal Pavilion at Brighton, machine-made, mass-produced furniture flooded the market and 'thin veneer' became a pejorative term.

One way or another, the Victorians reproduced and copied practically every style and every period, sometimes well, sometimes atrociously. In many ways 19th-century versions of 18th-century furniture are more solid, more soundly constructed than the originals. Good 'Victorian Chippendale' is exact in proportion though slightly differently constructed. It is often veneered instead of being cut from solid wood, and all the joints are regular because they are machine-cut. Bad Victorian Hepplewhite or Sheraton is awful, both in its failure to follow the right proportions and because the wood is cut across the grain. Eighteenth-century originals used the natural spring of the wood for strength; weaker Victorian versions are stretchered, which ruins the line.

The longing to return to the feel of natural wood and genuine craftsmanship of the Pre-Raphaelite Movement and the Victorian aesthetes, headed by William Morris and John Ruskin, led to 'Victorian Tudor' or 'Mediaeval', which is perfectly correct in its construction on the frame principle with mortise-and-tenon joints, except that both the holes and the pegs are machine-cut and neatly symmetrical instead of being hand-cut and oddly shaped. The same can be said of their rustic turned furniture, carved oak settles and refectory tables as they too were made by machine. A comparison of a genuine Tudor piece with a Victorian imitation will quickly show the difference in feel.

Imitation may indeed be the sincerest form of flattery, but too much of it debases the original and eventually renders itself practically worthless. At almost every sale, in almost every junkshop there is at least one piece of Edwardian satinwood furniture, a pale, sad reflection of the Adam original. There are Sheraton sideboards in every furniture store, made yesterday from thinly veneered chipboard, and Hepplewhite-style chairs by the hundred. But in antique shops there are country copies of fashionable furniture made perhaps 50 years after the original, beautifully constructed and with a resonance of the period which is unmistakable, though the proportions may not be quite right and the construction may be a little too sturdy.

Care and Restoration_____
Care

The chief enemy of antique furniture is central heating. Nothing will damage a good piece faster than bringing it into a fully insulated, centrally heated, double-glazed house without due precaution. Wood must have moisture to survive and improve, but efficient central heating produces a bone-dry atmosphere. The result is that wood shrinks and cracks.

The rule is to attune pieces slowly to their new atmosphere. Keep pieces in the coolest place in the house for months if need be, near

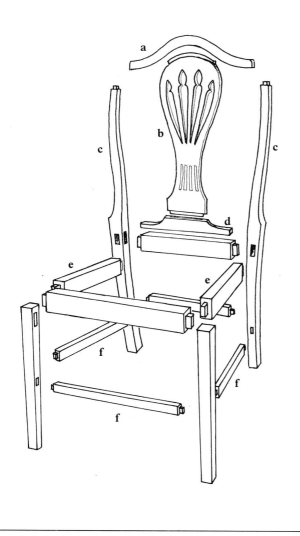

The construction of a chair. Note how every part is jointed – wooden blocks or metal brackets at the corners usually indicate repair or inferior manufacture. The parts are: a – crest rail; b – splat; c – side rail; d – shoe-piece; e – seat rails; f – stretchers. If the shoe-piece is made in one with the splat, the chair is quite likely to be a reproduction. The joints would normally be held with glue and wooden pegs for maximum strength.

windows (but out of direct sunlight and out of draughts) and away from heaters.

The two secondary enemies are sunlight and worm. Direct sunlight bleaches wood and can raise veneer. Worm will first make furniture unsightly and then destroy it. It is however unrealistic to assume that you will always be able to buy pieces that have suffered from neither light nor worm, but make sure that you do not pay top price for something damaged in either of these ways. If you have any suspicion that the worm in a piece you buy may be still alive (fresh-looking wood and powder in the holes, sharp edges to the holes), treat it thoroughly and immediately with a proprietary woodworm killer and again the following summer. It is not just the new piece you are protecting but all your other furniture too. Sunlight damage can be improved a little by polishing and careful staining, but consult a book on restoration for this.

Wood needs feeding and you feed it by polishing. A lot of elbow grease and a little beeswax is the recipe. Too much wax and you are left with a dull finish that attracts dirt. Sheepskin buffers attached to power drills are seductive, but useless. They rotate so fast that they melt the wax and disperse it.

Restoration

Just about anything can be restored, but the question is whether it is worth it. Buying a chair cheap at £10 because it is damaged, spending £40 on it and finding that at the end the chair is worth £25 is counter-productive. Many repairs however are relatively easy and cheap, and as long as the cost of repair is reflected in the purchase price there is no reason why you should not buy.

Many chairs and tables in time will come apart at one or more corners. The glue may have given out (particularly on stripped furniture) and the piece simply then needs re-gluing. Joints sometimes break, in which case the solution is usually dowelling the parts back together. Upholsterers will often do this work on chairs, for a flat charge of a few pounds per wobbly corner. You will often come across pieces with blocks or metal angle brackets screwed into the corners. This works, but is not approved of on good pieces. If it has already been done, leave it, but do not add any more such repairs.

Veneers often bubble or lift, crack or become crazed. The skilled amateur can do a lot to improve these problems and professional restorers can put them right, with the exception of crazing, which should be left as an attractive feature and a good sign of age. It is fine to buy pieces with damage to veneer as long as the price is right.

Marks are really of two kinds: dents and stains. Quite a lot can be done about both, but it is necessary to be realistic. A piece that may be 200 years old is going to be marked from normal use and it would be foolish to pretend that it won't. That is why modern reproduction furniture is sometimes 'distressed' – pitted, stained and dented – to add a phony appearance of age. If the overall appearance of a piece is pleasant, leave it. If it is dirty, badly dented or badly stained, pay less if you are buying and get to work if you own it already.

Dents can be eased by placing a damp rag over the spot and applying the tip of an electric iron set at the coolest temperature. The warmth and moisture cause the wood fibres locally to swell. Work carefully and expect an improvement, not a total cure.

Stains are of various kinds, requiring different treatments. All of them require follow-up polishing.

Water stains: white rings left by glasses or bottles; carefully rub in linseed oil, turpentine or butter.

Heat stains: similar effect and similar treatment.

Grease marks: cover the mark with blotting paper or several layers of tissue and press with a cool iron; you want just enough warmth to get through to soften the grease and let the paper take it up; a sprinkling of talcum powder under the paper can help.

Alcohol stains: on polished surfaces treat as water stains; alcohol dissolves varnish, so on varnished surfaces rub down the affected area and re-varnish; on French polished surfaces you have to get the piece repolished.

The things to look for in a chest of drawers. Tops have often been scratched in use or bleached by sunlight; veneer may have lifted, cracked or been replaced – the thinner the veneer, the later the piece. Drawers can tell a lot about the date and authenticity of a piece. Look for wear on the runners. Look too at the dovetail joints – if they are perfectly regular they are machine made and therefore probably Victorian. If the grain of the drawer bottoms runs front to back it is likely to be pre-1730. In later pieces the grain runs from side to side and the bottom is likely to be in two or three pieces. Drawers run the full depth of chests from about 1770. Damaged moulding round drawer fronts is easy to replace. Handles and scutcheon plates (keyhole surrounds) are sometimes damaged or changed. An original undisturbed fitting will have a build-up of wax and dirt round its edges. If in doubt about the authenticity of handles, look on the inside – spare screw holes will indicate that a change has been made. Finally, the feet of an old piece will almost certainly show signs of scuffing, though if it is very bad on a veneered piece, the veneer may quite legitimately have been renewed.

Ink stains: if fresh, swab with water and then work in lemon juice carefully; if old, paint the stain only with vinegar, using a fine brush, and follow up with a solution of 1 part Milton (from a chemist) : 10 parts water; dab off and repeat as necessary; expect improvement, not cure.

Blood stains: bleach out with a solution of 1 part Milton : 10 parts water.

Burn marks: the only real cure is to sand out the burned wood; if you are (understandably) reluctant to do this, you may be able to bleach out some of the stain with 1 part Milton : 10 parts water, but do not hope for much.

Cleaning

So much for the obvious things. What affects a great deal of old furniture though is dirt, and you should always consider cleaning any wood that is not in obviously good condition. The first stage is to wash the piece with soapy water – ordinary washing powders are fine. If this is not strong enough use a mixture of 1 part methylated spirits : 4 parts turpentine : 4 parts white vinegar : 4 parts linseed oil. Wipe the dirt off rather than rubbing it in.

You may think that cleaning in this way will damage the patina. It will not. Dirt and patina are quite different things and the patina will be much more obvious and pleasing if the surface is clean.

Stripping

The extreme of cleaning is stripping off unwanted paint or varnish. It is not only cheaper furniture that has been maltreated in the past: some excellent pieces have been disguised with paint and given rougher treatment than they were meant to take. Pine is the most familiar wood for stripping at the moment, but any wood that has been inappropriately painted or varnished can be stripped.

A simple piece can be stripped at home – an old kitchen table or kitchen chair, for example – with a proprietary paint stripper such as Nitromors. The job is messy and time-consuming but manageable. Home-stripping, if it is done thoroughly and well finished, looks better than stripping in a bath, which is the alternative way of doing it.

Professional furniture strippers usually have a large bath or tank of caustic soda in which they immerse pieces. It is a very effective way of doing the job quickly and of getting into difficult corners and round carved or turned parts. It is also relatively cheap. The professionals, however, rarely take the trouble to finish their work well, and if a piece comes back looking clean but dull, it will pay to wipe it over with vinegar (to neutralize any vestigial caustic soda) and then to polish deeply with beeswax until the wood glows. One thing to watch for is whether the joints have been loosened in the course of dipping: the caustic soda often dissolves the glue and can stay in joints and rot the wood; it pays to go to someone whose finishing is thorough. If you have got a piece with weakened joints make sure it is really dry and then repair it or have it repaired as described above.

Incidentally, pine strippers today are as skilled at making up pieces as any of the craftsmen of the past. Pine is not a very durable wood and so cannibalization of the good bits of damaged pieces to make up whole ones is rampant. There is nothing wrong with this as long as it is well done and the result is good-looking, serviceable and sensibly priced. What you are buying in many cases is furniture made with mellowed old wood, not authentic antique pieces.

Stripping of quality pieces is a delicate task and you do need to know what you are doing. A lot can be done at home, but only after experimenting on cheap pieces and reading everything you can find on the subject. The better the piece, the more certain it is that you should go to a professional antique restorer.

And a word about restorers. Good restorers are fully capable of making new pieces of high quality that are perfect matches in craftsmanship and materials to Queen Anne, Georgian or whatever. They understand construction and decoration as well as the old makers did. A lot of people who work as restorers however are skilled at joinery and turning but little more. Their achievement is to make pieces serviceable again rather than restoring them to their original condition. Choose your restorer according to the quality of the piece.

Dealers' Restoration

If a piece has any real value and age, the chances are that it has been restored in some way at some time. It is quite likely, if you are buying the piece in good condition that the dealer from whom you are buying has had the work done.

Good restoration is entirely legitimate, but a lot of not so good work – some of it downright peculiar – is done. Misleading restoration is one of the tricks of the trade, which you can come to understand only by learning – and, very possibly, by getting caught at some time. Dealers get caught too.

There are literally hundreds of rules to learn, the wise application of which will tell you with reasonable certainty whether a piece is what is claimed or whether it has been restored. They can be learned, with assiduity and patience, over a period of years. The people who know them best are the dealers and restorers. If you can develop a good relationship with a good dealer you will not be deceived and you will learn a lot. Failing that, look at each piece from *every* angle to see if it is harmonious. If it is, it is either perfectly authentic or has been well restored – probably. Either way, it doesn't matter too much as long as the piece functions properly unless you are buying very expensive pieces, and do not do that until you know very well what you are doing.

Periods and Styles

We start early in the 18th century, with Queen Anne, because furniture from the earlier periods is both relatively rare and on the whole rather expensive. Tudor, Elizabethan, Jacobean, Restoration and William & Mary styles were however revived in the 19th century, but clear indications are given in the sections on the Victorian period to help you tell copy from original.

Period: 1702–27 – Queen Anne

(The prevailing style did not change much under George I, 1714–27)

Influences: Cabriole legs adapted from French; otherwise style of this period is pure English.

Materials: Walnut, walnut veneer, marble, gilt gesso, English lacquer (japanning); elm, beech, yew; yellow Baltic pine for carcases.

Characteristic types of furniture: Dressing tables, dressing mirrors, knee-hole desks, chests-on-chests, chests-on-stands, tallboys, lowboys, bureaus, desk-and-bookcases, glazed china cabinets, corner cupboards, chests-of-drawers, long-case clocks, tea caddies, side chairs, dining chairs, dining tables, kitchen dressers, carved walnut-framed mirrors, drop-leaf tables, card tables.

Construction: The main development was the cabriole leg, which depended for its strength on the natural spring of the wood and made stretchers unnecessary. The shape was found in the wood, meaning that sometimes pieces of considerable girth were used. Tongue-and-groove joints on folding tables and cabinet doors made edges join with a hairline crack. Wooden hinges with flexible dovetail construction produced card tables of great elegance with folding tops, rounded corners for candles and dished cavities for coins and counters. Joints were customarily hidden.

Chairs: Cabriole legs, some stretchers, drop-in seats or over-stuffed seats, central back splat slotted into shoe-piece separate from back seat-frame. Side chairs still made on the old frame principle, with over-stuffed seats. Matching sets of dining chairs now made in quantity.

Chest and case furniture: Chests-on-stands with turned legs and bun feet giving way to chests-on-stands with X-stretchers and chests-on-chests with bun or bracket feet. Some glazing of display cabinet doors.

Drawers: Oak sides with rounded top edges made shorter than the length of the carcase to allow for ventilation inside. Around 1710 small lip mouldings were introduced to project round drawer edges to protect the veneer as the drawers were opened and closed.

Design and detail: Immaculate finishing to complement elegant, flowing shapes of furniture. Glazed doors and block-front doors to case furniture; architectural pediments to cabinets; pigeon holes and finials to desks; bun feet; ball-and-claw feet towards the end of the period; pad feet; friezes or aprons to conceal hingeing legs; rounded edges; crossbanding, feather-banding hid veneer edges; shell and scallop motifs; English lacquer, which is duller than oriental, particularly in red and gold with Chinese dragons for bureaux, dressing mirrors, chairs, small furniture; brass bail handles with solid backplates secured by iron pins split and flattened on insides of drawers; brass locks, keys and escutcheons.

Period: 1727–60 – Early Georgian

Influences: Classical, chinoiserie, rococo, Gothic. William Kent, John Adam; Thomas Chippendale senior published *A Gentleman and Cabinet Maker's Director* in 1754. It was used all over the country as a pattern book and Chippendale-style furniture was made for the next 50 years. Even after that date, country-made chairs with definitely Chippendale lines and proportions were still made and are legitimately within the period of direct influence.

Materials: Walnut, mahogany (San Domingo plain, Cuban curled or figured, Honduras 'baywood'), Virginia walnut; imported American red pine, white pine and Baltic yellow pine for carcases.

Characteristic types of furniture: Reading or 'cock-fighting' chairs, corner chairs, pillar-and-claw and tripod tables, console tables, hanging corner cupboards, tallboys, lowboys,

secretaires, serpentine-fronted commodes or chests-of-drawers, rococo mirrors and brackets, fireplace mirrors and overmantels, piecrust tables, tripod tables, broken pediments to cabinets, glass-fronted bookcases and bureau-bookcases, tea tables, teapoys, tip-top tables, drop-leaf tables, knee-hole desks, writing tables, library tables, settees, sofas and couches, Windsor chairs, upholstered wing chairs.

Construction: The strength of mahogany, which now became the most fashionable wood, allowed construction to become far simpler. Mahogany did not warp, was immensely strong and was able to be cut in considerable widths of plank. Joins were unnecessary, table tops could be supported on a central column into which tripod legs and feet (known as pillar-and-claw) could be dovetailed; leaves of tables could be unsupported except for bolt-and-fork fastenings to secure them, glazing bars were more slender, surfaces were unbroken and, with the arrival of figured mahogany, undecorated. Bookcases, cabinets and display cabinets could be built of great height and beds could be made with slender columns to support canopies.

Chairs: Square-sectioned legs, drop-in seats. Chairs with cabriole legs terminated in paw or pad feet and were more slender. Overstuffed seats for some chairs; country and provincial chairs with wooden seats were shaped to take squab cushions.

Chest and case furniture: Bow-fronts or serpentine fronts, particularly commodes or chests-of-drawers. Spider joins replace tongue-and-groove for even more smoothly joining surfaces.

Drawers: Cockbeading fitting flush round sides and lip, drawer bottoms made of a single piece of wood, grain running front to back until *c.* 1730, when bottoms were made with the grain running side to side.

Design and detail: Classical architectural silhouettes of desk and case furniture softened by broken pediments; serpentine- and bow-fronted furniture; asymmetrical flowing shapes adapted from French rococo with almost every straight line broken, curved or ornamented; heavy use of gilt and ormolu, giving way to more subtle furniture inspired by oriental design. Cabriole leg refined to delicately curving lines; other legs severely square-sectioned; development of pillar-and-claw pedestal supports for tables, with fluting and reeding much in evidence; marble tops for centre tables, console tables; bracket feet replace bun feet; castors with brass arms and leather disc rollers on small tables and some chairs; pierced backplates and bail handles secured at either side by screws through the thickness of the wood; cast brass rococo mounts and handles on grand furniture.

Period: 1760–1811 – Late Georgian

Influences: French and classical: the great age of classicism; Robert Adam *d.* 1792; George Hepplewhite *d.* 1786: his *Cabinet-maker and Upholsterer's Guide* published 1788; Thomas Shearer: *Cabinet-maker's London Book of Prices* 1788; also his *Designs for Household Furniture*; Thomas Sheraton's *Cabinet-Maker and Upholsterer's Drawing Book* published 1791–4; Thomas Chippendale junior *d.* 1822; Angelica Kauffmann. Manufacturers: Morgan & Sanders, George Seddon, Thomas Butler, William Ince, John Mayhew.

This was the greatest period of English furniture design: a closer study of the individual works of Adam, Hepplewhite, Sheraton and Shearer is essential in order to train the eye to all-important proportion and detail, both of which have often been bungled by later reproductions. Briefly, Robert Adam introduced classical symmetry, refined the cabriole leg to its ultimate grace, reintroduced inlay for swags, anthemions, urns, Greek key pattern. Hepplewhite was responsible for extremely graceful bow-fronted and serpentine chest furniture with curved aprons, bracket feet, and for the mercilessly copied shield-back chair, straight tapered legs and a wider use of marquetry employing satinwood and other pale coloured woods. Sheraton favoured square and rectilinear shapes, corner moulding and inlaid or veneered stringing, ornamental glazing bars to bureau-bookcases, display cabinets and corner cupboards. Sheraton probably influenced English furniture more than any other designer – as witness the endless reproductions of his work down to the present day. Sheraton also designed many ingenious multipurpose pieces in order to adapt to the severe shortage of both materials and money caused by the Napoleonic Wars (1793–1815). Thomas Shearer, though less of a household name, produced many items adapted from 'campaign furniture' designed for the houses of average families. Again, bear in mind the time-lag of around 50 years between London and the provinces: furniture made to the designs of the masters was still being made from their pattern books until well into the 19th century and cannot strictly be called reproduction.

Materials: Mahogany (flame-grain Cuban), satinwood, tulipwood, kingwood, harewood (stained sycamore), birch, chestnut, oak, beech, cheap 'baywood' (Honduras mahogany); imported Scandinavian red and white pine for carcases and built-in cupboard furniture. Gilding and gilt ornament; ormolu; revival of marquetry and parquetry.

Characteristic types of furniture: Clothes presses (wardrobes), Carlton House desks, cylinder desks, kneehole desks, pedestal desks, dining room furniture: sideboards, side tables, wine coolers, knife boxes; bachelors' chests, bonheurs du jour, campaign furniture, cane-seated painted birch and beech chairs, ladder-back, lyre-back, wheel-back and shield-back chairs, hall chairs, serpentine-front chest and case furniture, library steps, two-seater chair settees en suite with drawing room chairs, envelope tables, work tables, games tables, sewing tables, Pembroke tables, demi-lune side tables, draw tables, sofa tables, drop-leaf tables, bow-front commodes and chests-of-drawers, chiffoniers, Tunbridge ware, wash stands, side cupboards, pot cupboards, pine dressers, kitchen furniture.

Construction: The two principal constructional innovations in this period are the result of Matthew Boulton's Birmingham Brass Foundry which began making brass fittings and ormolu mounts from 1762, rendering it no longer necessary to import expensive brass fittings from the continent. The advent of lathe-turned screws and cast brass hinges produced a mass of furniture designed to conceal its function. Small furniture of all kinds appeared. Lighter construction of chairs, tables etc. brought back H-shaped stretchers for all but the finest mahogany shield-back chairs whose construction eliminated the central back-splat and shoe-piece.

Chairs: Tapering legs, straight, round or square in section, sometimes fluted, ending in spade feet or small plinths; towards the end of the 18th century horizontal back-splats replaced vertical back-splats. Hepplewhite chairs favoured over-stuffed seats, Sheraton chairs drop-in seats.

Drawers: In chest and case furniture they had bottoms made from oak with grain running side to side, usually in two or three pieces, fitting into grooves in drawer side from 1770. Drawers ran the whole length of the piece of furniture from about the same time.

Design and detail: Popular decorative motifs were lyre and shield, festoons, swags, masks, medallions; light-coloured woods used for small furniture of all kinds, much of it inlaid, painted or stained; marble tops inlaid with classical themes on more slender console tables, often fixed to walls so that the delicate supports did not bear the weight; lavish use of brass and ormolu.

Period: 1811–30 – Regency

Influences: French Empire, Graeco-Roman, Egyptian; Thomas Hope's *Household Furniture and Interior Decoration* published 1807; George Smith's *Cabinet Maker and Upholsterer's Guide* published 1828; Brighton Pavilion. Manufacturers: Gillows, Pratt & Sons, Morgan & Sanders.

Materials: Dark glossy woods: mahogany, calamander, amboyna, zebra-wood, Brazilian rosewood; imported Baltic pine (red and white) for carcases; French polish, imitation bamboo, japanned beech, ebonized wood.

Characteristic types of furniture: French sofa beds and couches, Grecian couches, bed-steps, Canterburys, Davenports, dumb waiters, fitted wardrobes with door mirrors, brass trellis-fronted bookcases and cupboards, brass inlaid writing boxes, sewing tables, work tables, card tables, foot stools, gout stools, music stools, pedestal desks, hanging bookcases, 'quartetto' tables, X-frame music stools, X-back chairs, sabre-legged chairs, lyre-back chairs, square-back chairs, S-arm chairs, marble-topped console tables and side tables, lyre-ended tables, sofa tables, leather-covered desks, writing tables, library and drum tables.

Construction: Changes lie in the increasing use of machines for planing, turning, moulding, grooving and brass inlay. Machine-cut veneer reduced the thickness from $\frac{1}{8}$in or more to less than $\frac{1}{16}$. Machine-cut dovetail joints are regular and uniform in size, with longer narrower tails. Evolution from pillar-and-claw to splayed feet from central pedestal or reeded column; round-topped tables on fluted pillars and tripod legs, massive monopodium central supports.

Chairs: Construction changed (with Thomas Hope 'Trafalgar' chair) to side-frames entirely flush; return of drop-in seat or square-edged cushion on cane seat; scoop-backed upholstered chairs; turned legs, stretchers and crest-rails.

Chest and case furniture: More massive, architectural in concept with broken pediments; breakfront bookcases; drawers uniformly made with machine-cut dovetail joints, cockbead, bottom runner now reaching full depth of carcase.

Design and detail: Typified by Egyptian, Graeco-Roman low lines to furniture; curves, scrolls; classical architectural pillar shapes (Doric, Ionic, Corinthian) echoed in furniture. The overall impression is one of flowing lines in dark woods highlighted with brass ornament, sometimes overdone and foreshadowing the excesses of Victorian ornamentation. Much Boulle work. Ebony and ebonized wood used to accentuate this very distinctive style. Particular to the Regency period are the nautical 'Trafalgar' or 'rope' motifs, commemorating the great naval victories of the day. Reeded, turned legs to tables and chairs; lion's paw brass feet, lion's head and ring handles, stamped brass backplates and keyplates; cast brass shoes to curved feet on sofas, couches, tables; much brass inlay, trellis, galleries, detail; square brass handles with two small backplates screwed through thickness of wood; brass rosettes and stringing.

Period: 1830–37 – William IV

(Late Regency or Early Victorian)

Influences: Continuing Regency, Louis xiv style, Pugin and the Gothic/Tudor Revival, late French Empire style; J.C. Loudon's *Encyclopaedia of Cottage, Farm and Villa Architecture and Furniture.* Manufacturers: Gillows, Holland & Co. (later '& Sons'), J.G. Crace & Sons, Pratt & Sons.

Materials: Veneers, French polish, brass decoration, padded upholstery, plain polished rosewood, solid mahogany, cast iron for conservatory furniture, beds and hall furniture; shell and mother-of-pearl inlay; imported Canadian/North American pine for carcases and kitchen furniture.

Characteristic types of furniture: Balloon-backed chairs, 'Grecian' chairs, couch-beds, prie-dieu chairs, button-back and upholstered spoon-back chairs, conservatory furniture, whatnots, plant stands, brass beds, decorative wrought iron beds, marble-topped washstands, side tables, servants' pine furniture, papier mâché chairs, small tables, trays, tea caddies, embroidered fire screens, pole screens, pier tables, console tables, marble-topped library tables.

Construction: This hitherto neglected period marks the divide between hand-made furniture and cabinet-makers' work and the beginnings of mass-produced machine-made furniture of all kinds. Improved steam-driven marble-cutting techniques brought pier tables and console tables into wider fashion. Coiled metal springs were patented by Samuel Pratt in 1828 and led to sprung seats for all kinds of seating furniture during this period. Thin machine-cut veneer now common.

Chairs: From the Thomas Hope flush-sided chair evolved a shape with a broad crest-rail over-running the frame and decorative horizontal splat with straight, turned or reeded legs; variations on this design had hooped backs and more decoratively carved horizontal splats, some chairs with 'waisted' back. Machine turning allowed the reproduction of 'Jacobean' chairs with swash-turned stretchers and uprights to backs, but with padded upholstered centres instead of cane. Return to over-stuffed seats for early balloon-back chairs.

Chest and case furniture: Bow-fronted or serpentine, as machine methods of shaping wood improved. Drawers were in cheap Honduras mahogany or oak-sided with mahogany fronts. Cheaper veneered furniture had pine runners.

Design and detail: William iv furniture styles overlap both Regency and Early Victorian, with heavy, solid woods, a tendency to over-ornamentation, the use of Greek and Egyptian motifs, heavy cast-brass ornament and rounded shapes as a result of the growth of the padded upholstery trade. Regency purity of line suffered, as upholstery caused Grecian lines to swell into over-emphasized curves. Stylized brass rosettes, used in the Regency with restraint, were added wantonly as were heavy cast-brass ornaments for mounts. The Victorian mania for copying shows with reproduction Restoration chairs, 'improved' by the substitution of upholstered panels in place of cane. Much veneering, use of tapestries, Berlin woolwork and printed fabrics of all kinds.

Period: 1837–60 – Early Victorian

Influences: Romantic, Gothic and Tudor, Louis xiv style, oriental, Indian, neo-Greek; William Morris, A. Pugin, E.W. Godwin; Strawberry Hill; Great Exhibition 1851; Scottish baronial style. Manufacturers: William Watt, Gillows, Collinson & Lock, W. & A. Smee, J.G. Crace & Sons, Holland & Sons.

Materials: Mahogany for dining-room furniture, rosewood for drawing rooms; beech, birch, yellow-coloured ash, bird's eye maple; painted white and gilt furniture for bedrooms, boudoirs and ballroom chairs. Veneering, French polishing, japanning, papier mâché, ebonizing, stained birch, ash, bentwood; oak for 'Tudor' revival; imported North American softwoods for carcases; iron frames for some seating furniture after the Great Exhibition; iron strap hinges for 'romantic' oak furniture.

Characteristic types of furniture: Machine-carved 'mediaeval' chests, cabinets, Chesterfields, pegged and carved 'romantic' chairs, 'Bible boxes', dressing boxes, 'Tudor' cupboards, 'Jacobean' chairs, Walter Scott-inspired 'romantic' Abbotsford chairs, slab-topped 'refectory' tables with pegged stretchers, button-back tub chairs, deep-buttoned leather or upholstered framed sofas and settees, conversation seats, ottomans; painted deal servants', kitchen and cottage furniture; reclining neo-Greek chairs, flat-fronted chests of drawers, Sutherland drop-leaf tables, military chests, Wellington chests, work tables, sewing tables, loo tables, music stools, Canterburys, Windsor chairs, smokers' bow chairs, cutlery stands, butlers' trays, wine coolers, teapoys, tea caddies, fitted travelling boxes, writing boxes.

Construction: Characterized by two opposing trends: the harking back to romantically mediaeval methods of construction and the increasingly machine-made mass-produced ranges. Wooden dowels and pegs used in great profusion on suitably romantic furniture, which can be easily detected from originals by the fact that both dowels and dowel-holes were machine-made and uniform in size. Machine-turning brought a revival of swash- and bobbin-turned furniture, the former often proclaiming its late origins by the Victorian passion for symmetry resulting in opposing twists: 17th-century twists all turned the same way. Machine-turning is noticeably shallower than hand-turned. Lathe-turned steel and brass screws with sharp points used on almost all furniture, including one-piece bottom boards for drawers screwed to side-pieces. Cheap machine-made

furniture was veneered with paper-thin veneer over coarse-grained softwood carcases; better furniture with knotty red pine or cheap imported Honduras mahogany carcases veneered with machine-cut Cuban mahogany or rosewood.

Design and detail: Heavy late Regency furniture lost its crispness by having corners rounded, pedestals made circular instead of triangular. Early modest turning on chair legs became more accentuated and bulbous. Balloon-back chairs developed more nipped-in waists and, for drawing rooms, were made with cabriole legs of short unhappy proportions. Lighter, beechwood, cane-seated bedroom balloon backs are more elegant than elaborately ornamented bulbous-legged parlour versions. Tendency to heaviness in all furniture. Heavy cast-brass ornament, oriental inlay, Berlin work, tapestries, Anglo-Indian ivory inlay, machine-grooved brass inlay, Victorian machine-cut Boulle. Carcase woods and thickness of veneer determine quality. Some fine detail and carving in solid woods. Great Exhibition of 1851 and subsequent exhibitions in Paris, Chicago etc. promoted 'novelty' furniture: cast-iron frames to upholstered seating furniture and papier mâché chairs for example. The Great Exhibition also led to a profusion of Indian-inspired use of fabrics: detailed study of articles from the Great Exhibition is rewarding. In contrast to the overstuffed look of almost all domestic furniture of the period, the clean simple lines of 'campaign' furniture are remarkable: strictly functional, brass-bound chests, desks and canvas-seated chairs in solid wood, unlike the veneered, French-polished drawing room furniture of the period.

Period: 1860–1920 – Late Victorian and Edwardian

Influences: Early Victorian influences continued – almost anything could be and was copied; strong element of 'art furniture' from Arts and Crafts movement, later from Art Nouveau which ran parallel but separate; William Morris, Bruce Talbert, E.W. Godwin, C.R. Ashbee, Ernest Gimson, C.F.A.

Voysey, C.R. Mackintosh, C.R. Eastlake's *Hints on Household Taste in Furniture* (1868), Ambrose Heal. Manufacturers: William Watt, Collinson & Lock, W. & A. Smee, J.G. Crace & Sons, Holland & Sons, Waring & Gillow, Liberty's, Heal's.

Materials: Light oak, stained oak, walnut for drawing-room furniture, ebonized woods, satinwood, machine-cut inlay panels, machine-made Boulle; ceramic and marble tiles, shell inlay, ivory, bone, mother-of-pearl, japanning, bird's eye maple, bamboo, cane, beech, ash; brass galleries, mounts and binding for campaign furniture. As period progresses, more incorporation into furniture of leather, metal, glass, mirrors and ceramics.

Characteristic types of furniture: Military chests and campaign furniture (Colonial and Crimean wars), pine chest furniture with oak-lined drawers, specimen chests, surgeon's fitted chests and cabinets, credenzas, bedside cupboards, pot cupboards, secrétaire-bookcases, bureau-bookcases, display cabinets, oriental lacquered display cabinets, serpentine-fronted inlaid glazed display cabinets, roll-top desks, Davenports, pedestal and ladies' kneehole desks, furniture 'en suite' for drawing rooms, bedrooms and dining rooms, pine washstands, fitted workboxes and travelling cases, writing slopes or lap desks, tantaluses, tea caddies, music stools, bedroom stools, bamboo and cane chairs, stands, conservatory furniture, garden furniture. Country ladder-back, wheelback, stickback, William Morris rush seat and bentwood chairs, Windsor chairs, dressers, Chesterfields. Eccentric furniture purpose-built in strange 'architectural' shapes for redesigned and new houses.

Construction: A schizophrenic period, with a huge output of machine-made furniture and a modest output of hand-made. On the one hand there was little change from the first half of the Victorian period, except for a general tendency to heaviness, bulbous turning, thin veneers and machine-made furniture. Campaign furniture and military furniture soundly constructed on traditional principles; handles and backplates, though machine-made, of fine quality. Tendency towards plain undecorated surfaces with the fashion for draping cloths and antimacassars over tables and chairs. Less sturdy, poorer quality woods for mass-produced carcases and drawers; furniture was screwed together with additional blocks where legs joined seats or table tops, producing an unstretchered line at the expense of durability. Wood was cut in any direction of the grain that suited the machines and much of it soon broke, cracked or warped: there was no time for timber to season. Much poor quality deal or pine furniture for servants' rooms. Hand-made furniture of the period was honestly and well constructed, though use of machine-cut joints and screws was common. Dowelling was frequently used, but its regularity shows the use of machines rather than hand-boring and cutting.

Design and detail: The late Victorian and Edwardian periods cannot be properly separated. Traditional designs, that is, yet more 'Queen Anne' and Regency-style pieces, flourished in the mass market while a design revolution, which is still having a direct impact on today's furniture, was taking place in parallel. In the mass market there was a whirlpool of design trends, in which there is a definite echo of Chippendale's chinoiserie, mixed with the overall design philosophy of the Adam period. Furniture was designed more to embellish and decorate the room than for its function, often resulting in pieces which, divorced from their original surroundings, seem to be made in extraordinary shapes. The mass-produced furniture of this period is characterized by a general decline in quality and design, with the original good intentions of early manufacturers sinking under the growing demand. With the establishment of the Empire, fragments of every culture were incorporated into designs of smaller furniture and used as motifs for decoration. Mother-of-pearl inlay, ivory, tassels, fringes – few things could be left alone, most were over-ornamented and exaggerated. Cast-brass ornament now often replaced with stamped copies in thin metal; ceramic knobs to pine furniture, turned wood knobs for bedroom furniture; ceramic rollers to castors. The best designed and made pieces were those in the oriental manner, though cheap British-made copies quickly debased richly ornate designs from India, China, Korea, Japan and Malaya. The use of ebony and ebonized wood, black lacquer and mourning cherubs' heads in sentimental grief was much in evidence for a considerable period after Prince Albert's death in 1861. Some good existing furniture was stained or painted black as the nation went into elaborate mourning.

In the same year William Morris founded a factory to produce furniture and ornaments with clean, clear lines and honest, simple traditional construction. This was in direct reaction to the mish-mash of derivative, heavy, veneered designs that swamped the market. The influence of Morris and his many collaborators in the Arts and Crafts and Aesthetic movements was powerful upon their successors in 20th-century design, but did little to influence contemporary mass-produced furniture. The inclusion of metal, glass, tiles and painting all into one piece did have some influence however, especially on bathroom and kitchen furniture. It is not properly accurate to label this design revolution Art Nouveau, which was properly a continental phenomenon. English Art Nouveau was much more restrained in its lines, at least in furniture. The decorative motifs of French and German Art Nouveau were however adopted with increasing frequency from continental models after about 1890. The simple 'country' styles reintroduced by the Arts and Crafts movement were to emerge, debased, in mass-market furniture with the Tudor taste of the 1920s.

The Late Victorian and Edwardian periods are interesting, if complex, and although the majority of their products are by definition not antique they are rapidly becoming so.

Price Guide

Chairs (£20–1,500)

Jacobean, Restoration, William & Mary. Oak: twist-turned legs, uprights and H-stretcher, carved front stretcher and crest rail, cane back and seat; often found with upholstered back panel, which means either a later replacement or Victorian copy. Singles in oak with cane backs, about £260; set of eight: £1,500. Set of six 19th-century copies from £620 up to £1,000.

William & Mary country versions in beech, walnut, mixed woods, less elaborately carved with plain barred back instead of carved surround and cane back; in oak with wooden seat and plain flat stretchers can be found for £200–300; country walnut £600 for six. Watch out for Victorian and later copies, machine-twist turned with upholstered backs: Victorian machine-twists usually are symmetrical – one leg twists one way, the other in opposite direction: originals have the twist going the same way on all legs.

Single chairs without arms about 70% less.

Pairs more than double price of single chairs. Sets very rarely found: should be well outside price range if genuine.

Queen Anne. Walnut: spoon-back, centre splat fixed to backframe with shoe-piece, drop-in seat, curved back, crest rail discreetly carved, cabriole leg, ball-and-claw feet, no stretchers: singles well outside price range.

Mahogany singles about £220. Good country walnut versions: pairs £1,200–1,800. Fruitwood, country-made, good quality, much less expensive at about £1,400 for six. Nineteenth-century walnut copies with ball-and-claw feet if they are of good quality will now be outside the price range for a set of six.

Georgian. Pre-Chippendale, (Virginia) walnut, with pierced splat, shoe-piece and drop-in seat, straight or slightly shaped crest rail, provincial made: £140 for singles.

Country-made oak-and-elm with wooden seats: about £50 single to £200 for pairs. Set of six in beech, ash or fruitwood over £1,000, but their size is rather against them.

Mahogany versions well outside price range. Nineteenth-century copies in mahogany can be found, often with unsightly back stretcher: around £825 for a set of six.

Chippendale: Mahogany well outside price range. High quality Victorian copies valued at £200 for six only ten years ago now fetch £1,050–1,600 depending on quality. Telltale drop-in seats: Chippendale designs were over-stuffed. Contemporary country Chippendale: elm, fruitwood, provincial in mahogany; set of six well outside price range. Wooden seats, elongated shoe-piece – set of six: £400. Surprisingly low appreciation so far. Oak with fretted back-splat – set of six: around £420.

Chippendale ladder-back: well outside price range. Country made, from original design, made around the turn of the 19th century, elm or oak with rush seats, set of six: £540; ash and elm with wooden seats: £200–300. Gothic designs – their size can be a drawback – go for about £200.

Hepplewhite: Mahogany, early wheel back, *c.* 1790, pierced splats, shoe-piece, over-stuffed seats, slightly tapered leg, pair: £300–380. Not popular so low appreciation.

Wheatsheaf design, drop-in seat, shoe-piece, untapered legs, set of six: £1,800. Recent good appreciation.

Camel-back country Hepplewhite 'wheatsheaf' in elm originally stained or varnished to look like mahogany, have probably been recently stripped, set of six: £1,200.

Oak, wooden seat, full-width shoe-piece, untapered legs, country-made Hepplewhite, set of six: £1,200. Considerable appreciation over recent years.

Many copies made up to mid-19th century: beware Hepplewhite wheel-back reproductions; originals had dished or bowed seats and shoe-piece. Reproductions should not be more than £600 for six.

Shield-back: legs should be unstretchered, back frame supports shield; spade feet, curved front seat frame, over-stuffed seats, well

outside price range. Even good 19th-century copies are fetching over £1,200 for set of six.

Note: Correct proportions set out in Hepplewhite pattern book: depth of seat 17ins, front width 20ins, height of seat frame 17ins, total chair height about 37ins.

Sheraton: Mahogany, square shape to back, slightly curved and tapered legs, drop-in seats and stretchers, some reeding on crest rail and uprights: outside price range. Simplest provincial-made: around £900 for six, low appreciation. Oak-and-elm, country-made: around £380–400 for six with better appreciation.

'Suffolk' chairs with horizontal back-splat, plain or bobbined in mixed woods; elm seat with oak or sycamore can be found for around £850–1,000 for six with high appreciation. Rush seats less at £780–800 for six.

Sheraton X-back, unstretchered, square-sectioned, tapered front legs, reeded backs, over-stuffed seats: well outside price range. This design has been put together with Sheraton's delicate cane-seated painted white-and-gilt chair with round section reeded legs and X-stretcher to produce many later versions of the X-back, which was a far more solid chair. Victorian and Edwardian copies and reproductions abound with bad propor-

Good plain late Georgian country-made Hepplewhite chairs. Part of a set of one elbow chair and five singles, of consistently dark laburnum wood. Made about 1780, perhaps in Scotland.

tions and over-turned front legs and H-stretchers.

Modern reproductions in ebonized wood, turned spindle leg and H-stretchers cost from £97–175 each; S-arms from £167–200; the best are hand-made, in the upper price range.

Late 18th-century transitional design with tapering turned legs, broad crest rail and horizontal splat, often rope-twist, unstretchered round-section legs, slightly tapered with over-stuffed seats: now well outside price range with recent surge of appreciation.

Elm and beech wheelback Windsor chair with turned legs and arm supports, mid-19th century.

Thomas Hope 'Trafalgar': Mahogany, sabre-leg, flush-frame construction, rope-twist crest rail, unstretchered square-section tapered legs, drop-in seats: sets now well outside price range, though uneven rise in value, actually depreciating in the first five years of the last decade, then rising sharply.

Modern reproduction rope-backs are around £600 for a set of six, but note that sabre-legged chairs involved the careful cutting of timber, using natural spring; reproductions seldom have the same original thickness of timber from which the leg is cut, and legs break easily down the grain.

Lyre-backed chairs: with reeded legs and curved side-rail: example of vagaries of taste – sets of six rose in value early in 1970s to £650, now out of fashion and a hundred pounds less. If your heart is set on Regency chairs, consider making a harlequin set: the flush-frame construction and even height lends itself to near matches. Singles can be found at about the same price as modern reproductions: around £100. Sets of six are well outside price range except for the now unpopular lyre-back.

Quantities of 'rout' chairs in beech, birch and pine, painted, of X-back derivation were made for Regency balls and social functions. Singles of these with recaned seats are around £20.

Windsor chairs. Yew, yew and elm, early Windsors with curved centre stretcher and cabriole legs rare. Front and back legs usually bobbin-turned around 1725. Construction of solid, saddle-shaped seat into which legs and back were fixed. From 1755 attempts to make design grander by incorporating simplified versions of Chippendale, wheatsheaf, Prince of Wales feathers and wheelback. All chairs with yew arms are more expensive. Yew and elm, cabriole leg, curved stretcher: around £390–450 with considerable recent appreciation. Simple stick-back, elm and fruitwood: £150–180.

Late 18th-century yew and elm with decorative centre splat: £390–450. Original wheelback in yew, recent huge appreciation, now up to £800; plain comb-back yew have recently soared towards £450.

Nineteenth-century straight stretchers with reel-turned legs: from £125–200 depending on wood.

Smokers' Bow, 19th-century, with arm-hoop made from several pieces screwed together and not in a solid piece – correct construction of the period; elm, pine, beech: £125–190.

Single chairs: plain stick-back: £20–25; sets of six: around £200.

Lancashire slat-back or turned stick-back, sets of six: £140–170.

Plain Victorian bar-back, matching sets of six if they can be found: £500–800.

William IV. Rosewood, simulated rosewood, mahogany; crest rail over-runs chair frame of flush construction; legs were round-sectioned, unstretchered, reeded and turned; drop-in seat; carved horizontal splat: a recent and, to some, surprising increase in value has brought sets of six nudging the top of the price range. There was a time when the rather clumsy front legs were replaced with sabre legs to increase their value but this period seems to be doing very nicely in its own right today. Many versions of these chairs with original legs and undecorated horizontal splats can still be found for as little as £280–350 for six and rising. But watch for those with replaced legs and consequent low price: £150–300 for six.

If the crest rail over-runs and they are sabre-legged, examine closely as they may have been remade. Provincial-made genuine articles with original legs and with stretchers are a bit cheaper than London-made (no stretchers), at £920–1,200 for six.

About 1830, more fluid, French-inspired chair with curving crest rail and upholstered back, seat often upholstered in leather: £500–700 for six; rather cheaper if needing new upholstery, cleaning off and polishing. Hoop backs £200–300 for six.

Awkward cabriole leg or heavier reeded leg, often with castors: £500 for six; mahogany or rosewood (but watch for early veneering as opposed to solid wood), plainer versions, often with happier scrolled feet or turned legs still have upholstered squarish seats; open-backed without upholstery are more expensive: around £500–800 for six, depending on quality of wood and carving.

Early Victorian. Early balloon-back with mildly nipped-in waist, curved seat frame and turned or cabriole leg with scroll feet, sets of six: rather over £1,000. Look for manufacturer's name 'Gillow' on good ones, but expect to pay more.

Later balloon-back with well-rounded, waisted backs and increasingly bulbous legs, decreasing in value according to design and proportion. Light plain versions in beech, originally for bedrooms, with stretchered legs, can be found for as little as £200–300 for six.

Round-backed chairs with circular panels of Berlin-type woolwork and seats are identifiably Early Victorian and, if needlework is original, value is increased. Singles around £200; sets of six (unusual as they were parlour chairs): £1,500.

Prie-dieu high-backed chair: usually in not very good condition, but quite fun to have around in hall or living room; recent considerable appreciation, £70–80 in poor condition, £200 if perfect.

Late Victorian and Edwardian. William Morris stained beech with rush seats, no appreciable investment value, since these chairs have been made continuously since mid-19th century. Current prices for new ones best guide to a straight second-hand bargain.

Art Nouveau high back curiosity in inlaid oak, four for up to £700 with recent appreciation.

Clean-cut versions of classical mahogany dining chairs with dipped top rails, *c.* 1910, going up fast to around £1,100 for eight. If interested in this period, study works of movements, individual designers listed (on page 26) under this period and use a crystal ball. Investment value depends on fashion to a large extent.

Tables (£30–1,200)

Dining Tables

Mediaeval, Tudor. Oak: early oak refectory tables have soared well outside the price range from their modest prices of ten years ago. The only available tables of this design are Victorian 'Tudor' with heavy bulbous legs and even they are nudging £800 or more. With some searching, country-made work tables can be ferreted out, plain trestle-type tables or plain square-stretcher tables for between £130 and £500 depending on size, the bigger the cheaper. Look for good stout worm-free timbers and good-condition top surfaces with few joints in the width. Ideally this type of table is made from as few planks as possible and for this reason they tend to be rather narrow for their length. Wood contracts across the grain, not along it: a guide to age for tables with a cross-piece at either end is that the width of the table has contracted with age: flush clamp ends and sides could mean that the top is new or has been cut. Tables in elm or fruitwoods such as apple are less expensive.

Jacobean. Gate-leg tables in oak: here the price depends to a great extent on convenience of size: six-seater gate-legs being well outside the price range if they are of any quality. Smaller ones, measuring about 4ft across when closed, opening to 5ft × 4ft are around £400, rising to £900 depending on the quality of the turning, age and condition. Watch for replaced leaves: there should be signs of wear where the gate has held up the leaf, and handling will have caused parts of the underside to be darker with a slight patina compared with the rest of the underside which should be untreated, paler and slightly dusty. Best examples over £1,000.

Queen Anne. Walnut, veneer, quartering, marquetry: well outside price range.

Georgian. Drop-leaf mahogany: well outside price range. Larger country period Georgian drop-leaf tables in oak can be found for £500–600, but watch for signs of restoration.

The tops should be pegged, not screwed, through the underframe.

Late Georgian drop-leaf tables of smaller size, about 4ft × 4ft 6ins, can be found, also in oak, at £215–235. Late 18th-century pine cottage tables, 7ft × 3ft, plain, £250. 5ft × 3ft proportionately less, at £180–205. *Note:* Modern reproduction veneered drop-leaf tables 'in the Sheraton manner' cost over £400.

William IV and Early Victorian. The 19th century saw a proliferation of cheval-constructed drop-leaf tables known as 'Sutherlands' with tops which are often very attractive, in burr-walnut veneer or figured walnut. The ardent efforts of the Victorians to achieve 'authenticity' often resulted in swash-turned or bobbin-turned legs, albeit machine-turned, which may be preferable to the end-pillar legs, where turning, reeding and fluting is often on the heavy side. Still a good buy for £100–150. Appreciation has been considerable over the last five years.

Breakfast tables, supper tables, 'tip-top' tables, loo tables

Tilt-top tables suitable for use as small dining tables.

Late Georgian and Regency. Rectangular in solid mahogany with splayed legs and brass paw feet fetch just under £1,000 with plainer versions at £460–550.

Late Regency, Early Victorian in rosewood or amboyna veneer, still just within the price range at around £1,200. *Note:* Copies of Regency splay-foot circular-topped tables made around 1900 are fetching £675–750.

Victorian. The most spectacularly decorated marquetry tilt-tops have already slipped out of the price range. In burr walnut, rosewood, flame walnut, coromandel, mahogany veneer they are £400 upwards, depending on quality. Ovals fetch less than circular.

Loo tables in plain veneers of the same woods also show recent appreciation and are currently in broad band of £400–620 depending on quality, lightness of style and decoration.

Round tip-top breakfast tables, measuring about 5ft across, are between £800 and £1,000. Oval or rectangular are less.

Centre tables

Not usually suitable for dining tables because of their deep frieze below the table top. Some ornately decorated 'oriental' Victorian examples lack this frieze and though the tripod base may be over-ornate are good value at about £500.

Side tables

All side tables have blank backs because they were designed to stand against the wall.

Georgian. Fine quality side-tables with walnut frames and marble tops, originally one of a pair, can be found as singles for around £600–900.

Late 17th- and 18th-century with turned legs and stretchers, in elm, oak, usually good proportions and solid craftsmanship: £280–350.

Country oak furniture following grand designs of Chippendale and Hepplewhite; side tables are still excellent value at around £100–150 but must be in prime condition with original tops for any investment value.

Mahogany, with plain square or chamfered legs, £300–400. Plain, in oak, same period, from £150.

Georgian pine functional side tables, often pleasantly proportioned and hard-wearing, £30–50. Beware Late Victorian softwood side-tables with replaced legs. Strictly kitchen pieces, they had turned bulbous legs and were made of inferior pine. Second-hand value only.

Victorian. 'Sheraton' side tables usually thinly veneered and too spindly for anything but display, which is what they were intended for. Often serpentine-fronted and quite elegant, fetching considerable prices nevertheless: £320–380. D-shaped or 'demilune' side tables, usually in pairs in satinwood veneer were made from Late Georgian to Edwardian. The catch is the Edwardian copy,

Oak tip-top tripod table, late 18th century.

imported in quantities from France, with machine-cut inlay which lifts very easily, warps, and is poor quality. Genuine Late Georgian satinwood, £650–700.

Pembroke tables

Two-flap tables with side drawer.

Georgian mahogany, very handsome and elegant, £650–700.

Late 18th-century mahogany or rosewood with some inlay decoration surprisingly still between £240 and £300.

Sheraton period in fine satinwood: £1,000 +.

Early 19th-century in plain mahogany, undecorated, solid and stable: £280–350.

The Victorians preferred 'demilune' and reduced the pretty Pembroke to an uncompromising two-flap, often with castors, all-purpose household table.

Card tables

In general, anything before mid-18th century well outside price range, and 'demilune' or

Late 18th or early 19th century elm two-flap table in a simple country form.

halfmoon card tables can be more expensive than square.

Chippendale period: with straight chamfered leg and foldover top in solid mahogany just within price range with considerable escalation in last five years: £800–1,000.

George II. Cabriole leg with pad feet and concertina action pull-out supporting legs are at the very top of the range, justifiably because of their beautiful craftsmanship, but can still be found for £950–1,500; more if it is a pale wood.

Versions of this neat and elegant table were made as tea tables with polished surfaces. If new baize has been added, suspect poor quality surface and examine closely: all the same, they may cost as much as £550–650.

George III. Rectangular Hepplewhite and Sheraton designs in mahogany with spade feet: good value at £100–150, but suspect interior surfaces as above.

Regency. Fine satinwood veneer, opening to a square shape, were much sought after ten years ago but became unfashionable until recently; now experiencing considerable appreciation: £650–720.

D-shaped, demilune: often originally made in pairs with fine satinwood cross-banding on mahogany veneer, not much under £1,000.

Good Regency card tables have soared outside the range, particularly those with fine design and inlay on both inside and outside surfaces. Even the late Regency splay-foot is now over £1,000.

William IV. Regency revival pillar-and-claw, noticeably heavier than originals, at a reasonable price of around £550, with quality marks added for fine figured wood veneer, mahogany veneer, carved solid rosewood centre pillar.

Victorian. Heavy pillar-and-claw pattern. Carving detail on the pillar and scrolled or paw feet increase value. Also quality of veneering, which can be fine, and in a variety of woods: burr-walnut, figured walnut, rosewood. Machine-cut marquetry used to good effect, and prices still reasonable at £350–370.

Edwardian. Satinwood reproductions, inlaid or painted in the manner of Sheraton's finest work, were mass-produced over a long period and are easily identifiable by paper-thin veneer and unstable spindly legs. The only interesting revival was the envelope card table, first made in the 18th century. Some Edwardian versions were quite well designed and made and have recently appreciated quite considerably to lift them into the £290–500 bracket. However, many of them were made of unsuitable wood which tends to warp, thus lifting the thin veneer.

Sideboards (£550–1,000)

Sheraton: Genuine period sideboards well within price limit because of their enormous size, over 6ft 6ins long: around £850–1,000. Victorian 'Sheraton' often same price. Do not be misled by lead-lined drawer, apparently a sign of genuineness: the Victorians used them too. Look for paper-thin machine-cut veneer, spindly legs, wrong proportions of the latter. No reason to pay same price for a 19th-century copy.

Smaller bow-front genuine period Sheraton well outside price range if dated before 1800.

Nineteenth-century Sheraton-style small mahogany bow-front at around £550–750; so ceaselessly copied that reproductions in veneered chipboard are still being manufactured today.

Dressers and Dresser bases (£180–1,200)

James I-type oak dressers, £400–500.

William & Mary oak dresser base and others from 18th century with original tops missing, still very handsome, can be found for £500–600.

Eighteenth-century oak low dressers measuring about 5ft 6ins with single drawer, around £900–1,000.

Georgian oak low dresser with three drawers: £800–1,000.

Welsh dressers: by definition country pieces, though the best are extremely grand and expensive. Even relatively humble ones are towards the top of the range, at between £1,000 and £1,200.

Parlour pieces in oak, beech and ash of varying quality range from £450 to £900 for the very best. The lower prices often indicate considerable restoration.

Nineteenth-century heavy Lincolnshire-style dressers, usually on the large side, can be found in varying condition from £130 to £160.

Prices for pine dressers vary according to size, as with sideboards: the bigger the cheaper. 6ft wide × 6ft 6ins high with fielded panel doors below: £350–400. 6ft 6ins wide × 8ft high considerably less at £200–350. Plain 18th-century pine kitchen dressers with three drawers and two plain cupboards: £180–200. Good Georgian natural pine with moulding and decorations significantly more at around £450–500. Should be less though if it has been painted and then stripped. Useful sign of age is that scrubbing of kitchen floors will probably have rotted the base: if there is no visible rot, look for repair pieces let in.

Side cupboards (£100–190)

Pine, kitchen, passage or pantry pieces, but watch for remade dresser bases.

Nineteenth-century side cupboard with

A pine dresser, probably 19th century. Check the bottom corners for signs of wear indicating age.

Upholstered Furniture (£210–950)

Settees, sofas, couches

Settees, couches, daybeds and sofas, up to the late Regency period, with hard horse-hair upholstery, following designs in period pattern books, are outside price range because of their scarcity. This in part was due to their fragile construction, and in part to their wholesale scrapping with the advent of padded upholstery and sprung furniture.

Late Georgian settees with heavy restoration can be found at £400–550.

William IV and Victorian. The bulk of upholstered furniture within the price range comes from this period.

Most popular were the chaise-longue shapes in rosewood or mahogany with undulating back and scooped sides with serpentine front and cabriole legs. Solid walnut, rosewood or mahogany frames, considerably 'rescued' and reupholstered: £450–550.

Grecian-style daybeds of this period, often with splay feet and brass inlay have appreciated enormously over the last five years and are around £850–950, but not very comfortable with old-fashioned horse-hair upholstery. The deep plain shape degenerated with the addition of bulbous turned legs; they are around in battered condition for second-hand prices.

Chesterfields were also popular, but there is little merit in acquiring one other than for its second-hand value, since the same model has been in almost continuous production since the early 1820s.

Easy chairs and button-backs

As with balloon-backed dining, salon, parlour and bedroom chairs, the appeal of these button-backs is partly their amazing comfort.

Mahogany, walnut, rosewood carved frame with open arms, cabriole legs and stuffed back and seat. Enormous appreciation over the last five years, now cost around £350–420. The first of the button-backs and

flight of three drawers and single cupboard: £140–150.

60ins long with centre cupboard and two flights of drawers flanking: £150–170.

48ins long of similar design (better size for today's living), more at £170–190.

72ins long as low as £100–130.

not yet debased by reproductions.

With upholstered arms, carved frame, cabriole legs but with less decorative framework: £280–350.

'Grandfather' or salon chair with scooped back, plain rounded back frame of rosewood, mahogany or walnut, the best with block arms, short cabriole leg: between £410 and £460; the lower price for upholstered frame; appreciation as above but levelling out.

'Grandmother' spoon-backed ladies' chair without arms, decorative rosewood frame, still going up and costing anywhere between £400 and £500 depending on condition.

Horseshoe-backed 'smokers' chair' with open arms, turned rosewood supports and legs: £350–380; Edwardian versions with raised padded backs considerably cheaper.

Tub chairs, nursing chairs with low seats, padded spoon backs: around £210–250.

Iron-framed tub chairs made for the Great Exhibition are of curiosity value at a slightly lower price. *Note:* Reproductions of these popular little chairs with foam upholstery cost about £115.

Chest Furniture (£50–1,200)

Note: Study drawer detail, frame and carcase construction, carcase woods of the period, thickness of veneer, drawer handle detail. Appearances often deceive. Many pieces of plain and honest country chest furniture have recently received veneering to add appeal and increase prices. Watch too for 'marriages', particularly in early period of chest-on-chest or chest-on-stand: new tops on bottom halves of chests-on-chests, Victorian or later stands to chests-on-stands. Beware Victorian 'Tudor' at all times: its construction will give it away.

17th century. Small oak country-made chests from the 17th century are fairly common, usually with three flights of paired drawers (frame construction) but have been subjected to considerable restoration: new tops, drawers, feet. The best are in two halves, but marriages are common: between £350 and £400. Chest-on-stand in oak, 4ft 6ins high, stand replaced: £450–650. Country-made oak on restored original stand, same price.

Queen Anne and Early Georgian. Walnut: outside price range. '18th-century' chests at low prices have often been made up from larger pieces. Good value for around £250 but little prospect of appreciation. Early 18th-century pine clothes presses: built-in wardrobes with double doors over three drawers of varying size, often originally built without backs, large (72ins high × 57ins wide): around £350. Late 18th-century with poorer workmanship, about the same size: £250–320.

Georgian. Mid-18th-century flat-fronted chests of drawers in walnut or mahogany nudge £1,000. Lower prices most often indicate much restoration, replaced tops, new aprons and feet. Searching can be well rewarded with country pieces of good proportions made in elm, fruitwood, oak with pine-lined drawers for around £200–250.

Eighteenth-century chests-of-drawers may well be bottom halves of chests-on-chests or tops of chests-on-stands with new feet. If the former, the outer line often flares slightly to match the original top. Between £500 and £650, but not worth the price if new top is added to bottom half of chest-on-chest.

Late 18th-century walnut 'marriage' of well-matching chest-on-chest: £700–850. Intact survivals should be well outside the price range.

Late 18th-century bachelors' chests £1,000–1,200. *Note:* Reproduction bachelors' chests in 'yew wood finish' of thin veneer on chipboard are around £350–370.

Nineteenth-century reproductions of Chippendale-style chests-on-chests are up to £1,000, but markedly less graceful of proportion than original design.

Regency. This period is governed by size except for the finest pieces. Most furniture was large. A George III chest-on-chest would be around 70ins high × 48ins wide: in handsome bow-front mahogany with satinwood cross-banding, already up to £1,000. Smaller pieces by Sheraton and Shearer have been reproduced almost continuously; the originals are well outside price range.

Mahogany tallboys are around for low prices, not surprisingly with measurements of over 6ft tall and 3ft 6ins wide: £750 upwards, good value and appreciating recently.

Early mahogany wardrobes with mock drawers in doors to look like tallboys are interesting but large. 78ins high × 50ins wide with interior fittings still intact: high prices of £900–1,100. In order to accommodate full-length hanging space many have been stripped of interior fittings, bottom drawers have been removed and left false-fronted. Genuine bow-fronts and serpentine-fronts with handsome architectural pediments outside price range.

Military chests: flush-fitting drawer-handles, brass-reinforced corners, often made in two pieces fitting together: mahogany, teak, padouk, cedar and camphorwood. Prices of these soared in the early 1970s but reproductions and made-up pieces have brought values down. Best prices up to £800 for fitted details, helmet drawer, secretaire drawer etc. some still around £400–600; more for good woods, detail etc. An awkward size for everyday use.

William IV. Size keeps prices relatively low. Most linen presses, clothes presses, wardrobes are over 6ft tall. Preference for fitted built-in cupboards in today's houses keeps price down: between £550 and £650.

Victorian. Small furniture fetches more than more cumbersome though well-made Victorian chest furniture. Best value are plain bow-fronted mahogany-veneered chests-of-drawers on solid imported Honduras mahogany carcases for £130–150 with turned wooden knob handles and two top drawers. Slightly more for ones with finer detail: ivory escutcheons, stamped brass handles. Watch as usual for replaced tops due to cracking in over-heated rooms or re-veneering. Better quality: £250–350. Drawers with bottoms of one-piece pine – keep an eye out for veneered oak country carcases. Knotty red pine and mahogany were the only timbers used at that period. Oak carcases means new veneer almost invariably. Pine chests mostly date from this period, porcelain handles or turned wood, some quite prettily made with bracket feet, shaped aprons, often with new brass handles but none the worse for that: £65–100. Good modern reproductions are slightly more expensive. More functional and less pleasing to the eye with bulgy turned legs: £50–90.

Late 19th-century pine wardrobes or linen presses: £250–350. Modern reproductions: about £300. (*Note:* Excellently made solid pine reproduction furniture recently on the market threatens the appreciation of less well made earlier pieces, although the reproduction is likely to cost a little more than the original.) Wellington chests; specimen cabinets with hinged side-pieces to prevent drawers opening in transport. From the

Victorian mahogany veneer bow-front chest with original handles.

1850s in walnut veneer, plain rosewood, mahogany, maple and oak; value increased by specially fitted drawers, decorative veneers, bracket detail: big recent appreciation, probably because of their usefulness for storing papers: best between £600 and £800.

Fin de siècle, Edwardian. Mostly reproductions of 'Sheraton' in unlikely satinwood veneer or characteristic mahogany veneer cross-banded with satinwood. Thin veneers a giveaway. Also imported satinwood veneered furniture and considerable use of ormolu mounts. This period is generally easily recognizable by its over-refined and wavering line. Good quality workmanship and materials against contemporary prices best guide. Even the pine furniture of this age is poor.

Case Furniture (£50–1,200)

Display Cabinets

Earliest within price range are William IV or Victorian. Smaller pieces in these periods already climbing fast out of reach.

Victorian. Standing display cabinets, probably one of their happiest and best designs, just under 3ft in height with brass gallery, ormolu or cast-brass mounts, glass doors and sides, in burr walnut, bird's eye maple or figured veneers in exotic woods: £600–700 with considerable recent appreciation. The most spectacular are Victorian Boulle or brass-inlaid rosewood or ebonized wood, with marble tops: still £1,000–1,200.

Also wide range of Indian and oriental small chest cabinets, trinket cabinets, notably handsome brass-mounted Korean in black lacquer with decorative strap hinges: £300–400. Many were mass-produced 'in the oriental manner' and are in poor condition, but some very decorative pieces are around for under £100.

Edwardian. Some of the best pieces of this period are the satinwood glass-fronted display cabinets, painted in the French classical manner with swags, drapes and medallions. The proportions are a little top-heavy because of the fashion for thin, tapered legs and most have been ignored until recently when good quality cabinets have become desirable and 18th- and even 19th-century pieces are out of reach. Take note of quality: best pieces over £1,000.

Later versions of Victorian standing display cabinets raised on the inevitable Edwardian spindly tapered legs, often with faint 'oriental' overtones; not so neat or so stable: £250–320 with higher prices for ornament and veneer decoration.

Curiosities of this period are numerous: watch for 'art furniture' with curious combinations of woods, metal inlays, lacquers, enamels, often with a distinct Japanese air. They need hunting for and recognizing; very high prices are being paid for the best, well outside the price range but with erratic appreciation. Even Edwardian curiosities are now going for £500-plus. Taste and pocket are the truest guides.

Corner Cupboards (£100–800)

17th century. Made extensively, usually large and carved in same style as dressers of the period. Standing, often two halves, many built into panelling in custom of the day. If they survive intact, with original hinges, fittings, backs, well outside price range. More elaborately carved tops alone have often been converted to hanging corner cupboards with considerable restoration. No glazed fronts of this period, therefore limited appeal, limited investment value: around £150, but at this price part of extensive panelled work and therefore not a 'whole' piece.

Queen Anne. Walnut with glazed doors well beyond reach. Country made, block-fronted, in oak, elm or fruitwood: lowest £360. More for original brass H-hinges, detail, patination, good woods. Some veneered walnut, often bow-fronted, around £375–420.

Bow-fronted English lacquer or japanning in chinoiserie taste of the day, probably the top halves of original tall standing cupboards; very handsome: £450–550.

Georgian. (Virginia) walnut, mahogany, fruit-wood, country oak, probably originally designed for stands if below £500. Watch for tell-tale bottom mouldings and flares to fit former stand.

Mahogany, elegant architectural shapes with fluted columns, moulded or broken pediments: with glazed doors outside price range. Block-fronted can be found, but expensive at £650–750. Watch for restoration, replaced backs. Late 18th-century block-front pine corner cupboards, often built in originally and therefore with replacement backs (indicates part of larger suite of built-in cupboards) £300–400; less if stripped.

Small 18th-century hanging corner cupboards with block-fronts £100–150 and about the same price for period country-made oak.

A full height pine corner cupboard, unusual in that it has just the one door. Probably 19th century.

Regency. Standing corner cupboards with brass grill-fronts are dubious. Many of them are French of a considerably later date. Also widely copied in ebonized wood and brass by Victorians. So too are the 'Sheraton' style mahogany corner cupboards inlaid with satinwood. Both should be viewed with suspicion if less than £300.

Pine corner cupboards with fan-shaped fluting, original shelves, often made with block-front doors for pantries, or plain glazed doors, between £350 and £425. This design has been subject to much plagiarism in a wide variety of sizes, which will tend to damage long-term appreciation.

Note: Small reproduction solid pine half-glazed standing corner cupboards: £150–265.

Victorian. Oriental lacquer flat-fronted corner cupboards, not to be confused with Queen Anne, usually over-ornate with lattice or decorated pierced hinges, block-fronted and decorative, many in the Anglo–Indian taste with inlaid ivory, mother-of-pearl, with good workmanship and materials: £170–200. Stripped pine: many hanging corner shelves, originally part of suite of kitchen or pantry fittings, without doors: £50 or less.

Note: Open-shelved solid pine modern reproduction corner cupboards: £59–69. Reproduction 'yew wood' finish glass-fronted corner cupboards from £150.

Country-made 19th-century oak corner cupboards in considerable quantities and varying qualities: glazed doors more expensive at £250–350; block front: £100–200. Also in fruitwood at slightly higher prices.

Edwardian. Most interesting are the 'architectural' or Japanese-style corner cupboards often of eccentric shape and mixed materials; prices vary wildly according to condition and design, and can be anything from £150–800.

Standing corner cupboards, glazed doors, satinwood, painted or machine inlay, as for display cupboards (see page 39).

Kitchen pine corner cupboards: craftsmanship and materials best guide against current reproduction prices. Glass-fronted modern reproduction solid pine: £150–170. Look for non-functional glazing bars and yellowish tinge to wood: plain pine has a soft golden honey colour.

Desk and Writing Furniture (£80–1,000)

Desks, Secrétaires and Bureau-bookcases

17th century. Fall-front escritoires on stands, often of beautiful marquetry work well outside price range. Those desks that are within price range seem incredibly cheap before close inspection, when they turn out to be 'marriages' of writing slopes or travelling desks on top of side-tables or chest-of-drawers of same period. Appreciation potential low. Around £300–450.

William & Mary and Queen Anne. Walnut desks and Queen Anne bureau-bookcases well outside range. Fall-front secrétaires of this period to be viewed with suspicion if within price range. Frequent marriages of Victorian 'Tudor' stands and fall-front top section.

Georgian. Secrétaires with shallow fall-fronts often concealed as mock drawer. Should have top flight of drawers, but frequently replaced with glazed door bookcase top or block-front door of later date. If less than £1,000 this is probably the case. True bureau-bookcases with sloping fall-fronts well outside range.

Eighteenth-century country-made oak, walnut, elm or fruitwood slope-fronted desks around £500–900 with little appreciation. Less convenient than kneehole desks of the period, which are well outside price range.

Plain late Georgian nine-drawer kneehole desk with original handles. The drawers are oak-lined and their fronts are cock beaded.

Late Georgian, Regency. Pedestal desks within price range, like other furniture of this period, are large. Country-made or provincial partners' desks also on the large side but reasonable at £400–800.

Best bet for small-sized desks (though hard to find) are early 19th-century campaign or military secrétaires at around £560–620.

Some nice later Georgian pine pedestal two-flight 6-drawer desks at around £400.

Regency rosewood writing tables: between £420 and £520; more with brass inlay.

Grand Carlton House desks, 19th-century reproductions recently overpriced and now about £850.

William IV. Most writing furniture large and sombre. Exceptions are ladies' pedestal desks of convenient size: £800–1,000.

Knee-hole desks with heavy ormolu handles and mounts, often inlaid, nudging £1,000. Plainer versions from £500.

Regency Davenports: compact low desks assumed to be designed for ladies, named after Captain Davenport who had this design made by Gillows in the late 18th century. It was repeated for 100 years or more. Earliest models straightforward with mock drawers at side, cupboard below, often with small brass gallery: veneered in satinwood, rosewood, mahogany, burr walnut: prices continuing to rise – already about £1,000.

Victorian Davenports more ornate and less well proportioned. Best piano tops around £900; later versions: £440-550.

Pine pedestal desks with two flights of four drawers: £300–340; lower ones with three-drawer flights: £100–150.

Victorian. Ladies' cylinder desks or tambour fronts in rosewood or mahogany have pleasing proportions at the expense of stability; not much investment value: still around £350.

Note: 4-drawer mahogany-finish writing desk modern reproductions: about £400. Reproduction modern 'yew finish' bureau-bookcase: £700.

Library Tables

Library tables of late Regency design, elongated rectangular on central stretcher and cheval support are a little large at 5ft but provide plenty of desk-space if no drawers. Appreciating recently: £225 six years ago, the best are now £600–800.

Victorian writing tables, grandly called 'bureaux-plats', rather despised but better proportioned, unostentatious pieces which provide writing space and two drawers in frieze, good value at £330+.

Edwardian library tables considerably less at £120–250.

Writing Slopes, Writing Boxes

Travelling desks, often erroneously called 'Bible boxes', few of which survived. Slope-fronted oak copies made in Victorian 'Tudor' period and still around for under £100.

18th century. Resurgence of popularity of travelling furniture, usually made to fold up like a box, fitted inside, usually with at least one secret drawer. Rare to find in genuine hand-cut Boulle and expensive.

Regency. Writing slopes in rosewood or mahogany, often with elegant scrolled supports and fitted pigeonholes along the back, recently appreciating: now £175–200.

Plainer versions of campaign-style writing boxes with brass-bound corners: £80–100.

William IV. Some very fine examples in satinwood veneer inlaid with ivory or mother-of-pearl: around £150.

Early Victorian. Anglo–Indian and lacquer with decorative shellwork, Victorian Tunbridge ware and machine-cut brass inlay varying from £80 to £100 depending on decoration and quality.

Brass inlaid rosewood, extremely decorative: £100–165.

Furniture Terms_____

Acanthus see **Decoration**

Anthemion see **Decoration**

Apron Panel immediately below frame of table-top or chair seat, or below chest of drawers between the front legs.

Arabesque see **Decoration**

Armoire Large cupboard of a kind originally made for storing armour, now used to describe many large cupboards with decorative panels, usually French.

Arts and Crafts Movement Movement away from mass-produced to hand-crafted designs, influential from 1860s under the aegis of William Morris.

Bachelor's chest Low chest of drawers, with top opening out to writing surface; from 18th century.

Back plate Brass or ormolu plate on to which the handle of drawer or cupboard is fixed.

Bail handle Half hoop like a slightly flattened miniature bucket handle.

Balloon back see **Chairbacks**

Baluster see **Legs**

Banding Strips of veneer set round the edges of tables, drawer fronts etc; when the grain of the banding runs at right angles to the grain of the main surface it is called 'cross-banding' and if the veneer is arranged in a herringbone pattern it is 'feather banding'.

Barleysugar twist Turned in the shape of twisted barleysugar; also known as twist-turned, swash-turned.

Baroque Ornate style, grandly ornamented, particularly of Restoration period and up to 1730s.

Baywood Mahogany.

Berlin work Pictorial embroidery in great popularity from 1830s almost to the end of the century.

Bible box Small lidded box, often oak, with some shallow carving, originally mediaeval but copied, heavily carved, by Victorians and Edwardians.

Block front Solid-fronted (cabinet, book-case, bureau-bookcase) as opposed to glass-fronted.

Block foot see **Feet**

Board construction see **Construction**

Bobbin see **Decoration**

Bolt and fork Brass or steel plate and socket used to join leaves of tables together.

Bombé Term used chiefly of commodes and chests to describe fronts swelling out in a curve towards the bottom: a D-shape when seen from the side.

Bonheur du jour Small writing desk of light, elegant construction, with long tapered legs.

Boulle (boule, buhl) Originally tortoise-shell inset with brass or silver; later versions usually rosewood.

Bow front Convex shape of fronts of chests, commodes, etc.

Bracket foot see **Feet**

Breakfront Bookcases, display cabinets, etc. with centre section set forward from two side wings.

Chairbacks

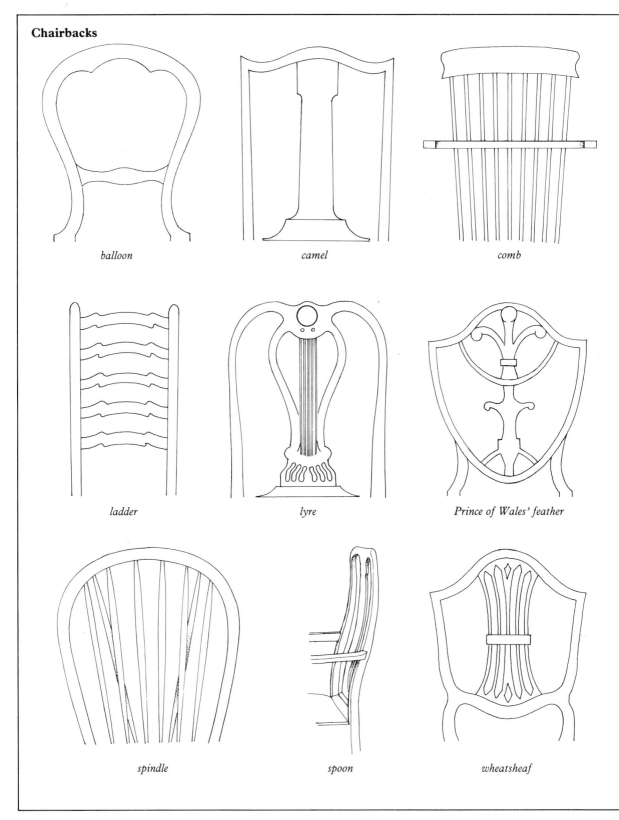

balloon

camel

comb

ladder

lyre

Prince of Wales' feather

spindle

spoon

wheatsheaf

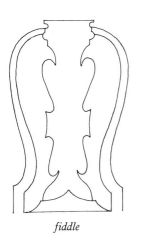

fiddle

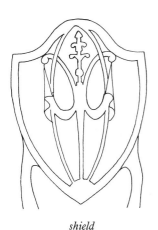

shield

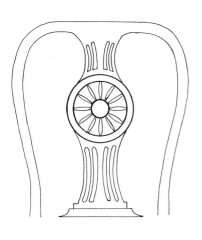

wheel

Broken pediment Top moulding to bookcases, cupboards etc, with symmetrical shape cut out in the centre.

Cabriole leg see **Legs**

Camel back see **Chairbacks**

Campaign furniture Portable furniture with straight lines, countersunk brass handles, particularly associated with Peninsular, Crimean Wars.

Canterbury Sheet music rack on castors, with divisions.

Carlton House desk D-shaped desk on legs with pigeonholes and drawers; late 18th century onwards.

Case furniture Any kind of cupboard, including bookcases and display cases.

Carcase see **Construction**

Chairbacks see illustrations, left.

Chest furniture Chests containing drawers as opposed to cupboards.

Cheval Type of construction depending on support at sides or ends only: large mirrors pivoting from standing frame, or tables supported at ends only.

Chiffonier Low moveable cupboard suitable as a sideboard, sometimes with shallow bookshelves above, sometimes with marble top; Regency examples often have brass lattice-front doors lined with silk.

Clothes press Early term for wardrobe.

Clout nail Iron nail with rough rectangular head.

Cockbeading Moulding which projects round the edge of drawers to protect veneer; from *c.* 1730.

Coffered panel   Panel sunk into frame.

Commode   Ornamental chest-of-drawers.

Console table   A table supported by brackets fixed to a wall.

Construction
Board: Carpenters' work of nailed planks, pegged bars, flush surfaces back and front.
Carcase: Box construction in common timber, on to which veneer is added.
Frame: A solid skeleton of strong timber.
Joined: Solid joiners' work using mortise-and-tenon joints.

Conversation seat   Two joined seats, facing opposite ways.

Pine chiffonier, showing appropriate signs of wear at the base, round the drawers, on the decoration and on the top. Probably Victorian.

Country furniture   Two meanings: cottage-type furniture of local plain woods – Windsor chair the most famous example; alternatively, copies of fashionable styles made in the country of local plain wood, without veneer or inlay, often simplifying the model but retaining the true spirit of its design.

Court cupboard   Two- or three-tiered display cupboard with heavily carved pillars: forerunner of both dresser and sideboard.

Credenza   Credence table, originally used for Holy Communion, later small cupboard on legs.

Crest-rail   The top rail of the back of a chair.

Cross-banding   see **Banding**

Cylinder desk   Roll-top desk, originally with one solid curved sliding top, not the later Victorian slatted construction.

Davenport   Small desk with slant or piano top and side-drawers.

Deal   Softwood.

Decoration   see illustrations, right.

Demi-lune   Half-moon shaped.

Desk   see **Bonheur du jour, Carlton House, Cylinder, Davenport, Knee-hole, Pedestal**

Distressed   Trade term for damaged surface; originally described badly cut veneer.

Dovetail   Joint in which fan-shaped wedge fits into corresponding wedge-shaped slot at right angles; through-dovetails with tail-ends projecting from 1600, lap-dovetails which do not penetrate drawer-front from late 17th century.

Draw table   Table with leaves that draw

Decoration

acanthus

anthemion

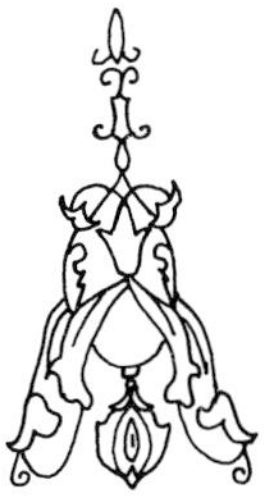

arabesque

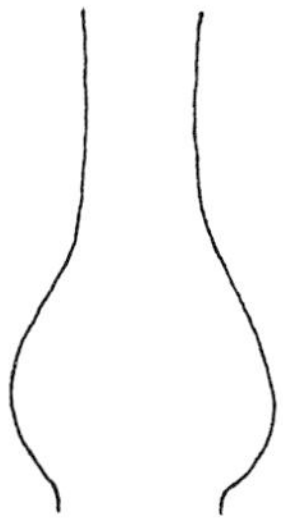

baluster

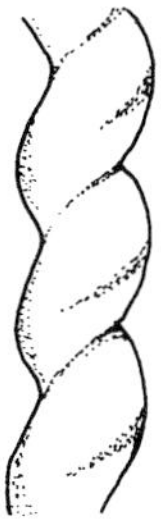

barleysugar

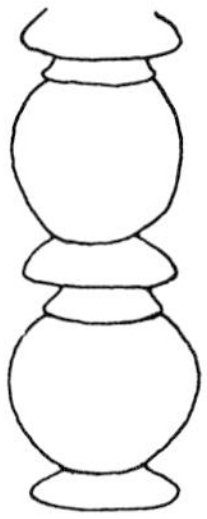

bobbin and reel

corinthian

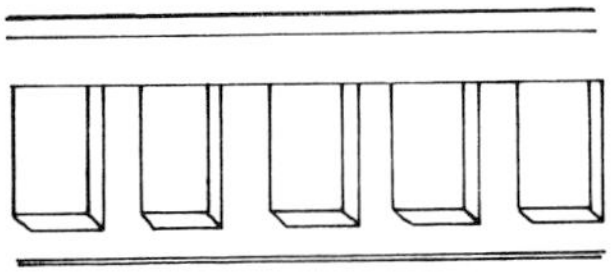

dentil

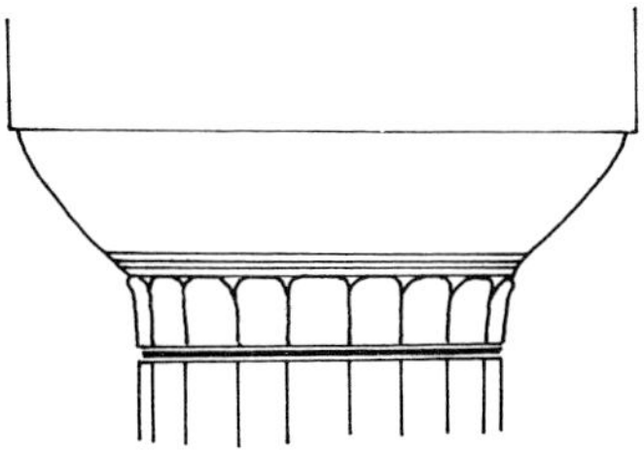

doric

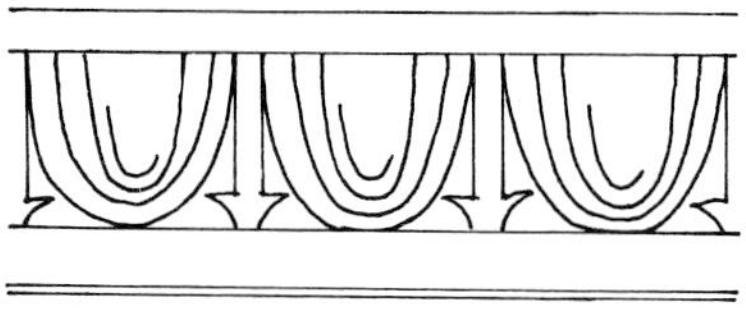

egg and dart

fluting

festoon/swag

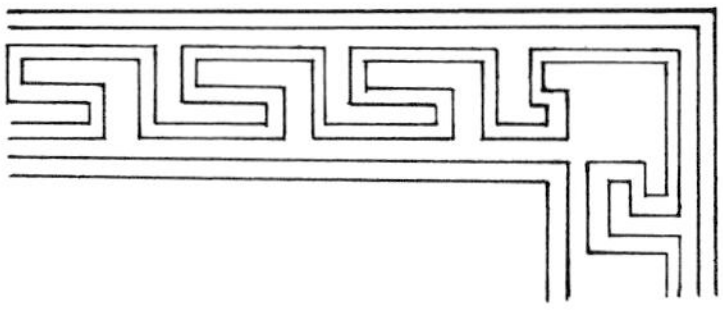

fret/Greek key

gadrooning

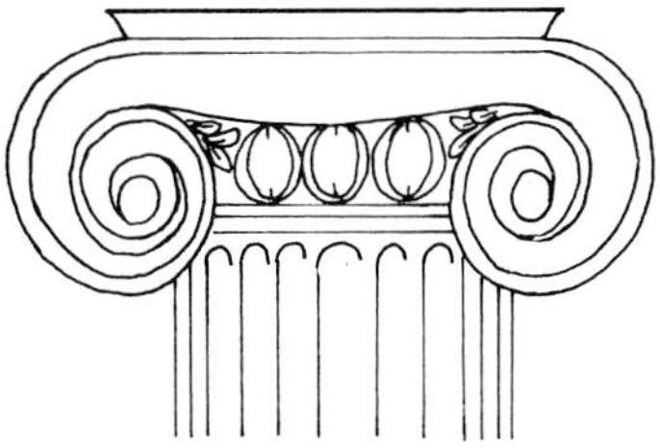

ionic

continued

Decoration *continued*

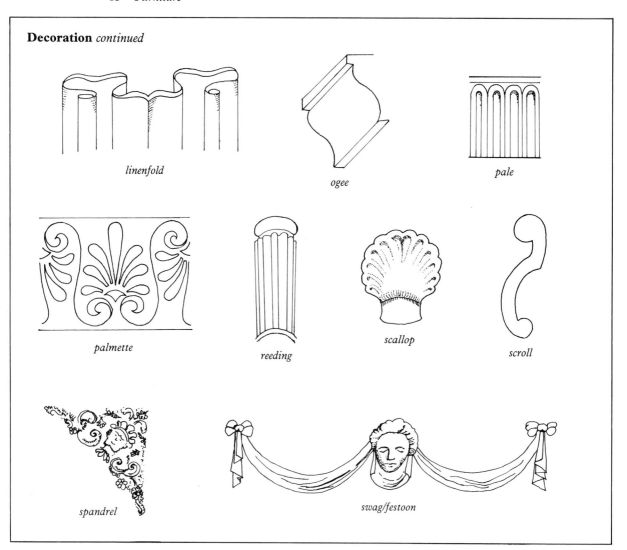

linenfold

ogee

pale

palmette

reeding

scallop

scroll

spandrel

swag/festoon

out from under the central section and are supported on their integral slides.

Drop front   see **Fall-front**

Drop handle   Brass tear-drop or pear-shaped handle hanging from backplate; late 17th century, much copied.

Drop leaf   Any table with hinged supported leaves.

Drum table   Round-topped table on centre pedestal with drawers in the frieze.

Dumb waiter   Circular two- or three-

tiered table on centre pillar with tripod legs; also a revolving drum-shaped stand for use in centre of dining table.

Egg and dart   see **Decoration**

Envelope table   Table with top which opens out from centre from small square to larger square.

Escritoire   Secrétaire; desk with vertical fall-front, as opposed to sloping desk top; made both with cabinet above and as desk, particularly in the 18th century.

Escutcheon   Originally shield-shaped

plate round keyhole; term used for all keyhole plates.

Etagère see **Whatnot**

Fall-front vertical flap to desk, opening outwards on hinges to horizontal surface, often supported by slides.

Feather banding see **Banding**

Feet see illustration below for some common kinds.

Fielded panel Opposite to coffered; with the central panel raised and bevelled.

Finial Decorative knob.

Fluting Concave grooves resembling those found on classical columns; the opposite of reeding.

Frame see **Construction**

Frieze Decorative border below cabinet cornice, table top etc.

Gate-leg Table with drop leaves supported on hinged swinging legs; usually oval or round with flaps up.

Harlequin A set of similar but not matching items: chairs, glasses, china etc.

Hinges
H-hinge: surface-mounted hinge on cupboards, cabinets, shaped like an H.
Rule: commonest kind of hinge for table-flaps etc. fixed to the concealed edges and invisible on surfaces.
Strap: long horizontal iron or steel basic hinge on face of doors to cupboards, often elaborately ornamental; typically 16th, 17th centuries.

Hutch table Cupboard with top which hinges down to form table.

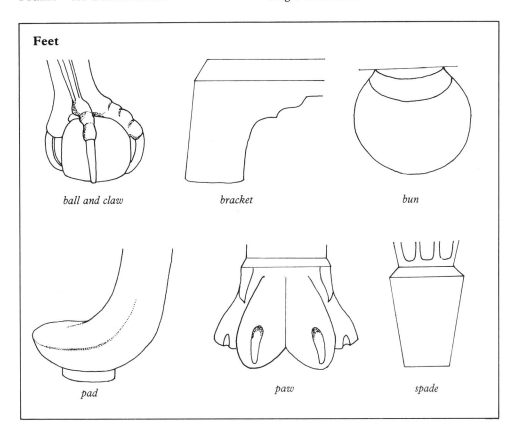

Feet

ball and claw   *bracket*   *bun*

pad   *paw*   *spade*

Japanning layers of varnish applied to form rich glossy surface, similar to but not identical with lacquering, which it imitated.

Knee-hole desk Desk with horizontal top and central recess to take the knees of the writer.

Knife box Veneered box with slots to take knives, sloping top for graduated sizes inside; from the 18th century onward.

Lap dovetail see **Dovetail**

Ladder back see **Chairbacks**

Legs see illustrations below.

Linenfold see **Decoration**

Linen press Old term for clothes cupboard.

Lip moulding Similar to **Cockbeading**

Loo table Tip-top table used for 'loo', a Victorian card game.

Lowboy Small toilet or dressing table without mirror (boy = *bois*, wood).

Lyre back see **Chairbacks**

Marquetry Inlaid veneers in coloured woods, when the veneer is cut and fitted together in decorative motifs.

Marriage A piece of furniture made up from two or more parts of other pieces.

Military chest The most commonly known piece of **Campaign furniture.**

Monopodium Table supported on single central pillar.

Mule chest Recent term for wooden chest with one or two drawers in base: forerunner of chest-of-drawers.

Ormolu Cast brass decoration gilded to protect it from tarnishing.

Ottoman Most commonly a backless box with upholstered seat.

Over-stuffed (stuffed over) Upholstered seat secured on the outside of the chair frame.

Oyster veneer Veneer cut from knotty wood; the knots show as elaborate irregular rings resembling oyster shells in their shape.

Pad foot See **Feet**

Parquetry Veneer cut in geometrical shapes.

Patina Sheen or bloom on old furniture, built up through years of polishing and use.

Pedestal Desk or sideboard supported by separate pedestals or plinths at each end, usually containing drawers or cupboards.

Pegged see **Construction.**

Pembroke table Small light table with flaps, small drawer beneath top, usually squarish but sometimes oval; from 1750s.

Piano top Curved top shaped like the cover of a piano keyboard.

Legs

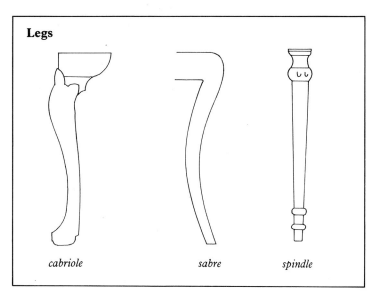

cabriole   *sabre*   *spindle*

Piecrust Frilled edging to small pieces of furniture, usually tripod tables.

Pier table Table designed to be placed between two windows; often made in pairs.

Pillar-and-claw Tables, from 18th century, supported on central column ending in three splayed feet.

Prie-dieu Prayer chair: chair with very low seat and very tall padded back, usually over-stuffed; crest rail padded too.

Provenance History of a piece of furniture, therefore proof of its authenticity.

Quartetto tables Nest of three or four small tables made for drawing rooms from the end of the 18th century.

Rail The struts of a chair, e.g. seat rails: the front, side and back members of chair seats; also back rails. See illustration page 18.

Reading chair Chair with seat shaped for man to sit astride facing the back, sometimes with leather-padded curved back to rest the arms on and with a small ledge for book.

Reel see **Decoration**

Refectory table Long narrow table with solid stretchers which almost touch floor.

Rococo From French *Rocaille* = rock and shell; light, fanciful asymmetric decoration in vogue during early–middle 18th century; can best be seen in English form in Chippendale mirrors.

Rope twist Cable twist to chair backs and uprights; in celebration of the Battle of Trafalgar, 1805.

Rout chair, rout stool Light chair or long narrow stool, usually with caned seat, painted or gilded, for occasional use during routs or balls.

Sabre leg see **Legs**

Saddle seat Seat shaped with ridge to prevent the sitter sliding forwards; usual on Windsor chairs.

Secrétaire Fall-fronted desk with flap dropping down to rest on two pull-out supports, or held by curved brass hinges; forerunner of slant-topped desk.

Serpentine S-shaped.

Shield back see **Chairbacks**

Shoe Brass casing, usually paw foot design, with small brass castors, fitted to pillar-and-claw tripod legs.

Shoe-piece Separate, often shaped, slot-piece to house bottom of back splat on chairs, made separately and attached to back seat rail through 18th century; in one piece with seat rail on reproductions.

Smoker's Bow Variation on original Windsor chair, but with low hooped back in one piece with arms.

Spider join Matching concave and convex mitred edges, used in particular for hair-crack joins of gate-leg and flap tables, often continued right round edges.

Splat Piece of a chair, often decorated, connecting the back seat rail with the top or crest rail.

Spoon back see **Chairbacks**

Squab seat Loose padded cushion, originally fitting into depression in chair seat.

Stick back see **Chairbacks**

Stretcher Horizontal support between legs, used to strengthen construction and/or as foot rail.

Stringing Narrow inlaid strips of wood

(brass much used in Regency), sometimes chequered.

Sutherland table Narrow space-saving gate-leg table with deep flaps; from 1860s.

Swash-turned see **Barleysugar twist**

Tallboy Double chest-of-drawers, the upper one slightly narrower than the lower; made from 1700s (boy = *bois*, wood).

Tambour Roll-top or roll-front.

Tantalus frame for two or three square-sided decanters with bar to lock them up; Victorian.

Teapoy Originally a small tripod table in Georgian period; by Regency days applied to small tea-chest on tripod stand.

Tongue and groove Joint for two planks, one with groove, the other with shaped ridge, with the grain.

Trafalgar motif see **Rope twist**

Tunbridge ware Form of veneering in which different woods are bunched together and cut to show the endgrain; these small sections of variegated veneer are then applied to small wooden objects in highly intricate patterns.

Twist turned see **Barleysugar twist**

Wellington chest Tall narrow chest-of-drawers with hinged flap to prevent drawers from falling open in transit; originally a piece of **Campaign furniture.**

Welsh dresser Term used loosely for any kind of oak dresser. Properly there are three variations in dresser design native to Wales just as there are local variants in other parts of Britain.

Whatnot Etagère; small stand with several shelves or levels for displaying ornaments.

Wheelback see **Chairbacks**

Wine cooler Lead- or zinc-lined container to keep wine bottles cool; often in brass-bound mahogany from late 18th century; sarcophagus-shaped in early 19th century; zinc-lined only from early 19th century.

Writing slope Originally a box with sloping front to stand on table; with its own stand (forerunner of the desk) from late 17th century; portable 'lap desks' from 18th century often folding into brass-bound box; revived in many variations in Victorian period.

X-frame Two curved, often carved X-shaped frames for back and front legs of chair; seat, often leather, slung from side-rails joining the two back and front pieces; commonly associated with Carolean and Cromwellian periods.

X-stretcher X-shaped stretcher to chairs, stands for chests, often with central finial.

Further Reading

Joseph Aronson, *The Encyclopaedia of Furniture*, London, 1966

Therle Hughes, *The Country Life Collector's Pocket Book of Furniture*, London, 1968

Geoffrey Wills, *English Furniture 1760–1900*, London, 1969

Elizabeth Aslin, *19th Century English Furniture*, London, 1962

Nancy A. Smith, *Old Furniture: Understanding the Craftsman's Art*, New York, 1975

Glass
Up to £400

Ale glass of standard
form engraved with
hops and barley; folded
foot and plain stem,
c. 1740.

Introduction

Dating and Authenticity

The dating of drinking glasses by identification of certain features such as stem and bowl shape, knop shape and position, or certain types of decoration such as air twist or engraving can be hazardous. Although general guidelines can be given there are numerous variations which bear witness to the individuality of the craftsman who made the piece. Weight, colour and workmanship are the best criteria for identification, but of course one needs to have some experience in order to be able to make the comparisons which indicate 'fine workmanship', 'good colour'.

There was a great deal of persuasive copying by the Victorians of 17th- and 18th-century pieces and, of course, copying continues today. Jacobite commemoratives, for example, with their characteristic and beautiful decorations of roses and legends extolling the Stuart cause are much sought after and expensive. Many originally plain 18th-century glasses were engraved with Jacobite motifs and passed off as authentic. It is very difficult for anyone other than an expert to spot this sort of clever doctoring.

The pontil mark is also taken as an irrefutable dating mark. Up to 1750 the pontil, an essential part of the making of drinking glasses, was left unground. It was not part of the piece being blown but was later attached to the blown but still molten piece while the mouth of the glass was cut and smoothed. In order that the uneven break point of the pontil would not affect the stability of the glass a raised foot was formed by folding or doming the foot in order to contain the pontil. Between 1750 and 1830 there was a tendency to grind off the jagged pontil of finer pieces

while leaving lower-grade glasses unsmoothed in order to save production time and costs. With the introduction of blown moulded glass in about 1830 the pontil was again left unground, especially on copies of older styles. As the 19th century progressed most glasses lost their pontil mark. As such an obvious sign of age it is not surprising that the pontil has been used by many copyists in a misleading manner.

Wetting the rim of a glass and rubbing one's finger around it to make a musical note is no more a reliable test of 'good' glass than 'pinging' the rim with a finger-nail. Genuine crystal, heavy with lead (24% in 'half lead' and 30% in 'full lead' crystal glass), will make a fine, clear sound but so will a lot of non-crystal glass because the frequency depends, to a great extent, on the shape of the bowl. Even the common glass found in pubs can sound melodious.

Historical Background

English glass, and more specifically the drinking glass, owes its history and development as much to politics as to design and invention. In 1575 Elizabeth I granted a patent to the expatriate Venetian, Jacopo Verzelini, to make glass which would compete with the imported Murano drinking glasses which, hitherto, had dominated the market. George Ravenscroft (1618–81) was the first man to come up with a formula for making 'flint glass' of 'glass or lead'. His experiments at the Savoy, by the Strand in London in the early 1670s, and later at Henley-on-Thames as the offical glassmaker to the well established Glass-Sellers Company of London, resulted in English glass of a brilliance and hardness which quickly halted foreign imports. Once Ravenscroft's license had run out glass houses all over Britain began to make glass to his formula and quickly the old soda glass, with its characteristic bubbles and imperfections, was superseded.

Wine bottles in dark green or brown glass were made in England from about 1650 onwards. The coloured glass was partly the result of impurities in the raw 'metal' and partly because it was found that wine kept better if protected from the light. With the arrival of port wine in England as a result of the Methuen Treaty of 1703, which favoured Portuguese wine over French with 20% less duty, the shape of decanters changed and in order to keep port in good condition, stoppers had to be airtight. Unlike claret, which was often cloudy, port was a deep ruby colour which merited clear glass instead of dark-coloured bottles.

In Bristol, blue 'zaffre' or cobalt from Saxony was added to glass, thus producing the famous 'Bristol Blue', though Bristol was by no means the only place to make blue glass. Stourbridge also made it, as well as many other glass houses all over the West Country and the West Midlands. With the introduction of the cut Silesian stem from Germany around 1714, English glassmakers began to perfect the art of glass-cutting and faceting which reached its height in the luxuriously heavy glassware so typical of the Georgian period.

The swingeing tax on glass of 20% by weight which was imposed in 1745 proved to be both a blow and a stimulus to the British glass industry. The quality of glass was lowered because of the quantities of 'cullet' – scrap glass – added to the melting pots. Engraving and enamelling took the place of cutting for decorative purposes, since the glass could be thinner and lighter. Coloured glass, easily obtainable from the bottle houses and exempt from tax, was used for wine glasses and tableware, and flat-cutting was introduced to glasses as well as airtwist and colour-twist stems.

The Irish glass houses, hitherto a small and unremarkable industry mainly making tableware for the wealthy Anglo-Irish, now assumed an enormous importance, for Irish glass was free of tax. From the 1760s Irish glass became the synonym for heavy, deep-cut glassware of all kinds. By the 1780s Waterford and Dublin were paramount. Perhaps their most famous creations were the cascades of pendants, peardrops, icicles and fingers of cut glass – Waterford and Dublin chandeliers. The production of Irish glass continued in all its magnificence until 1825 when the Irish imposed their own tax on glass.

The production of English enamelled glass also petered out after a heavy tax was imposed on it in 1777. Yet again, though, the glassmakers found a way round the restrictions by combining splash-enamel with coloured glass, producing the highly distinctive Nailsea-type glass full of milky swirls and patterns, first made at the enterprising Nailsea glass houses near Bristol and then throughout the country as 'novelty' and 'fancy' glass became more and more popular.

The glass excise tax was finally removed in 1845, freeing the manufacturers from control and the designers from limitation. As with every other branch of antiques, the Victorian era is a mixture of the grandest and the worst. The Royal Pavilion inspired richness and decadent 'good taste' and a mass of cheap gimcrack copies of practically every style and period. In the field of glass, taste and fashion pursued two very different paths: the mass-produced products of the new industrial techniques, and the fine craft-made objects which drew their inspiration from the purity of the Arts and Crafts Movement, William Morris and John Ruskin.

British glassmakers and the British public in general were a conservative bunch, and though there was a rather vulgarized British version of Art Nouveau, most of it was imported from France, Austria and Bohemia. Yet one English glassmaker, Thomas Webb, was the inventor of one of Art Nouveau's most recognizable characteristics: the curiously metallic finish, originally known as Webb's Bronze, which had been inspired by the discoveries of chemically changed fragments of glass in the archaeological expeditions of the day.

Despite Ruskin's condemnation, cut glass not only survived but flourished at the end of the 19th century. 'Rock crystal cutting' had a tremendous vogue in the 1880s and 90s. With the inexorable march of progress, machines took over from craftsmen and by Edwardian days, slice-cut glass was monotonously decorated with deep daffodil-leaf shaped cuts in designs that were as mechanical as the machines which made them.

Care and restoration

Care

Carefulness is synonymous with care when dealing with glass. Glass is at its most vulnerable when it is being washed – not because of hot water (if it does not hurt your hand it will not hurt glass) but because of putting glass down clumsily or drying it carelessly. Many good drinking glasses have ended their days being washed up after a good evening's drinking. Rinse them after washing and put them on a drying rack or on a towel – never straight on to a hard surface. Do not economize on time by piling them higgledy-piggledy with plates and pans. Wash and dry them first.

Drying is important, as damp can spoil glass. A whitish cloudiness in glass is usually the result of not drying it properly or of storing it in a damp place. There is nothing that can be done, as the stain is the result of a chemical change in the glass itself.

Some stains however can be removed. Wine stains and stains in glass flower holders can be removed with a solution of one part nitric or sulphuric acid (from the chemist) to 20 parts water; use rubber gloves and rinse the glass very thoroughly. What appear to be cloudy stains at the bottom of old decanters can sometimes be loosened with a weak solution of domestic bleach.

Stoppers stuck in necks can be removed in one of two ways. First hold the neck and stopper in hand-hot water for a minute or so; different rates of expansion may loosen the stopper. If this does not work, mix glycerine (from the chemist) and methylated spirits in approximately equal parts, pour the mixture round the stopper and leave overnight.

Store glass in as dry conditions as possible. Wrapping it in newspaper is not a good idea as newspaper attracts damp.

Restoration

It is possible to repair broken glass after a fashion, but on the whole the pieces should go in the bin. If however you are very fond of the object and wish to keep it at all costs, epoxy resin is the normal answer, provided that it will dry and stay clear. You will have to resign yourself to having lost the value of the piece and you will probably not be able to use it again without being conscious of the repair.

When glass breaks it has smooth edges to which adhesives do not bond as easily as to rough surfaces. It is therefore necessary to support the piece perfectly while the adhesive works – you cannot simply push the pieces together and hold them for ten minutes.

If you are repairing a broken bowl use adhesive tape to hold the pieces in place while the resin sets. Drinking glasses can be treated the same way if the break is in the bowl, but if it is in the stem you will need to build a Plasticine cradle to support the glass until the adhesive has gone hard. Stems of very special pieces can be joined with glass dowels, but this is a difficult and highly professional job.

The old way of repairing broken glass was with white of egg; it will not stand up to use or hot water, but it dries clear and holds.

Glass is occasionally ground down to eliminate a chip in a rim or foot – this accounts for some of the eccentric shapes one occasionally sees. Grinding down is to be counted an alteration (lowering the value), not a repair.

Do not buy cracked or chipped glass. Be particularly careful, when buying decanters, that the rim has not been ground to eliminate small chips. Check too that the stopper matches and is a correct fit.

Periods and Styles

Glass dating from the 17th century is not only rare but very expensive too. We therefore start with the earliest 18th-century styles, though some of these are almost identical to those of the end of the 17th century.

Period: 1685–1714 – William & Mary, Queen Anne

Influences: Dutch, French, Huguenot. Glass tax of 20% weight levied 1695–98. Treaty of Utrecht 1713 permitted import of German glass. Glassmaking centres at Bristol, Stafford, Stourbridge, Newcastle, King's Lynn, Henley and London. More robust wheel-engraving used to fine effect on stronger, thicker English glass for commemoratives, royal and loyal.

Drinking glasses: Change in drinking habits as a result of the Methuen Treaty of 1703, allowing Portuguese wines into England at 20% less duty than French wines. Small heavy balusters, wine glasses with triple-ringed knop, plain knop, mushroom, cylinder and collar. Spiral-ribbed bowls ('wrythen'), multi-knopped and inverted baluster. King's Lynn peculiarity: ribbed rings and knops. Brief use of coloured glass, exempt from tax, for tableware. Bristol making blue glass from imported 'zaffre' (cobalt oxide) from Saxony.

Wine bottles, decanters: Distinction between claret jugs with handle, lip, cork, and clear-glass port decanters to show deep ruby-coloured wine. Wine bottles dark green to exclude light made in vast quantities. In 1695 it was computed that 240,000 dozens of bottles were made in England every year. Decanter jugs from 1685.

Other table, glassware: Beakers, fluted ales, tall flower holders, vases, tall small-bowled cordial glasses, bowls, dishes in silver shapes, applied decoration, stringing, punch bowls, stirrers, flattened cup-shaped tazzas or salvers, small finger bowls with folded rims, candlesticks in metal baluster shapes, taper sticks, plain dome-footed two- and four-arm standing candelabra, water jugs, ewers. Open lattice-work baskets, bowls, rims to plates, similar to salt-glaze patterns, often attributed to Bristol because of sapphire-blue edge.

Period: 1714–27–George I

Influences: 'German George' and introduction of Silesian stem. London Distillers' monopoly broken on sale of spirits and wines. Establishment of Newcastle-upon-Tyne as prime centre for wine glassmaking. Increased use of wheel-engraving, Newcastle glasses sent to Netherlands for diamond-point engraving.

Drinking glasses: Principal design change with introduction of four-sided pedestal-stemmed Silesian pattern. Widespread drinking of cheap spirits: sturdy 'tots', 'drams'. Tavern glasses and 'firing glasses' for rapping on tables at political meetings and clubs. Ale glasses plain-stemmed, trumpet-shaped, often engraved with hops, barley. 'Deceptive' glasses with thick glass at base of bowl for holding very small quantity of liquor. Tumblers with thick bases, broad mouths, tall-stemmed small-bowled cordial glasses for 'champaign' – still red wine, not sparkling white. Light balusters from 1724, particularly from Newcastle, centre for wine glass trade, many glasses of the period being called 'Newcastle glasses'. Distinctive for tall baluster stems, thin bowls, very clear with high surface brilliance. Goblets, rummers with solid stems and broad footed for drinking hot rum and beer.

Wine bottles, decanters: Shouldered shape for wine bottles. Claret jugs with glass stoppers, port decanters with almost air-tight ground stoppers for better storage, many without handles.

Other table glassware: Sweetmeat glasses with Silesian stem, hexagonal, octagonal, popular over next 45 years. Candlesticks with variation on Silesian stem and wider drip pans. Jelly glasses, custard glasses with tall bowls on flat feet, no stems, one or two handles. Tazzas, fruit and punch bowls, small cream jugs, milk jugs, ewers, water jugs.

Period: 1727–45 – Early Georgian

Influences: Classical, Adam brothers, some Jacobite, some Continental. Government regulations on spirit, alcohol measures 1736. Silesian stem shape encourages use of stem faceting. Air twists from 1740.

Drinking glasses: Light baluster glasses made in sections: bowl, stem and foot. Feet often double-thick, sometimes cut, sometimes scalloped or 'sewn', sometimes domed. Folded foot rarer than in earlier 18th century. Trumpet bowls, plain bowls, often with ridged foot, made in such quantitites they were sold by weight. Characteristic bowl-shapes: round funnel, ogee, cup, drawn and tapered, lipped cup (rare) and double ogee. Engraved festoon ornament echoing Adam designs. Cut stems increasingly fashionable: elongated diamond, close-scale faceting and grooving. Sometimes 'rose' continued to base of bowl as fluting to make pattern from inside bowl. Air-twists from 1740, at first with drawn bowl and air twist often not quite reaching base of bowl. Twists: mercurial, corkscrew, coil, silver rope. Also variations such as 'wrythen' or spiral grooves on outside of stem, similar to Venetian. 'Amen' glasses engraved with crown and Stuart legend, etc.

Wine bottles, decanters: Wine bottles with squarer shoulders and straighter necks. Plain

Early 19th-century fluted half ale glass.

glass decanters, mallet- or club-shaped, sometimes faceted, some with bullseye stoppers, all with ground glass close-fitting stoppers. Engraving themes: festoons, swags, floral, bird, butterfly, landscape, sporting.

Other table, glassware: Sweetmeat glasses, pedestal bowls with cut 'Vandyke' rims, serrated, looped, toothed. Small custard glasses, jelly or syllabub glasses, circular stands with galleries to hold fruit in pyramid with sweetmeat glass at top. Centrepieces, snake arms, baskets, cut-glass 'rose' bowls, plain or flat-cut cream jugs, water jugs, candle and taper sticks. Cut-glass designs: shallow flat diamonds, hexagons, vertical fluting, slice-cutting. From Bristol, imitation of soft-paste porcelain in opaque white glass for candlesticks, tea caddies, oriental-shaped flower holders, spill holders.

Period: 1745–60
– Mid-Georgian

Influences: Jacobite Rebellion 1745. Brierley Hill Glassworks opened 1740, at Stourbridge. William Beilby, glass enameller at Durham, then Newcastle. Glass excise duty imposed 1745. Chippendale's *Directory* 1754. Lighter weight glass to cut payment of tax, increasing use of 'cullet' or waste broken glass, less lead content. Growing use of green, blue bottle glass (exempt from tax) for tableware. Ruby red introduced in 1754.

Drinking glasses: Wine glasses with opaque spiral twists, mixed air and opaque, seldom with domed foot, nearly always folded. Standard bowl patterns: tapering or funnel, round funnel, bell, rectangular bell, bucket, waisted bucket, lipped bucket, ogee, double ogee, ovoid, trumpet, rounded or cup-shape, thistle, hexagonal, octagonal. Jacobite themes of rose and one or two buds, oak leaf, oak tree, star, thistle, compass, Bonnie Prince Charlie, many Latin tags such as 'Fiat', 'Audentior ibo', 'Reverescit', 'Redeat', etc. Jacobite loyalists' toasting glasses incriminating, hence symbols hidden beneath foot or in floral designs. From 1750s green glass for wines, blue for cans (tankards).

Wine bottles, decanters: Wine bottles more elongated, mallet-shaped. Decanter stoppers hollow, domed, with ribbed tops, button finial to 1750, spire-cut from 1750s. Label decanters from 1755 with vine, grape, fruit decoration round engraved 'Port', 'Marsala', etc. Engraving themes: hunting, sporting, landscape, birds, floral, classical buildings, architectural, masonic, vine leaf, hops, barley. Bristol blue-glass decanters usually half-pint size for cordials and other strong spirits.

Other table, glassware: Punch bowls, toddy lifters, ladles, tazzas with flattened rim, hollow stem and domed foot. From 1750s salt cellars, dishes, plates, bowls, basins, cruets, sugar casters, 'lining plates' for delicate porcelain. Water glasses, finger bowls from 1750s tumbler-shaped, straight-sided. Epergnes with snake-arms holding baskets, candle-holders. Candlesticks with air-twist stems, sweetmeat dishes with bucket-bowls, air-twist stems known as 'Master', 'Orange' or 'Captain' glasses. Sweetmeats with flat bowls, Vandyke or saw-cut edges, from 1760, sets of cruet bottles in stands, mustards, salts following boat-shaped silver designs. Ceiling chandeliers in metal shapes with flat cutting to arms and spheres.

Period: 1760–1800 – Late Georgian

Influences: Classical, Adam, Hepplewhite, Sheraton. Development of Irish glass houses outside jurisdiction of English excise tax: Dublin 1764, Belfast (Benjamin Edwards) 1776, Waterford (George & William Penrose) 1783. William Edkins, glass enameller at Bristol, Beilby family at Newcastle. Nailsea glass houses opened 1788. Tax on enamelled glass 1777. This period marks the height of English glassware, decorations, cutting, imaginative use for lighting, architectural detail and decoration. Decline of Bristol with tax on elegantly decorated enamelled ware.

Drinking glasses: Bowl shapes unchanged, but feet ground flat without pontil for most good glassware. Colour twists: combined transparent blue, pink or turquoise and air-twist, then opaque and colour-mixed twist. From 1770s cut and faceted stems. Fine green glass for wines, usually with baluster stem, some air-twist, Silesian cut. Champagne glasses deep with folded rim to bowl. Other air-twists: mercurial, corkscrew, coil. Enamelled heraldic, armorial, full colour or white by Beilby.

Wine bottles, decanters: Recognizably bottle-shaped bottles with almost straight sides and short necks. Decanters with diameter of base increased, drum-shaped, squared, or gently sloping shoulders, short necks, two to four neck-rings, flared mouths. Elaborate cutting for best quality, plain-shaped labelled decanters, also in sets, coloured glass with silver frames like cruet stands. Bristol blue labelled, decorated with gilding by William Edkins. Cutting: shallow flat diamonds, hex-

Left: Clear glass triple ringed mallet-shaped decanter, c. 1800, delicately engraved with grapes and birds around the sides; bullseye stopper.
Right: Tapered clear glass club-shaped decanter with bevelled stopper, c. 1790.

stands, coloured, labelled or flute cut. Water glasses, finger bowls with curved sides. Bristol blue straight-sided, often with Greek key patterns. Wine-glass coolers, similar to finger bowls with one or two notches in rim to hold inverted stems of wine glasses. Flat-bowled sweetmeat dishes closely resembling today's champagne glasses, but many of them with serrated, decorated or saw-cut rims. From 1770 flat-cut geometric, diamond, with serrated, fan-cut, scalloped and Vandyke rims to boat-shaped fruit bowls, salts, sweetmeat and sugar bowls. Blue glass rolling pins, spirit flasks from Bristol.

Nailsea: Ingeniously using dark greens, browns, 'blacks' of bottle-glass free of tax, decorated, embellished with white splash-enamel, trailing, crinkling for purely ornamental glass, inspired by 'friggers' or small curiosities made for extra money by glass-blowers, sold to visitors. Rolling pins in coloured stripes, flask-shaped bottles, mugs, jugs, tumblers, jars, walking sticks, gemmel flasks, always with decoration in slight relief. Similar, less refined wares also made at Warrington and Midlands without relief effect. Dark green, blue 'witch balls' for superstitious sailors, gaudy polychromatic or blue splashed white for visitors.

Irish glass, Waterford glass: With the doubling of the glass tax in 1776 and the granting of free trade to Ireland in 1780, tremendous incentive for English glassmakers to set up business in tax-free potential export country. Most Irish glass, including Waterford, made to old Stourbridge formula and designs from England. Distinguished by excellence of workmanship, precision in cutting, particularly broad panels of miniature diamonds covering entire piece. Classical forms, Greek urns, boat shapes, turn-over rims to pedestalled fruit bowls, celery vases. Compared to contemporary English glass with lower lead content and lighter weight, Irish glass is heavier, richer, more brilliant; the cutting more profuse and precise. Today the long-held opinion that Waterford has a smoky metallic blue colour has largely been discounted, but nevertheless some pieces of undoubted provenance have blue-grey tinge.

agons, vertical flutes or slice-cutting, elongated diamond, close-scale facets, strawberry, hobnail. Ships' decanters ('Rodneys' for example) from 1780 with wide flattened bases and bodies. Spire-cut stoppers, partially cut flattened spheres, plain upright discs.

Lighting: High-quality cut glass stimulated idea of lustres, pendants, drops, prisms to increase reflection and refraction. Moulded glass candlesticks with wide drip pans hung with polished icicles, shallow-cut buttons, pear-shaped lustres. Table candelabra with glass arms, lustres, embellishments.

Other table, glassware: Sets of cruet bottles in

Period: 1800–30 – Regency

Influences: Classical, Thomas Hope. Egyptian. Graeco-Roman. Height of popularity of cut glass, Waterford, Irish until Ireland imposed its own tax, 1825. Brighton Pavilion rococo an influence from 1817.

Drinking glasses: Cut and faceted stems, wheel-engraving to wines as well as ales, flutes and goblets. Return of the original 'roemer' shape with baluster stem as cider or beer glasses. Tumblers, beakers, considerable use of coloured glass, in particular deep blue and green, now made in many glassworks other than Bristol. Introduction of services or sets of glasses, same pattern, different sizes, with matching decanters. Square bases, hobnail cutting to large goblets, tumblers with rose-cut bases and fluted sides. Emphasis on using glass as material in its own right to add sparkle to dark woods of furniture.

Decanters: Whiskey decanters, square-shaped, often square-cut, with silver collars and faceted ball stoppers. Experiments with mixing patterns of strawberry, diamond, fluting, step-cutting on same piece. Applied neck-rings for easier grip while pouring. Rose-cut mushroom stoppers, flute-cut mallet, club shapes.

Lighting: Old methods of construction abandoned for ceiling chandeliers, now made with cascades of hanging drops, dramatic falls of close-set cut buttons, drops to conceal central shaft supporting gilt metal ring into which short, glass-embellished candle arms were set. 'Fingers' of cut crystal, diamond-shaped icicles used to great effect, following example of Royal Pavilion, Brighton. Girandoles, wall-lights, candlesticks, all dripping with lustres for refraction, glitter. Silvered witch-balls also used to great effect.

Other table, glassware: Straight-sided finger bowls with mouths slightly smaller than bases, wine coolers in plain cut glass rich dark green, amethyst, blue with gilded Greek key patterns. Complete sets of dishes, cruets, plates, urns and covers, fruit bowls on short stems with low pedestals, all heavy, deep-cut and lustrous. Decanter jugs, paperweights, scent bottles, toiletry articles, silver-mounted desk articles, rose bowls, punch bowls. Silvered glass salts, sugar bowls. Green glass 'floral' patterned solid door stops, sugar crushers, stirrers, Nailsea ornamental glass, coloured glass hand bells with clear flint-glass clappers, gemmel or twinned flasks, looped elegant decoration. Walking sticks, rolling pins, miniatures, sulphides or 'crystallo ceramics'.

Period: 1830–60 – William IV and Early Victorian

Influences: American press-moulded glass introduced to England 1825, commercially manufactured 'stained' glass, removal of excise duty 1845. Gothic, pseudo-Chinese, oriental, 'Venetian', 'Bohemian', 'Egyptian', 'Etruscan', 'Grecian' and proliferation of coloured glass.

Drinking glasses: Netherlands 'roemers' with hollow stems, prunts, copied in many sizes. Copies of 'façon de Venise' winged goblets, revival of Murano glassworks. Elegant flutes, flat cups both for champagne (now sparkling white) and 'foaming' wine. Wine glasses with coloured bowls, clear stems and feet, cranberry, green, ruby. Increasing manufacture of services, sets of glasses for individual wines, cordials and spirits. Ostentatious goblets, loving cups with trailing vine pattern, romantic themes. Cut, serrated edges to foot, return of domed foot for romantic-style goblets and glasses.

Decanters: Square-sided spirit decanters in sets of three, guarded by 'tantalus' frame with lock. Decanters with simple spire-shaped stoppers or hollow balls. Moulded square-sided square-cut decanters from 1830s. Cased glass stained over, then cut away to show clear; most popular in red. Neck rings tend to disappear. Cutting excessive, shapes more bulbous, heavier, though good-looking ships' decanters, many finely-cut Irish, in use during reign of 'Sailor Billy'. Fine pouring decanters on pedestal base with handle; embellished with delicate engraving.

Other table, glassware: As with furniture, taste extremely uneven with contrasting styles of simplicity and ostentation, excellent copies of early shapes, exuberant use of new techniques. Press-moulded glass first made in England at Newcastle 1833 and Stourbridge same year. Development slow until lifting of tax. Early English press-moulded glass excellent quality, almost as clear as true cut glass from which it was copied. Fire-polished to give crispness. Early press-moulded tumblers, goblets, glasses with pontil mark, but from 1850s bases held with claws, though pontil marks deliberately added to give authenticity to 19th-century copies of early Netherlands glass. With social changes and growing prosperity, increase in demand for glass of all sorts. Wine glasses, goblets, tumblers, sugar basins, butter dishes, coolers, salt cellars, honeypots, door and drawer knobs, domestic articles, kitchen articles. Coloured glass, cased or stained, gilding, enamelling, early machine-engraving, all much in evidence. 'Bohemian' and 'façon de Venise' both made in Birmingham. Stourbridge making 'Egyptian', 'Etruscan' and 'Grecian' and coloured. Ruby, oriental blue, chrysoprase, turquoise, black, rose, cranberry, opal-coated blue, cornelian, opal-frosted, pearl opal, mazarine blue, both plain gilded and overlaid, particularly red and brown overlaid clear. Accidental production of orangey 'carnival glass' due to imperfect staining. From 1851 injection of new ideas from Continent: black 'Etruscan' boxes, urns, opaline or milchglas, fashionable 1824–30. English 'millefiore' paperweights first made *c*. 1845, in Birmingham.

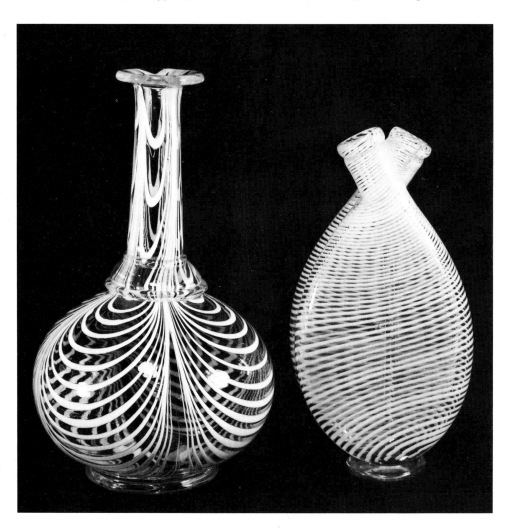

Left: Carafe of clear, colourless lead glass decorated with festoons or loops of opaque white glass common during the 19th century. Right: 'Gemmel' or double flask of clear lead glass decorated with trails of opaque white glass typical of the Nailsea style, c. 1845.

Period: 1860–1900 – Late Victorian

Influences: France, America. Lalique, Emile Gallé. 'Façon de Venise', Bohemian, archaeological discoveries, American Tiffany glass. Reaction from heavy 'static' cutting and shapes to flowing, blowing to show texture. Leaves, swirls, pale tints, copied by Powells of Whitefriars from work of Salviati at revived Murano glassworks. Squared shapes from 1870s. Pressed glassworks of Sowerby, Gateshead, largest in world by 1880s. Greeners of Sunderland, Davidsons of Gateshead also producing pressed glass in quantity. Reintroduction of soda glass for copies of high technical skill and artistry.

Drinking glasses: Many mass-produced table glasses blown-moulded in ribbed, 'wrythen' and other earlier patterns. Drinking glasses with moulded stem, foot, blown bowl, joined after being made separately. Acid-engraving from 1870s. Machine-etching same date. Straw-coloured, greenish-tinged soda glass for 'Venetian' 'façon de Venise'. Some high-quality cut, engraved flint glass.

Decanters: Pressed glass blurred shadows of cut originals, 3-set square decanters for spirits in tantalus. Surprisingly good revival of Regency square shapes, elegant decanter jugs copied from 'Elgin' jug with pouring lip, narrow neck, handle, elegant engraved body on pedestal foot. High Gothic ecclesiastical shapes for ewers, claret jugs, many silver-mounted with silver lids.

Lighting: Distinct new departure with use of paraffin for domestic lighting in 1860s. Large production of oil lamps, shades, bowls, chimneys, inventive and decorative night-light holders. 'Queen's Burmese Ware' originating in America and also made at Stourbridge for lampshades, nightlights, small vases. Proliferation of moulded glass 'lustres' on light fittings of all kinds, wall, ceiling, standing, poor version of cut crystal with little reflection and dingy sparkle. Cut glass used excessively for lustres on better-quality light fittings.

Other table, glassware: 'Queen's Ivory Ware' by Sowerby's Ellison Glassworks *c.* 1870 as

Press moulded Victorian custard cups.

imitation of the pierced, lattice-rimmed salt-glaze and Wedgwood's 'Queensware'. Less happy developments included opaque 'vaseline' green glass for pierced, lattice, basket-weave, later in translucent pale pink, and blue from 1870s. 'Pearline' glass from 1889 in blue, greeny-yellow and brown. Milk-white opaque glass for pseudo-porcelain shapes, vases, flower holders, oriental vases. Also for fine pierced plates with grape design, loving hands, dishes, 'cow' butter dishes, little baskets. Transparent coloured glass made in blue, green, amber, puce, brown, black majolica, malachite, but lacking any subtlety, except for cranberry ranging from deep ruby to pale pink, rose. Artificial iridescence and 'metalling' used with abandon during the craze for Egyptology. All manner of novelty glass in their press-moulded millions: pin trays, cigar trays, spill holders, inkwells, candle- and chambersticks, nightlight holders and covers, decorative knick-knacks, 'bonnet' glass baskets, covered butter dishes, animal shapes, commemorative plates, figures, bottles and containers. Sowerby's 'Vitro-Porcelain' *c.* 1880 with new range of opaque white domestic, kitchen and tableware, opaque white and tinted dessert plates, dishes, 'fish jugs', shell-shaped covered basins, butter dishes, cream jugs. Press-moulded butter-dish covers, biscuit jars, water jugs, carafes and tumblers. True 'Bristol blue' and 'bottle green' relegated to the pharmacy as medicine bottles. Fashion for mixing clear and frosted glass for novelties, vases, celery vases, some tableware. 1885 Thomas Webb & Sons of Stourbridge got the licence to manufacture Queen's Burmese Ware, a tinted glass ranging from rosy-pink to pale yellow, which had first been produced in America. Webb & Sons also produced American 'spangled' or 'spattered' glass (given its name by the glittering effect of mica).

Period: 1870–1920 – Art Nouveau, Fin de Siècle, Edwardian

Influences: William Morris, Lalique, John Ruskin, 'Guild of Handicrafts', Arts & Crafts Movement. Ambrose Heal, Waring & Gillow, Liberty's.

Drinking glasses: Mass market supplied by Czechoslovakia, Bohemia and mass-produced, press-moulded, blown-moulded table glass. The Aesthetic Movement returned to clear, simple shapes of early Netherlands and Murano glass in classical shapes, little or no decoration except stringing and faded soda-glass colours. Slim tankards, beakers, flutes, hock glasses on tall thin stems, 'Elgin' shapes for glasses to match decanters. Sherry sets, plain well-proportioned whiskey tumblers, thistle shapes, some with cut bulbs. Use of rock crystal cutting, deeper than engraving with clear-cut line, intaglio cutting for similar effect. Some singles, sets using combined cutting, engraving and intaglios of impressively high artistic, decorative merit.

Decanters: The same applies, with elegantly-shaped decanters, decanter jugs made in matching sherry sets, whisky sets with outstandingly pure line and shape. Some heavy, hand-made, hand-cut decanters with flat rose-cut bases, fluted necks, rose-cut stoppers and return to traditional Waterford designs.

Other table, glassware: Main idea of Art Nouveau absorbed into English Arts & Crafts Movement, harking back to 'source' material. Marbled, agate glass similar to Whieldon/Wedgwood styles for vases, jugs, ewers, decorative spire-handled glass bells, tall tulip vases, loving cups, use of thickness of glass alone to shape and underline design. At the other end of the period, opulent sets of table glasses, finger bowls, side plates, rather stilted engraving and stiff daffodil-leaf slice-cutting, wide-mouthed, heavy-based iris vases, flower vases, toilet sets, writing sets, bathroom tumblers, carafes, powder jars, scent bottles. Domestic ware, kitchen ware, ovenproof 'Pyrex' from 1915 in America, 1919 in England.

Lighting: Imported Art Nouveau shades by Liberty's for oil lamps and electric lighting. English oil-lamp shades in frosted, engraved, opaque and frilled glass. This field is the only one which Art Nouveau proper penetrated, together with Tiffany glass lamps in petal shapes, bells and flowers.

Price Guide

Wineglasses (£30–400)

Plain teardrop stem, drawn trumpet, folded foot, 7ins, *c.* 1730, £110–150.

Light baluster, bell, teardrop, knopped stem 6½ins, *c.* 1740, £170+.

Simplest Jacobite, *c.* 1745, £300–400.

Plain Newcastle with drawn trumpet bowl, 7½ins, *c.* 1750, £130–150.

Bell-shaped bowl, mercury corkscrew air-twist, domed foot, 7ins, *c.* 1750, £80–100.

Large tavern glasses with double knop, domed foot, 7ins, *c.* 1750, £100–140.

Large output of early Georgian glasses, 5ins mid-*c.* 1750–60, surviving in quantities and extremely good value at £30–40.

Mixed opaque and colour-twist, funnel and trumpets, rarer and not usually in mint condition, about £60.

Singles, pairs, late 18th-century bell-shaped with corkscrew air-twists, 6ins, also made in considerable quantities and to be found for

£85–95 a pair, less than half for singles.

Heavy 3-piece baluster tavern glasses, heavy quality, 6½ins, *c.* 1750–60, very usable and solid from £65–75.

Same size, date, waisted bucket-shape with opaque double twists, from £50–70.

Small, 4¾ins, ovoid bowl, with faceted, flute stems or twists, late 18th-century, £100–130.

Set of six early 19th-century blown-moulded, 5 ins, from *c.* 1830–50, recent appreciation to £100–130.

Set of six Edwardian 5½ins wine glasses with dolphin stems, £75–100.

Coloured wineglasses. Late 18th-century rummers in blue with prunts, 5ins, hollow stems, £60–70.
Set of six, plain green Georgian glasses, 5ins, £140–160.

Set of six, Victorian cranberry bowls, 5ins, plain stems, £60–75.

Set of six, Georgian cup-shaped bowls, ribbed stems, *c.* 1750, £240–260.

Ales, Rummers (£35–150)

Mid 18th-century ale glass with vertical fluting, double opaque twist stem, 8ins, £50–60.

Ale glass, with barley, hop engraved motif and cut stem, 6ins, *c.* 1770, £120–150.

Tall elegant ale glass, with double air-twist, round funnel-shaped bowl, *c.* 1750, £80–100.

Engraved loyal and commemorative, 'deceptives', £150 upwards.

Firing glasses, dram glasses, 4½ins, *c.* 1740, £95–105.

Thick heavy cordials, with folded foot, 5¼ins, *c.* 1730–60, £60–80.

Set of four, Victorian ale glasses, 7ins, £120–140 the set.

Plain rimmed-foot rummer, with engraved sailing ship, *c.* 1855, £120–150 (Sunderland 'nauticals' more, at over £180).

Regency capstan, cut-stem rummers, *c.* 1810,

very reasonable at around £35–60 depending on quality.

Late 18th-century nautical port glasses, 5ins, around £60–70.

Tumblers, Water Glasses (£60–180)

Wide-mouthed, engraved Jacobite motif rose and two buds, 3½ins diam., late 18th century, £150–180.

Flower-engraved finger bowl, 3¾ins diam., 18th century, £65–85.

Commemorative finger bowl, 4½ins diam., early 19th century, £60-90.

Regency gilded key pattern, 'Bristol blue' wine coolers, £160 and up. Greens, simple bowl-shaped with or without lips, at £150 but many reproductions around.

Decanters (£50–350, singles)

Bottle decanter, with cork stopper, handle, body decorated with 'nipped diamond waies' design, *c.* 1680, £350 at least.

Pair late 18th-century shouldered decanters with stoppers, £120–180.

Pair late 18th-century club-shaped decanters with mushroom stoppers, £290–320.

Set of three 'Bristol blue' decanters with cut stoppers, probably originally with silver stand, *c.* 1790–1820, £230–250 without stand. Single, green, £50–70.

Single ale carafe, jug, engraved hops and barley, *c.* 1770, £280–340.

Single mid-Georgian early lime glass decanter with hollow stopper, £75–85. More than double for pairs.

Pair of Irish decanters, three applied neck rings, mushroom stoppers, *c.* 1800, £260–290.

Late 19th-century heavy cut glass with square-cut stopper, £125–175.

Pair 19th-century imported Bohemian pinched glass with gold decoration, £95–120.

Bowls, Salvers, Tazzas (£20–240)

Pair of bowls and covers, early 19th-century, strawberry, fan cut with faceted stems, 8ins, £180–210.

Cut-glass fruit bowl, mid-19th century, with turn-over rim, detachable raised pedestal stand not mint condition, £110–150.

Mid-19th-century heavy cut-glass two-handled cup and cover, probably Irish, £185–200.

18th-century Irish cut-glass bowl with scalloped rim, square-cut pedestal base, 10ins, £100–125.

Plain tazza, with flattened rim, domed and folded foot, 10ins diam., *c.* 1790, £50–60.

18th-century jelly stand or tazza with domed and folded foot, 14ins diam., £55–65.

Victorian dish in milk glass with frilled edge, £20–35.

Late 19th-century wide-mouthed glass vase in pink overlay with cameo mark 'Webb', 6¾ins high, £210–240.

Pair Victorian cranberry glass vases, flute-shaped, frilled edge, clear glass foot, 10½ins high £210–240 pair.

Jugs, Ewers, Water Jugs (£60–400)

Pair of late Georgian claret jugs with stoppers, 13¾ins high, £265–300 the pair.

Victorian silver-mounted claret jug, engraved with scrolls, foliage, 1865, by Messrs Barnard, 11ins high, £380–400.

Mappin & Webb silver-mounted cut glass claret jug, 11ins high, 1902, £350–400.

Cut-glass ewer, with ribbed handle, pedestal foot, in Neoclassical style, 10½ins high, *c.* 1830, £200–300.

Heavy George III cut-glass water jug, 6½ins high, £75–85.

Heavy cut-glass ewer, with plain handle, decorated rim, foot, Neoclassical style, 10¼ins high, *c.* 1830, £160–190.

Nailsea baluster cream jug, with opaque white decoration, applied blue band to rim, 3½ins high, *c.* 1820, £130–160.

Stourbridge 'satin glass' ewer, in two shades of amber, 5½ins high, *c.* 1870, £60–70.

Glass terms

Acid engraving Nineteenth-century method of shallow line-engraving on glass using hydrofluoric acid.

Ale glass Drinking glass usually with deep funnel or bucket bowl, often on tall stem, decorated with hops, barley, for strong ale.

Amen glass Drinking glass *c.* 1745 with large trumpet bowl, a Jacobite engraving and the word 'Amen' beneath.

Air twist From *c.* 1740 threads of air bubbles drawn and twisted for stems of drinking glasses, later made with prepared rods or canes combining air, opaque and coloured glass. See **Stems.**

Baluster see **Stems.**

Blown-moulded Shaped, patterned vessels formed by blowing molten glass into metal mould. Widely used from the 17th century onwards for one-piece moulds, two-piece from 1800s, three-piece from 1820s. Unlike pressed glass, surface indentations are noticeable inside as well as on outer surface.

Bonnet glass Little baskets shaped like old-fashioned poke bonnets, in pressed glass from 1860s, known also as fancy glass or novelty glass.

Bowl shapes   see illustration below.

Bullseye stopper   Upright shaped disc similar in shape to a target, often crinkled, fluted towards the centre.

Burmese glass   see **Queen's Burmese Ware.**

Captain glass   Sweetmeat glass which topped elaborate pyramids of salvers and tazza of

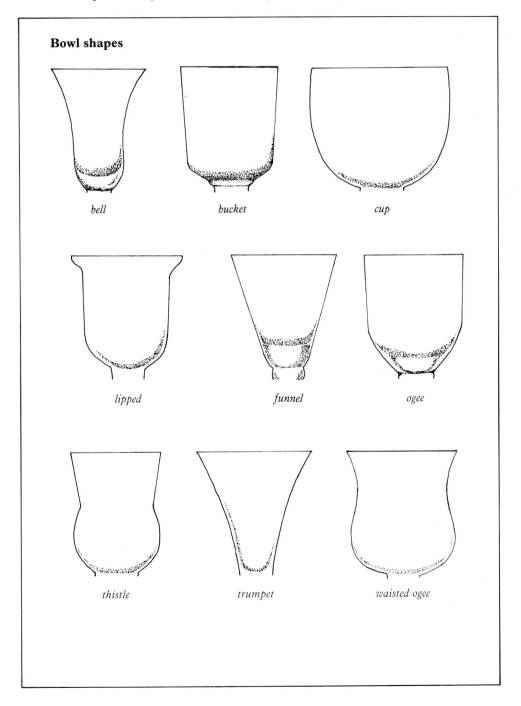

Bowl shapes

bell

bucket

cup

lipped

funnel

ogee

thistle

trumpet

waisted ogee

fruit. Known also as Orange glass, Master glass.

Cased glass From 1845 onwards in England, coloured and opaque glass overlaid and fused together, then cut away to form facets outlined in oblique stripes cut through layers. High quality 19th-century ware should not be confused with poor, coarse quality imported from Continent in 1920s and later.

Caudle cup Two-handled cup with cover and saucer, made in pairs as presentation sets for mother and child for rich warm drink. To Victorians, display pieces only.

Cordial glass Tall-stemmed glass with small bowl for strong liqueur-type drink.

Crisselling Network of fine cracks characteristic of 17th-century lead glass.

Crystallo-ceramic Crystal cameo. Patented in England 1819 by Apsley Pellat, developed at his Falcon Glassworks. Minute cameos embedded in clear flint glass.

Cullet Waste glass, scrap, broken glass, added to new meltings.

Deceptive glass Drinking glass with extra thickness in base of bowl, thus holding smaller quantity than it appears to.

Diamond point Engraving on glass using diamond 'blade' and tools. Highest craftsmanship achieved by Dutch in 17th, early 18th century, often on plain imported English glasses.

Domed foot see **Feet**.

Dram glass Heavy-footed stubby glass, often with no stem or short thick stem, holding 2oz of spirits. From 1736, after government regulations on spirit, alcohol measures.

'Elgin' shape Elegant decanter jug on

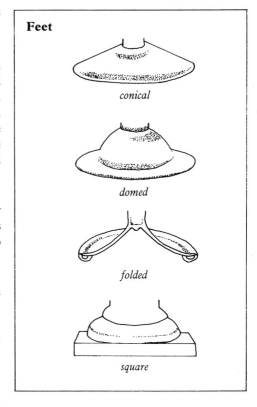

Feet

conical

domed

folded

square

classical lines inspired by the archaeological finds of the Victorian era.

Epergne Table centrepiece with elaborate arms for candleholders, sweetmeat dishes, radiating from central tiers of bowls. Also in silver, less common in glass, ceramics.

Ewer Large water jug, usually to accompany basin for washing hands.

'Façon de Venise' Venetian glass from Murano and other glass houses, straw-coloured, yellow-greenish soda glass. Typical are glass goblets with elaborate covers and winged stems. Also gilded glass, coloured glass and white-opaque. Famous from 13–17th centuries after which English clear flint glass ousted it for most purposes. Romantic revival in 1850s–60s.

Faceting Facet cutting. Shallow hollows forming diamonds, triangles, to add refraction, brilliance. Shallow from 1720–40, then more elaborate until largely superseded by deep diamond cutting from 1790s.

Fan cut   Cutting in the shape of a fan, often on scallops of rims and feet.

Firing glass   Stubby dram glass with thick heavy foot to applaud toasts by rapping on tabletop with sound resembling firing muskets.

Flint glass   see **Lead crystal.**

Flute glass   Tall drinking glass with deep conical bowl to allow sediment in cider, ale, to settle.

Folded foot   see **Feet.**

Feet   Base of stemmed drinking glass. See illustration opposite.

Frigger   End-of-day glass made up by glassworkers from odds and ends. Now used as term to cover all Victorian, Edwardian novelty glass, including Nailsea.

Gemmel   Twinned flasks (less commonly other objects) as Nailsea spirit flasks, oil-and-vinegar bottles fused back-to-back.

Girandole   Lustre-hung branched candle brackets, candlesticks, candelabra. Extremely ornate, often with mirror backing from 1750s, more functional from 1780s.

Heavy baluster   Solid knopped stems to wine glasses taking lines from candlesticks and furniture of the 17th and 18th centuries in new quicker-cooling lead glass whose properties differed from soda glass. From *c.* 1673–*c.* 1715.

Hobnail cutting   Deep cross-cut diamonds cut again into eight-pointed stars, from 1780s in heavy Irish glass, later in English after lifting of glass tax.

Intaglio cutting   Incised design.

Kick-up base   Pushed-up dome in base of bottles, decanters.

Knop   Originally the ring connecting the bowl to the stem, changing to a decorative element in the design of drinking glasses. See below for the types of knop most commonly

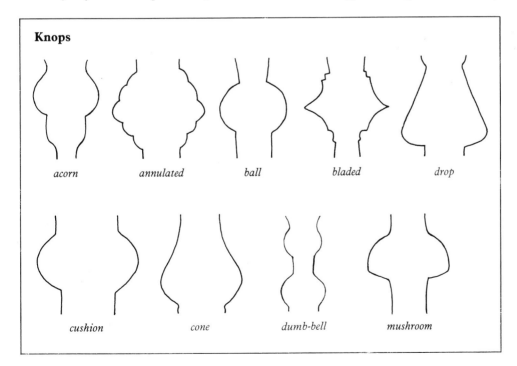

Knops

acorn   *annulated*   *ball*   *bladed*   *drop*

cushion   *cone*   *dumb-bell*   *mushroom*

found, sometimes in conjunction with each other. 'Knop' is the old spelling of 'knob'.

Latticino Technique invented, perfected, by Venetian glassmakers: lace-like threads of white or coloured glass enmeshed in clear glass, used most successfully by Nailsea at end of 18th, early 19th century as well as Sunderland, Newcastle, Stourbridge and other glassmaking centres.

Lead crystal Lead glass, flint glass. Developed by George Ravenscroft *c.* 1673 by replacing lime with lead oxide for more brilliant, stronger glass and widely used by end of 17th century.

Light baluster Refined version of heavy baluster, particularly in Newcastle glass from *c.* 1724 onwards.

Lustres Polished, cut pendant drops, icicles, beads, usually hung from chandeliers, girandoles, candelabra etc. to increase refraction and reflection.

Master glass see **Captain glass.**

Milchglas Opaque, almost white glass imitating porcelain, made in Germany and France by adding tin oxide and decorating with enamel or transfer-printing. Similar ware also made in Bristol and Stourbridge.

Milk glass Not the same as the milchglas of Germany. Practically indistinguishable from slagware or vitro-porcelain.

Moulded see **Press-moulded, Blown moulded.**

Nipped diamond waies Bands of applied glass wound in diamond pattern over body of decanter-bottle and while still molten, pinched with disc-ended pinchers into raised diamond shapes.

Opal glass Semi-opaque ornamental glass much favoured by Victorians, in white and milky colours.

Opaque glass see **Milchglas.**

Orange glass see **Captain glass.** No political connotation as an orange was often used to top pyramids of fruit, dessert.

Pontil, punty Uneven mark left on base of glass vessel where dab of glass had attached it to iron rod used to hold the glass during finishing and shaping. Ground off from 1750. Reappeared for a while in early press-moulded glass *c.* 1830 and used to advantage in fakes.

Press-moulded Pressed glass. Cheap method of making decorative functional glass, originating in USA and taken up by English manufacturers *c.* 1830. Molten glass was pressed into a patterned metal mould with a plunger, giving characteristic smooth inner surface, unlike blown-moulded glass.

Prunt Applied ornamental glass disc, often stamped with strawberry, raspberry, lion's mask, often decorating hollow stems of Netherlands glass 'roemers'.

Queen's Burmese Ware American patent for heat-tinting opaque glass coloured pale yellow to deep orangey pink with uranium or gold. Made in England for some tableware, but principally for nightlight covers, light shades, lamp shades.

Queen's Ivory Ware Opaque glass known as vitro-porcelain, also made in other colours, between 1870 and 1890 by Sowerby's Ellison Works.

Rock-crystal cutting Deep wheel engraving in lead crystal glass with pattern polished free of matt engraving finish to a brilliant clarity. From 1878, associated particularly with West Midlands.

'Rodney' decanter Type of ship's decanter with wide flat bottom, named after Admiral Lord Rodney in 1780s.

Rummer, roemer, romer Originally

Stem shapes

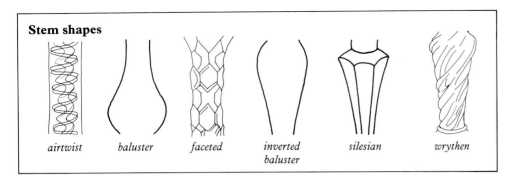

airtwist   baluster   faceted   inverted baluster   silesian   wrythen

German, Netherlands pale green drinking glass with wide hollow stem, often decorated with prunts. The roemer or romer developed into the first English round-bowled thick-stemmed 'rummers'.

Salver   Originally a flat dish with low raised edge standing on a low foot. Later simply a flat tray, usually silver, on three or four small feet.

Sconce   Bracket candlestick, i.e. wall sconce.

Sewn foot   Shape of glass foot which has been held, minutely gathered, by claw as opposed to pontil during shaping and finishing.

Ship's decanter   Flat-bottomed decanter, fashionable from 1780s. See **Rodney decanter.**

Silesian stem   Hexagonal or octagonal vertical cut stem for wine glasses introduced to English glassmakers from the beginning of Georgian period with German fashions, customs, designs imported with the Hanoverians. See **Stems.**

Slag glass   A trade name of Sowerby – the so-called vitro-porcelain which incorporated steel slag, the waste from iron furnaces, to give a purple or green mottled effect.

Slice cutting   Deep cuts tapering at one or both ends.

Soda glass   Quick-cooling fragile glass characteristic of pre-17th century European glass, superseded by English lead or flint glass (q.v.). Revived by Victorians for romantic 'façon de Venise' winged goblets, drinking glasses, etc.

Spire cut   Of decanter stoppers cut like a church spire.

Splash enamel   Opaque glass incorporated into clear or coloured glass in random decorative splashes. Typical of Nailsea and its imitators from the end of 18th century.

Stem shapes   see illustration above. The distinction between shapes and knops can at times be slight – as for example with baluster stems.

Stringing   Glass threads wound round mould to make hollow stems for Netherlands 'roemers' and for decoration in all periods. Particularly favoured by Victorians as decoration to handles and stems of glass vessels.

Tantalus   Set of three square decanters in wooden frame with locking bar.

Tazza   Similar to the original salver shape – wide shallow bowl on low foot used as table centre-piece for fruit.

Tear   A tear-shaped air-bubble trapped in the stem or base of the bowl.

Toddy glass   Similar in shape to rummers for hot toddies (rum or whisky, lemon, nutmeg, sugar, hot water) from 1770s. Also giant goblet on thick stem, often square foot, for mixing and serving toddy.

Toddy lifter Small long-necked decanter-shaped glass instrument with hole at each end, operating on pipette principle. One end immersed in bowl, filled, top hole covered with thumb to retain liquid to be released into drinking glass.

Vandyke rim Lace-edged, taken from collars of Vandyke portraits of the time.

Wheel engraving From *c.* 1730, glass engraved with pattern cut by abrasive action of revolving wheel and sand-based powders.

Wrythen Surface twisting of stem, lower part of glass bowl in swirled ribbing, faintly distorting clarity of contents thus masking cloudy wines. See **Stems.**

Zaffre Prepared cobalt, originally imported from Saxony, for colouring enamels, glass and ceramics.

Further Reading

Harold Newman, *An Illustrated Dictionary of Glass,* London, 1977

E. Barrington Haynes, *Glass Through the Ages,* London, 1970.

G. Gross-Galliner *Glass, A Guide for Collectors,* London, 1970

D. C. Davis, *English Bottles and Decanters 1650–1900,* London, 1972

Geoffrey Wills, *The Country Life Pocket Book of Glass,* London, 1966

Pottery and Porcelain
Up to £1,000

Liverpool creamware jug printed with a harvesting scene with Palemon and Lavinia depicted in the foreground, c. 1790.

Introduction

Buying

Old pottery and porcelain might well be reckoned the most complex area of all antiques. The literature, vast and impressively scholarly, is evidence of the collecting passions and historical detective work stimulated by this, somehow the most genteel of all the areas of antiques covered in this book.

Over the centuries, and particularly in the 18th, techniques changed quickly as an expanding middle class demanded more refined wares of different kinds. Manufactories rose and fell, sometimes to be resurrected by different owners (Royal Crown Derby is an example) with a change of emphasis on their products. Potters moved from factory to factory trading expertise, literally leaving their mark before moving on or setting up independently (the perambulations of William Billingsley of Nantgarw and the complicated story of Nantgarw-Swansea is a good example).

The documentation of old pottery and porcelain is often sketchy as many craftsmen, quite understandably, were much more concerned with making a living than ensuring that their records would be conveniently ordered for future historians.

Marks, which would seem to offer such an unequivocal way of dating and identifying a piece are not always as straightforward as they at first appear. Unlike silver hallmarks they were and are not legally regulated and enforceable and, as with the pontil mark on old glass, it is precisely because they are taken to be such an important means of dating and identification that they have been and are subject to copying. It is not wise, in a guide such as this, to attempt to explain the intricacies, the similarities and changes seen in the marks of the makers. Simplification can all too easily lead to confusion, and it is far better for the potential buyer to check marks in one of a number of excellent specialist publications listed on page 100. The range, diversity and complexity of the subject are precisely what make old pottery and porcelain such a good area for buyers and collectors at all sorts of levels. Here we are concerned primarily with pieces which, though special, are not too precious to use. Not many of us can afford or feel comfortable with a Chelsea cream jug of 1753 recently sold at auction for £2,860, or would be entirely relaxed pouring our coffee from a Worcester pot of 1760 sold for £3,520. But to build up a harlequin set of early 19th-century cups and saucers at £30 each, or to buy a Ridgway blue-and-white transfer-printed plate *c.* 1820 for £40 or an unmarked late Victorian willow pattern meat dish for £16 is within reach.

Damage will reduce the investment value of old pottery and porcelain considerably in all but the very early and rare earthenware where damage is almost inevitable, but it need not deter the buyer who really wants to build up, say, a dinner service of character which can be used rather than displayed, as long as the damage does not jeopardize the piece in use or make it impractical to use. Collectors at the highest level are fanatically fussy when it comes to damaged pieces and it is possible to buy good things reasonably because they have often quite slight damage. Even though such damage does not impair their function, it affects their value. Be prepared to accept, though, that your gain on the roundabouts might well be lost on the swings if you are buying with an eye on resale. A dealer who may have made light of damage when he sold the piece may suddenly announce that there just isn't a market for such pieces when you come to sell it back!

The vast production of enormous dinner, tea and dessert services from about 1820–1910 also provides a happy hunting ground. A 200 piece dinner service intact will be lucky to find itself a home, whereas it can profitably be split up by dealers (or even the private buyer who goes to a country house sale knowing unwanted pieces can be parcelled out to friends) into manageable parts.

Historical Survey

The very earliest history of pottery-making belongs more to the historian than those who want to buy things for use in the home and it is documented more fully elsewhere than this *Guide* can hope to do.

As far as most buyers are concerned the story of English pottery becomes interesting in the 16th century with the tin-enamelled earthenware introduced from the Netherlands; hence its name: delftware. Although English potteries made their own wonderful delftware, this sort of earthenware (although solid and robust-looking) is fragile and thus rare and comparatively expensive.

During the 17th century the crude and brittle pottery was coated with a clay and water solution (slip) to give it protection and decoration. This slipware was made in quantity at Wrotham in Kent, throughout Staffordshire, Sussex, North Wales and the West Country. It was also in the 17th century that the trade with the Orient being energetically pursued by the Dutch and English East India Companies, introduced what must have seemed the miracle of porcelain: light, translucent yet amazingly strong and beautifully decorated. Immediately English potters (along with their European rivals) began the search for a home-produced porcelain.

The debates about who discovered what, when, first, rage among historians of pottery and porcelain but there seems to be a grudging consensus that John Dwight of Fulham

was the first to take out a patent in 1684 on something he called porcelain but which was, in fact, a fine salt-glazed stoneware resistant to hot liquids (unlike its earthenware predecessors, delftware and slipware). This breakthrough was quickly copied by other potteries and by 1715 the fine china clay of Devon and Cornwall was being used domestically and exported.

Continual experiment was spurred on by the increasing fashion for drinking coffee and tea which itself was part of the steady rise of a relatively wealthy middle class determined to cultivate 'taste' and refinement. Not for them the rough utility of coarse pottery, pewter or wooden plates and mugs of earlier and rougher times.

It was then discovered that if stoneware was fired at a lower temperature ($750°C$) than that previously used ($1,200°C$) a very adaptable creamware resulted which was lighter. It was then protected by a clear lead glaze. It began to replace other forms of pottery and was to be further developed in the 1770s and 80s by Josiah Wedgwood (who called his version Queensware). At about the same time Wedgwood was also foremost among a group of potters (including Miles Mason) in developing new forms of stoneware (a strengthening of earlier earthenwares) such as redware, brownware and saltglaze stoneware by adding vitreous – glass-like – materials and firing at very high temperatures. Wedgwood called his Black Basalte, Jasperware and Caneware whilst the company Mason founded in the 18th century was to market its Patent Ironstone China in 1813. Spode also made stoneware in the early 19th century.

All the foregoing are types of pottery, albeit pottery attempting to emulate the durability of porcelain, and the search for the secrets of porcelain is a parallel story. Porcelain is chemically different from pottery. It is a mixture of kaolin (china) clay (related to granite as a fine powdered form: hence strength and lightness) and china stone or petuntse (also related to granite). This paste is formed and fired first at $900°C$ and, having been glazed, is fired again at $1,300°C$. The strength of the component clays and the vitrifying effect of the high firing temperatures produce toughness combined with lightness and translucency. This sort of porcelain is known as 'true' or 'hard paste' and the secret of its manufacture known previously only in China was broken by the Meissen factory, near Dresden, Saxony, about 1708. It took another 60 years or so before a passable hard paste formula was found in England (William Cookworthy of Plymouth is usually given the credit but Bristol and New Hall also made it during the 18th century).

In England, soft-paste porcelain proved a popular and often cheaper substitute for true hard paste. Local clay reinforced with sand or flint to boost the vitreous content were substituted for kaolin clay and potash or lead replaced china stone. It was fired first at 1,100°C and then glaze-fired at 900°C. Soft paste, as the name implies, scratches more easily than hard and more easily develops surface cracks when filled with hot liquid. The colours applied to the under-glaze of soft paste sank deeper and produced a softer and very attractive effect.

In the second half of the 18th century soapstone was also substituted for the kaolin clay of hard-paste porcelain because it was found to make pieces more resistant to changes of kiln temperature and therefore a better business proposition.

The addition of bone ash from reduced ox bones (as much as 50% in some cases) to soft-paste porcelain (Bow about 1749) and then to hard paste (Josiah Spode, 1794) created what was to be by 1800 the staple of fine English chinaware: bone china.

Left: New Hall hard paste coffee can enamelled in blue, pink and gilt, c. 1795. Centre: Fluted Coalport china coffee can, c. 1820, painted and gilt with vines. Right: Crescent marked Worcester soapstone porcelain coffee cup, reeded and decorated in blue and gilt, c. 1785. Note the characteristic straight sides of the cans compared with the rim-footed cup.

Techniques and Terms_____

Agate ware Lead-glazed earthenware of brilliant-coloured glazes on improved cream-coloured salt-glaze body. Early Wedgwood/Whieldon partnership made agate, tortoiseshell and marbled stoneware while continuing to refine the body. Technically important as a turning point for English 'china'. In 1759 Wedgwood left the Whieldon firm and, using the refined earthenware body with cream-coloured glaze, began to make 'Queensware' or 'Creamware'. *Principal products:* tortoiseshell, marbled, plates, teapots, jugs, tureens, knife handles.

Applied relief Decorative shapes made separately and added to the basic shape, slightly raised on the surface.

Biscuit (or **bisque**) When pottery or porcelain clay has been fired once in the kiln it is hardened but porous and is still the original clay colour.

Black Basalt(e) ware Revived in the 19th century as Basalt or Black Basalte. Developed by Josiah Wedgwood in the 1770s and ultimately called 'Egyptian black' by him. Matt or shiny black stoneware made from ironstone and other ingredients. Extremely successful, highly prized during 18th and 19th centuries for vases, cabinet ware, tablets, plaques and as a silver substitute for writing and toilet articles. *Principal products:* teapots, cream jugs, sugar bowls, coffee pots, chocolate pots, medallions, plaques, cabinet-ware, articles for writing and toilet tables, vases, urns. *Principal producers:* Josiah Wedgwood's 'Etruria' works, E. Mayer & Son, Palmer & Neale, Thomas Whieldon, Lakin & Poole, Eastwood, John Turner, E. J. Birch, Joseph Twyford, Charles Green, H. Palmer of Hanley, Josiah Spode, David Dunderdale of Castleford. *Decoration:* Moulded, applied relief, classical and commemorative. Regency Adam style.

Blue-and-white The very high demand for imported Oriental blue-and-white porcelain stimulated the search for home-produced copies. Dr Wall, a Bristol merchant-chemist, succeeded in making a blue dye from cobalt (the supplies of which were previously dependent on Germany) and this breakthrough was commercially exploited by Dr Wall's Worcester Porcelain Company (which had started at Bristol). Other makers of pottery and porcelain also produced blue-and-white ware in the oriental manner.

By the last quarter of the 18th century transfer printing (introduced by Robert Hancock, 1756) on to pottery (Minton's fine Nankin ware is an outstanding example) was being developed. Much blue-and-white china was printed in underglaze blue whereby a pattern would be engraved on a copper plate, the plate treated with cobalt blue and an impression taken onto tissue-thin paper, and then transferred to the unglazed biscuit; the piece was then fired and glazed with the border being added separately (if one looks closely, some border patterns are seen not to meet accurately). Transfer-printed blue-and-white ware was immensely popular throughout the 19th century.

Willow-pattern blue-and-white is probably the best known. It was supposed to have been introduced by Thomas Turner of Caughley and then copied by Thomas Minton about 1785 when he left Caughley. Minton sold the pattern to several factories, the first of which may well have been Spode. There are many variants of the willow pattern and it has been estimated that there were over 200 potters turning out willow ware by 1865. The number of people on the bridge, the number of birds and trees varies greatly but they are not a reliable guide to dating.

Body Potter's clay, strictly a term used for earthenware and stoneware, but generally applied to all basic mixtures used by pottery and porcelain makers.

Spode transfer-printed bone china Italian pattern blue-and-white platter, early 19th century.

Bone china   Adopted by most English potters at the beginning of the 19th century as an ideal formula for fine 'china'. Bone-ash from calcinated ox bones was added to hard-paste ingredients and was first produced commercially by Josiah Spode in 1794 from developments in 'bone porcelain' produced by Bow, Chelsea, Derby, Caughley, Liverpool. Due to its very white, translucent and durable characteristics it quickly became the standard English china. The great 18th- and 19th-century manufacturers made quantities of extravagantly decorated and gilded tableware for the nobility and by the middle of the last century were mass-producing many regular designs. *Principal products:* Tableware, tureens, vegetable dishes, dessert services, tea services, coffee services, breakfast services, ornamental and cabinet ware, vases. *Principal producers:* Derby, Rockingham, Minton, Liverpool, Coalport, Worcester, Copeland & Garrett (late Spode), Swansea, Davenport. *Decoration:* Initially copied from the French and German designs, but as technique improved, developed individual styles and colours of their own by which their wares are recognized.

Bone porcelain   Soft-paste porcelain body strengthened with powdered bone ash.

Brownware   Brown salt-glazed stoneware of the 17th and 18th centuries. Revived in the 19th century. It was made from sand-enriched clay, originating in Germany and known also as 'Cologne ware'. The first potter to make it in England was John Dwight of Fulham who also experimented with marbled effects, later taken up and developed by Thomas Whieldon and Josiah Wedgwood. *Principal products:* Jugs, mugs, functional bottles, spirit flasks, jars, harvest pitchers, Toby jugs, loving cups. *Principal producers:* Fulham, Lambeth, later Staffordshire, Sunderland, Derbyshire and many others. See also **Nottingham Stoneware.** *Decoration:* Turned rims, necks, incised flower, leaf decoration. Raised sporting, hunting scenes on buff-coloured body with dark-brown glaze to top half.

Cabaret set   Usually porcelain or bone china tea set for one or two people, including matching tray in same material.

Cabinet ware   Decorative pieces never intended for use but only for display and admiration.

Cane and bamboo ware   Made by Wedgwood from the mid-1780s of tan-coloured unglazed stoneware with cane and bamboo imitation in relief. Used much for tea sets, jugs, pot pourri jars and candlesticks.

Castleford ware   Late 18th, early 19th century. Moulded white salt-glaze ware with relief decoration and painted panels, usually landscapes. Castleford was near Leeds, the leading salt-glaze pottery of the period. Rare pieces marked 'Turner' for John Turner, or D D & Co. Castleford for David Dunderdale.

Caudle pot   Two-handled bowl with lid and saucer, porcelain in 18th century, bone china in 19th. Often specially made in pairs as presentation gifts.

Cobalt   Basic blue colouring, originally imported from Saxony in Germany (also known as zaffre or sapphire). Extremely important in early ceramics as it stood up to the extreme heat of the glazing kiln. Made in Bristol and Cornwall in the 18th century.

Combed decoration   Simple method of decorating earthenware by combing the liquid 'slip' into wavy patterns.

Left: 'Opaque China,' late 19th century with Chinese decoration on a white ground. Right: Brown Nottingham stoneware jug, c. 1800, from the Morley factory.

Early 19-century Staffordshire pottery lustre cow creamers. A matching pair in blue and black with pink noses and green bases.

Cottages Also includes churches and castles in which tablets (called pastilles) were burned in order to give off a fragrant aroma – quite useful in the days before adequate sanitation. There are many modern replicas.

Cow-creamer milk jugs modelled to resemble, not surprisingly, a cow. The tail would be the handle, the mouth the spout, and milk was poured into the body through an opening in its back. Cow-creamers without a base are usually 19th century and early 20th century imitations.

Creamware From 1750s to the present day. Some authorities suggest it was invented by the Astburys and Enoch Booth; it was first developed commercially by Josiah Wedgwood using liquid cream-coloured lead glaze over an improved earthenware body fired at a moderate temperature and very similar to that used for saltglaze. In the late 18th century it displaced delftware as the principal earthenware product. Called 'Queensware' by Wedgwood in 1765 after a commission from Queen Charlotte. In its early stages its main drawback was that it was not hot water-resistant and could not be used for teapots, coffee pots etc. Once developed, taken up by many Staffordshire potters many of whom shamelessly adopted the name 'Queensware'. Creamware usually means plain undecorated ware, but much of it had simple decoration. *Principal products:* Sweetmeat and pickle dishes, bowls, cream jugs, serving dishes, sauce boats, tureens, pharmaceutical jars, jugs, dessert plates, centrepieces, cabinet pieces and display pieces. From 1760s teapots, coffee pots, chocolate pots, night lamps, food warmers and many domestic articles: mousse moulds, jelly moulds, shapes, ice-cream moulds, bowls and dishes. *Principal producers:* Wedgwood, Spode, Minton, Swinton (later Rockingham), Leeds, Swansea, Sunderland, Liverpool and many Staffordshire potteries. *Decoration:* Much pierced and lattice work similar to white saltglaze, low-relief lattice and decoration, painted scenes, nautical motifs, commemorative, royal and loyal, local views, export wares to America.

Delftware 16th, 17th and 18th centuries. Tin-enamelled earthenware with a white glaze. Brought into England by the Dutch, and was an attempt after contact with the Orient to produce a white-surfaced pottery which resembled 'china'. Naturally much of it was decorated to imitate Chinese and oriental patterns. *Principal products:* Wine bottles, pill slabs, drug jars, plaques, large shallow serving bowls or chargers, barbers' bowls, bleeding bowls, posset pots, vases, flower bricks, apothecaries' pots and jars, sauce boats, wine cups, caudle cups, syrup pots, spouted pots, fuddling cups, puzzle jugs, tiles. From 18th century: tea, coffee and chocolate pots. *Decoration:* oriental designs, sprigs, flowers, leaves, royal and loyal, commemorative and similar themes to slip-ware. London: White on white, blue and white, manganese purple. Bristol: Blue and white, green, brick red, brown, yellow, purple. Liverpool: Blue and white – in particular nautical scenes for deep large punch bowls, also polychrome enamels. Wincanton: Blue and white, blue and manganese, often covering the whole ground.

Earthenware   Term used to refer to clay ware which remains porous after firing and for most purposes consequently requires glazing.

Engine turned   Finely-shaped line patterns originally engraved on metal as decoration, used by Wedgwood and other potters from 1760s to decorate fine hard stoneware.

Faïence   French tin-glazed wares originally named for pottery coming from Fayence.

Fairings   Mementoes of a visit to the fair, they were small porcelain groups of figures manufactured mainly in Germany in the last half of the last century and the early part of the 20th for the English market. Often inscribed with slightly titillating mottoes ('Kiss me quick,' 'Last in bed must turn out the light') they are one of the classic examples (along with Staffordshire dogs and figures) of working-class knick-knacks which are now collected avidly and hence much copied.

Famille rose   An exceptionally fine variety of Chinese decorative porcelain with a rose-pink glaze. The style was much copied by Meissen, Bow, Chelsea and Worcester, among others.

Felspar porcelain   Another soft-paste substance based, as its name implies, on mineral as opposed to 'bone' base, contemporary with development of the more universally accepted 'bone china'. Thicker than hard-paste porcelain and was used in particular by Spode as base for transfer-printed wares.

Firing   Baking clay-ware in kilns at high temperatures, baking glazed ware to fix the glaze. Twice-fired means fired again to fix the painting, decoration on once-fired ware.

Frit   A vitreous mixture consisting of sand or calcined flint and potash or lead, added to local clay to give soft-paste porcelain its characteristic toughness.

Fuddling cup   Three or more mugs, usually earthenware, joined together so that the liquid flows between them.

Glaze   Coating made from silicate or glass-based substances to decorate, enhance and make pottery and porcelain non-porous.

Green glaze ware   Tableware with a brilliant green liquid glaze over moulded shapes, first made by Whieldon in the 1740s, developed commercially by Wedgwood in the 1760s and popular ever since. Leaf-shaped dishes, cream jugs, serving dishes, dessert ware, tea ware, all with leaf theme. Made consistently by many imitators until the present day, as well as current Wedgwood products. Victorian green glaze was thicker, earthenware finer. *Principal producers:* Wedgwood and Whieldon. Imitated from 1860s by Poole, Stanway & Wood, Banks & Thorney of Hanley, Daniel & Son of Longton and many more recent imitators.

Hard-paste porcelain   Pure white, translucent porcelain approximating to oriental 'china'. Has a metallic ring when struck and is immensely strong in spite of its apparent delicacy. The strength is acquired by ageing the paste, kaolin and china stone (petuntse), before firing at high temperature. The Chinese stored their paste for decades; to the English potters seven or eight months was enough. Called 'hard paste' because it requires a 'hard fire', i.e. a high temperature. First made commercially in England by William Cookworthy at Plymouth in 1768 but Richard Champion of Bristol had a monopoly on the Cornish clay essential to its manufacture. 1770 Plymouth potteries transferred to Bristol where Champion's Hard Paste Porcelain was manufactured. *Principal English products:* Copies of Dresden figures, Four Seasons, Four Elements, etc. Vases, cabinet pieces, decorative ware, tea ware in the oriental manner. *Principal producers:* Plymouth, Bristol, New Hall. *Decoration:* Inevitably, much decoration in the Chinese manner, blue-and-white for articles associated with tea-drinking. Copies also from Bristol of Meissen ware, marked with Meissen crossed swords and the letter 'B'. See also **Soft-paste porcelain.**

Imari Name used by 18th-century English potters for export Japanese ware, with patterns derived from brocaded silks, hence considerably gilded.

Incised Decoration made by cutting or engraving into the body.

'In the white' Undecorated ware.

Ironstone Tough earthenware made from mineral base.

Jackfield ware A generic term for any ware glazed with a glossy black finish. Coffee and teapots, jugs etc. made by several Staffordshire potteries including Whieldon. Originally a variety of red pottery covered with a brilliant black glaze made at Jackfield in Shropshire in the 18th century (sometimes called 'jetware').

Lambeth earthenware (Majolica ware, Mintonware) Only superficially resembling delftware because of common roots in antiquity via Italian maiolica. Made in the 1850s by Herbert Minton for a line of cheap wares, mugs, jugs, platters etc. Adopted by the 'Art Movement' of the Victorians and made from 1872 at John Doulton's pottery, decorated by many artists from the Lambeth School of Art. Continued production until 1914. *Principal products:* Traditional ware, the ground colour is distinctly yellow, the painting more elaborate than delft ware.

Lead glaze Powdered lead ore sprinkled on ware which turned yellow when fired in the kiln, producing familiar greenish-yellow 'Tudor green'. Colourless lead glaze from 1750s.

Low relief Decoration slightly raised from surface.

Lustreware A form of ceramic decoration using very small amounts of gold (for 'copper' lustreware) and platinum (for 'silver' lustreware) in the pigment. Although developed in Sunderland in the 1740s, its main production dates from about 1800 when it was used to imitate gold and silverware, an intention frustrated by the introduction of electroplating in 1840. Modern reproductions abound (especially copper lustre jugs and wall plaques). *Principal products:* All-silver tea services, coffee pots, chocolate pots, candlesticks, silver pieces, tankards, goblets etc. Lustre decoration for tableware, cups, saucers, jugs, mugs. Copper lustre for large-lipped jugs in sets, commemorative ware, royal and loyal, local views, souvenir pieces, plaques, motto jugs and mugs. Very popular with Victorians. *Principal producers:* Wedgwood as silver substitute, Sunderland and many Staffordshire potters for copper, purple etc. *Decoration:* As with gilding to highlight and band pieces of tableware, silver on white ground for tankards, mugs. Copper lustre, purple lustre with medallions of views, mottoes etc.

Majolica English derivation of 'maiolica', majolica was colourful moulded ware with opaque buff-coloured or white ground vividly painted. Developed in Minton factory in 1850s.

Martinware Jugs modelled in grotesque animal forms with spooky human expressions or human heads with leering clownish faces made by the Martin brothers first at Fulham and then at Southall, London, 1873–1915 in salt-glazed stoneware. This distinctive grotesqueness has created a collector's market but also effectively puts off many others.

Mazarine blue Rich blue colour developed in France, imitated by Chelsea, Derby, Worcester.

Mocha ware From 18th century, but mainly 19th century. A range of cheap tableware principally made for coffee houses, taverns, public houses. Its name variously attributed to 'Mocha' coffee, and to the moss-like decoration which resembles trees. Early Mocha ware is highly collectable, but by the 19th century, it was thick, crude earthenware with a cream glaze and 'Mocha' decoration and jugs, mugs, tankards, coffee pots, plates of various sizes were made in great quantities. *Principal producers:* Edge & Malkin, Burslem; T. G. Green & Co., Derbyshire; Leeds Potteries, by 19th century most potteries in Britain, also in France.

Moulded Tableware and figures made from pressing the body (stoneware, earthenware, porcelain etc.) between two moulds, allowing great freedom of shape and variety of decoration which could be repeated identically.

Nankin ware Common name loosely applied to 18th century pseudo-oriental blue-and-white ware.

Nottingham stoneware A finer quality brown salt-glazed stoneware particular to this town, made throughout the 18th century. Peculiar to Nottingham was double-walled hollow ware made in late 18th century, with inner vessel to contain liquid and outer pierced wall, punched or perforated to give an illusion of lightness in weight not otherwise achieved in this heavy material. *Principal products:* Loving cups, puzzle jugs, mugs and punch bowls, 'Bear jugs' with surface covered with clay shavings to represent fur. Made again at the end of 18th century with bear squeezing Napoleon. *Principal producers:* Nottingham, also Chesterfield and Brampton. *Decoration:* Turned and incised.

Parian Primarily a fine-grained unglazed, white variety of soft-paste porcelain used for figurines by Copeland and Garrett, Minton and Wedgwood, its cheaper hard-paste variety was used for moulded jugs, vases and dishes. Differs from biscuit or unglazed porcelain by its characteristic silkiness. Biscuit has a chalky appearance.

Pearl ware A harder-bodied earthenware with a slightly iridescent appearance. Developed by Josiah Wedgwood, resistant to hot water and considered by him simply as an improvement on Queensware. *Principal products:* Dessert services, tableware of all sorts until 1770s. After that date, confined mainly to ornamental work. *Principal producers:* Many other potteries used pearlware while experimenting with basic creamware, including Josiah Spode, Leeds.

Piecrust ware Dates from 1790s and outbreak of Napoleonic Wars when a flour tax prohibited English cooks from making standing crust pies and raised pies. Josiah Wedgwood produced a range of vitrified stoneware to substitute for pastry cases, brought to the table as 'crock pies'. Elaborately decorated, often in the shape of a hare, pheasant, duck etc. with sprigged ornament, leaves and flowers in relief. Not heatproof, purely decorative. Chesterfield potters developed an ironstone ware which was less crisply decorated but withstood oven heat and boiling in water. By the 1830s this ceramic was being made by several potteries.

In 1850 Wedgwood developed a new range of ovenproof glazed stoneware pie dishes in four sizes designed to be placed inside the ornamental piecrust. *Principal products:* Imitation piecrusts with crisp relief modelling of game, birds' head finials to lids, leaves, ferns, swags, etc. *Principal producers:* Wedgwood, John and William Turner, Elijah Mayer, William Adams & Son, John Davenport, Swansea. *Decoration:* Relief moulded, uncoloured. Swansea decorated theirs with sprigs of fruiting ivy.

Pill slab   Tile, often delftware, used by pharmacists for mixing powders, potions and for rolling pills. Also used as shop signs.

Pipeclay   Fine white substance made from 'china clay' used as decoration, particularly by Wedgwood.

Porcelain   see **Bone china, Bone porcelain, Hard paste, Soft paste.**

Pot lids   The decorative tops of glazed stoneware jars which originally contained men's hair pomade, fish-paste spreads, toothpaste or shaving cream were first produced in the early years of 19th century by such makers as Mayer, Maling and, most notably, Pratt of Fenton who pioneered a multicoloured printing process. Many reproductions can be found, of which the collector should beware.

Posset pot   Two-handled, lidded, sometimes spouted pots made in slipware, delftware, stoneware in 17th, 18th centuries.

Prattware   William Pratt (1753–99) made a highly coloured Staffordshire earthenware of folksy charm made also by many other potteries. Tea caddies, teapots, plaques, jugs with rustic themes in high relief are characteristic, as are Toby jugs, cowcreamers, watchstands, commemorative busts and naive ornaments. Dessert and tea services with distinctive malachite borders of intricate oak-leaf pattern borders and colour-printed pots lids were made until the last

quarter of the 19th century.

Queensware   Name granted to Wedgwood's range of creamware, later adopted by many other potteries for similar ware of their own manufacture. See **Creamware.**

Red stoneware   Late 17th and 18th centuries. Developed by John Dwight of Fulham in imitation of Chinese red stoneware imported into England with cargoes of tea. Also made by John Elers of Vauxhall and by several early 18th-century imitators, among them Josiah Wedgwood. Unglazed hard red stoneware later improved upon by Samuel Bell of Newcastle-under-Lyme and polished to high gloss. Josiah Wedgwood in early 1760s produced attractive 'rosso antico' with engine-turned and 'famille-rose' enamel type decoration. Proved highly suitable material for tea, coffee, chocolate pots in mid-18th century. The red clay base later proved an ideal substance for Staffordshire lustreware. *Principal products:* Tea ware, pots, bowls, cream jugs, sugar boxes, teapoys. *Principal producers:* Fulham, Lambeth, Wedgwood, Coalbrookdale, Enoch Wood, Spode, Samuel Hollins, Robert Wilson and other Staffordshire potters. *Decoration:* Impressed, stamped, pierced and engine-turned. Applied raised decoration, imitation Chinese sprig ornament, decorative handles, spouts. Some with imitation Chinese stamps on base.

Relief   A raised decoration modelled on to the pottery or porcelain body.

Salmon scale   Fine gilt lattice decoration resembling fish scales, used notably by Worcester.

Saltglaze   First developed by John Dwight of Fulham in 1671, rock salt was thrown into the kiln, where it volatilized together with silicon and aluminium oxides in the clay to give a slightly pitted glaze. During the mid-18th century bright enamel colours were used to make striking contrasts with neutral-coloured body. It was moulded, and a high degree of intricacy was achieved in pierced ware, basket-work and low relief decoration. Being neither thrown nor turned, all manner of curious shapes were used for teapots in particular, including houses and animals. *Principal products:* Teapots, coffee pots, chocolate pots, dishes, plates, puzzle jugs, mugs, food warmers, night lamps, cream jugs, sauce boats, dessert baskets, serving dishes, tureens, chestnut dishes, domestic ware, flat ware. *Principal producers:* Burslem, Leeds, Liverpool, many Staffordshire potteries. *Decoration:* White pipeclay moulded relief, lattice, pierced, basket-work, moulded relief. From 1740s blue cobalt-stained clay was rubbed into incised decoration, known as 'Scratch blue'. Blue-and-white oriental enamelled overglaze with clear colours, crude painting. Agate, tortoiseshell and marbled also made for knife handles, teapots, ornamental figures, particularly by Whieldon and Wedgwood in 1740s.

Scratch blue   Scratches or incisions filled with cobalt blue powder before firing. 18th century.

Sgraffito   After the pottery has been coated with a creamy slip it is scratched ('sgraffito' in Italian) to make a pattern. The piece is then glazed. Although this is an ancient tradition it was particularly popular on Staffordshire mugs and jugs. When the scratched part was coloured in with cobalt it was known as Scratch blue.

Slip   A cream-thick mixture of clay and water which was either used to completely cover a piece or was dribbled over it for decorative effect.

Slipware   Plain earthenware decorated with slip and then glazed. Made in the 17th and 18th centuries, with country potteries continuing well into the 19th century. The ground colour of lead and manganese glaze is yellowish, or yellowish-green. The natural clay colour depends on the district, varying from light buff to dark terracotta red. Sometimes an entire piece is dipped in slip which is then cut away into patterns before

firing and glazing. *Principal products:* Jugs, posset pots, flat plates, dishes, chargers, pitchers, flasks, wine jugs, puzzle jugs, fuddling cups, tygs, naive ornamental pieces. *Principal districts:* Wrotham in Kent, Harlow in Essex, Staffordshire, Tickenhall in Derbyshire, Bolsover near Chesterfield, Buckinghamshire, Cambridgeshire, Hampshire, Nottingham, Somerset, Bristol, Warwickshire, Wiltshire, Yorkshire, Glamorganshire, Devon.

Soapstone porcelain   A divergence from earthenware in the search for white, hot water-resistant substances for tea ware, tableware, soapstone porcelain is a soft-paste porcelain which bridges the gap between earthenware and 'bone china' which was finally developed in the late 18th century. *Principal producers:* Worcester, Bristol, Liverpool and Caughley 1748–80.

Soft-paste porcelain   White-bodied base also known as 'bone porcelain' and transitional development before 'bone china'. First made at Bow in the 1750s, followed by Chelsea, Derby, Liverpool and Lowestoft. Early soft-paste porcelain was very fine and the nearest then yet achieved by English potters to oriental 'china'. It could not withstand hot water and was at first confined to cabinet pieces and ornamental ware. *Principal products:* Ornamental figures, candlesticks, writing and toilet table articles, decorative ware, bowls, boxes, figures. From 1760s when Bow developed a hot-water resistant soft-paste porcelain, dessert services, tea services, coffee services, breakfast services, flatware and tableware of all kinds. *Principal producers:* Bow, Chelsea, Derby, Liverpool, Lowestoft, Longton Hall, Worcester. *Decoration:* Early ornamental figures made at Derby, Chelsea, Bow, were influenced by Meissèn, Sèvres, Dresden, pastoral, animal, finely decorated and sculpted, though colouring was still relatively crude compared to European work.

Spill vase, spill jar   Wide-mouthed, often straight-sided jar to hold strips of wood, paper, etc. to light pipes from the fire.

Staffordshire blue   White earthenware, bone china, painted or transfer-printed, made in great quantities by numerous potteries in 18th and 19th centuries.

Stoneware   Stone or flint was added to the clay used to make earthenware and fired at a high temperature (1,300°C) to produce a hard non-porous pottery. Salt was thrown into the kiln at its highest temperature to produce salt-glazed stoneware.

Tazza   Originally from the Arabic for basin, they were dishes on a raised foot or pedestal which held fruit or sweetmeats. A necessary part of most Victorian and Edwardian dinner and dessert services, they were grandly positioned at the centre of the dining table or on the sideboard.

Teapoy   In ceramics, a lidded container for preserving tea.

Terracotta   Ancient, soft, unglazed, slightly porous ware, material for flowerpots etc. In 18th century developed by Josiah Wedgwood into intricate classical urns, plant pots, boxes, jardinières. Victorian terracotta highly popular for conservatories etc. made at Lambeth, Wedgwood, Doulton, Coalbrookdale, Lowesby in Leicestershire and F & R Pratt of Fenton.

Tin-enamelled, tin-glazed   Opaque substance with tin base, particularly associated with Delft.

Toby jugs   First produced about 1760 and made by many factories, they represent genre-types such as hearty squires, national heroes and historical characters. Although modelled with great vitality in the 18th century they had by the end of the 19th century degenerated into crude copies. Very early jugs tend to be unglazed with non-gaudy colours.

Transfer-printing   Stoneware, bone china, decorated by transferring pattern or picture from engraved and inked copper plate onto a sheet of tissue paper, a process which could be repeated many times with each engraving. See **Blue-and-white.**

Turned   Hollow ware shaped and made on a lathe.

Tyg   A drinking pot often with more than one handle.

Wemyss ware   Vases, mugs, tea sets bowls, candlesticks, with underglazed painting of fruit, flowers, cocks and hens, made at the Fife Pottery by the Heron family from 1817.

Willow pattern   See **Blue-and-white.**

Principal Pottery and Porcelain Factories

Belleek: 1857– present day

Established at Fermanagh, Northern Ireland, it specialized in a lustrous mother-of-pearl effect on rather elaborate openwork baskets, or dishes decorated with modelled marine motifs such as seahorses and sea-shells. Tea services were often decorated with finely modelled flower-clusters.

Bow: 1745–75

Soft-paste porcelain developed by Thomas Frye and others in competition with Chinese imports. Blue-and-white from 1753 for tea ware etc. Dessert services, tableware from 1759. Pastoral scenes, fruits, birds on useful and decorative wares. Octagonal plates and pot-bellied mugs were typical. Blue ground from 1765, then rose pompadour, rich cobalt blue, turquoise, copper red, yellow, tiny gold leaves. Its vast output varied in quality and appearance, making identification difficult sometimes. Some Bow soft paste has poor translucency, is heavy for its proportions and is strongly absorbent on unglazed areas. In the later years a decline was marked by increasing elaboration and gilding.

Bristol: 1600s–1770s

Tin-enamelled delft from 1600s. Buff tinted body, slatey blues, reddish-white glaze. Also 'quaker green', dull yellow, brownish orange, manganese purple and pale turquoise blue. Symmetrical flowers characteristic. Much Oriental-style blue-and-white. Soft-paste porcelain from 1750s. Firm acquired by Dr Wall of Worcester in 1752. See Champion's Hard-Paste Porcelain below for last period.

Caughley: 1775–99
(Pronounced 'calf-lee')

Established as The Salopian China Manufactory by Thomas Turner, formerly of Worcester. Soapstone porcelain, transfer-printed in black, sepia and blue. Much blue-and-white, blue with characteristic violet tinge. Plain tableware in all-over blue with gilding. Chinese-style landscapes, fisherman and pleasure-boat designs. Gilding for edge bandings, highlights, sprays of foliage picked out in gold. There is also a great deal of confusion with Worcester which worked closely with Caughley. 1799–1814: traded as Coalport/Caughley. Caughley manufactory acquired by Coalport in 1814.

Champion's Hard-Paste Porcelain: Bristol, 1770s–1782

Richard Champion acquired William Cookworthy's patent, improved on the hard-paste and adopted fashionable Sèvres neo-classical decoration. Champion concentrated on tea and coffee sets both for grand families and as 'cottage' ware but also made figures and small oval plaques modelled with flowers. Beset by litigation from rivals and the failure of his North American trade, Champion was forced to sell his patent to the group of Staffordshire potters who founded New Hall.

Chelsea: 1745–69

1745–49 Triangle period
1749–52 Raised Anchor period
1752–56 Red Anchor period
1756–69 Gold Anchor period
Leader in the field in fine porcelain in the Sèvres and Meissen style. The Raised Anchor and Red Anchor wares are most prized, the better the piece the smaller the anchor. Some oriental styles also produced. Colours are exceptionally brilliant and have been copied by almost every other pottery with greater or lesser success. Famous Chelsea claret and turquoise, mazarine blue, pea green, well-balanced gilding. Later ware fell in with the fashion for landscape, exotic birds, fruit and flowers.
Chelsea-Derby: 1770–84. See Derby.

Coalport: 1795 to present day

Considerable output of willow pattern and transfer-printed ware from 1814. 1822 felspar porcelain production for fine translucent tableware. Characteristic rich maroon ground colour; rich, ornate services, many in the Sèvres and Meissen manner. Great copyists: Derby mazarine blue, Sèvres turquoise and rose pompadour, Chelsea claret ground colour. In 1926 Coalport moved to Stoke, Staffordshire. See also Caughley.

Copeland
See Spode

Davenport: 1793–1885

Earthenware and moulded stoneware. Bone china in similar colouring and decoration to

Derby. Large table services, some fine decoration.

Derby: 1749–1848 (Royal Crown Derby 1876 to present day)

Under William Duesbury, mainly figures in the Meissen manner but also useful wares of variable quality, often thickly potted with pitted glaze. After Duesbury bought the Chelsea factory in 1770 there was an improvement in the production of both figures and useful wares, especially tea and dinner wares. Known as Crown Derby (1786–1811), it was during this period that the introduction of bone china meant an increased emphasis on tableware, quantities of which were decorated with the Japanese Imari pattern. Between 1811 and 1848 the factory was known as Bloor Derby and quantity replaced quality – opaque, heavy china with glazes tending to crack; poor, gaudy colouring and heavy-handed use of the Imari pattern to hide defects and appeal to a popular if vulgar taste for strident colours. Old Crown Derby China Works (1848–1935) was established by ex-employees using old Derby moulds. An entirely separate concern – the (Royal) Crown Derby Porcelain Co. – was established in 1876 and continues to this day.

Doulton & Co: 1815 to present day

Established as a manufacturer of sanitary earthenware, after the Great Exhibition of 1851 moved into 'craft' pottery in association with the Lambeth School of Art, producing ornamental pottery, grotesque heads, commemorative mugs. In 1872 production began of Lambeth faïence, based on the Minton series of majolica ware and very popular with Victorians. Royal Doulton from 1902. Work by many famous artists from this pottery: deserves further study.

Fulham 1671 – present

Founded by the remarkable John Dwight in 1671 to make, salt-glazed earthenwares, later developed by John Astbury and Ralph Shaw into white salt-glazed stoneware. The family remained in control until 1861 making a range of salt-glazed stoneware domestic and sanitary ware and tankards and jugs decorated with hunting scenes and celebrities of the day. In the 1860s the decoration changed to favour the Japanese style.

Leeds: 1760–1878

Salt-glazed stoneware. Creamware, blue-and-white in Chinese designs. Among the finest manufacturers of creamware which is particularly fine and light in weight. Lattice, trellis, patterns cut by hand with hearts, diamonds, circles, handles of inter-twined strips ending in flowers, leaves, berries. Pierced candlesticks, table centre-pieces. Also made agate, pearlware, tortoisehell and lustre. Engine-turned red stoneware.

Liverpool: 17th century – 1800

Tin-enamelled delft ware by 1710. Blue-and-white oriental teaware. Creamware from 1780s, light in weight, decorated in blue and other enamelled colours, and blue and black transfer printing. Soft-paste porcelain from mid-18th century to 1800. Soapstone porcelain resistant to hot water from 1756. Much blue-and-white Chinese design to 1770s. Some red and black transfer-printed ware, not very high quality. Excellent tableware in soapstone porcelain with high-quality enamelled decoration. Of the group of Liverpool potteries of the 18th century, the Herculaneum is the best-known, founded in 1796. Heavy quality fine tableware and flat ware with duck-egg greenish glaze from Herculanaeum is distinctive, also punch bowls decorated with brilliant blue enamel.

Mason's Patent Ironstone transfer-printed side plate in 'India Grasshopper' pattern, c. 1820.

Lowestoft: 1757–99

Soft-paste porcelain domestic wares, souvenirs, commemorative, blue-and-white and polychrome, also small flowers painted inside bowls as well as on the outside. Reds are very purplish, mauve-pink.

Mason's *c.* 1792 – present

Strong, hard plebian earthenware development by Miles Mason *c.* 1792 and patented 1813 but used in slightly adapted forms by many potteries. Mason's Patent Ironstone China was extremely popular, mass-produced, brought pseudo-Oriental polychromatic designs to the general public who had only been able to buy monochrome transfer-printed wares. By the mid-19th century designs were peonies, roses, birds of paradise, butterflies, all lavishly painted, the more expensive services embellished with generous gilding. Most typical are Mason's octagonal jugs with reptilian handles, sold in sets of three to 14. From 1848 until recently the firm traded under the name of Geo. L. Ashworth and Brothers, but has recently reverted to Mason's Patent Ironstone.

Minton: *c.* 1793 – present

Thomas Minton was a pupil of Thomas Turner of Caughley and at one time an employee of Jeremiah Spode. He founded his own firm about 1793 and by the turn of the century had begun production of bone china with fine blue transfer printing of 'Nankin' patterns. Regency Greek key patterns on simply decorated rims to 1820s; thereafter designs became more exotic with increasing use of gilding for foliage, vines and tendrils. Japan colouring introduced for patterns with blue and pink peonies and variegated leaves. From 1823 Minton cups had decorated inner rims and by 1825 scalloped edges to cups and saucers. Thomas died 1836 and was succeeded by his son Herbert, who produced a wide range of excellent transfer-printed ware from the 1840s. In the 1850s developed English 'majolica' resembling Dutch Delft with a warmer, creamier ground. From 1848 began new range of exotic cabinet ware and enormous output of dinner services and tableware from the most opulent to the humblest. Minton's used a year code from 1842 to 1943, continuing thereafter with last two digits of the year only.

Nantgarw-Swansea: 1813–20

After an abortive attempt to produce a soft-paste porcelain to rival Sèvres, William Billingsley moved from Nantgarw near Swansea to the better-equipped factory of the Cambrian Pottery at Swansea. A distinctive and fine duck-egg porcelain was one of the results of this period at Swansea (1816–17) but Billingsley went back to Nantgarw to produce his own soft-paste porcelain. Whether from Nantgarw or Swansea, the wares were famous for high-quality painting, especially of flowers. However, a lot of Nantgarw-Swansea ware was decorated in London from

Minton bone china teacup and saucer, late 18th century.

the white. Much faked and much copied, especially by Coalport.

Rockingham: 1745–1842

From 1745 making earthenware, tea and coffee services; from 1785 under the name of Swinton. 1787–1806 the firm was in partnership with Leeds and making identical wares under the name of Greens, Bingley and Co. Creamware, Queensware, Nankin blue, tortoiseshell, Egyptian black and brown china. From 1807 traded under the name Brameld, making brown domestic china, domestic ware, cane-coloured stoneware from 1820. 1826 with financing by Earl Fitzwilliam began trading under the name Rockingham for fine bone china. Rich clientele and consequently ornate rococo designs, heavily gilded, with superb colouring: opaque apple green particularly characteristic, also deep violet blue, deep pinks, deep yellow, maroon, peach and gilded pink. Relief-moulded edges to dessert services, dinner services in Georgian silver shapes. Tea-table ware with engraved views on base and sides. Massive table services were stock-in-trade but nobility deserted the firm after the death of William IV with catastrophic results.

Spode: 1770–1833

Copeland & Garrett 1833–47
Copeland 1847–1970
Spode Ltd 1970 – present
Creamware from 1770. Transfer-printing from 1780s. Pearlware from 1780s – richer, more lustrous blue than 'Staffordshire blue'. Felspar porcelain, ironstone china from 1800s. Fine transfer-printed ware with Oriental, pastoral, Indian, 'new Nankin', Italian and in 1826 'Blue Imperial'. Table

One of a pair of Spode's 'New Stone' sauce tureens decorated in famille rose *coloured enamels applied over a printed outline pattern,* c. *1825.*

*Brameld (which
later became the
great Rockingham
factory)* parroquete
*pattern. Twelve-
sided dish with
gadrooned edges,
1820–30.*

services, richly coloured and often gilded. Distinctive blue with splashes of scarlet, many of them in fashionable Japanese patterns. Early period to 1797 when Josiah Spode died most highly regarded. From Copeland & Garrett more run-of-the-mill table services as well as made-to-order, but did not aspire to the rich heights of Rockingham. Now trades as 'Spode Ltd.'

Wedgwood: 1759 to present day

Most prolific and inventive of all English potters, though the firm only ventured into bone china for a brief period. Original partnership with Thomas Whieldon experimenting with fine-quality stoneware, producing range of agate, tortoiseshell and marbled wares together prior to Wedgwood's independent firm. 1759 began to produce creamware and green glaze. Unlike most other potters who swiftly began to copy Wedgwood's creamware, Wedgwood's was usually decorated, at its most simple with rim band, leaves in relief, from 1770s transfer-printed decorative bands. Creamware named 'Queensware' from 1765 after commission by Queen Charlotte. Red stoneware, black

basalte from 1760s called 'rosso antico' and 'Egyptian black'. Cane ware or bisque porcelain from 1770s. Brown-glazed pie dishes from 1793. Piecrust ware from 1790s. Bone china from 1812 to 1822. First oven-proof pie-dishes from 1850s. Other products include terracotta urns, flower pots, jardinières, kitchen ware, jelly moulds, mousse moulds, ice-cream shapes, green leaf-shaped dessert ware.

Worcester: 1751 to present day

First Period (Dr Wall)   1751–74
Davis, Flight 1774–93
Flight and Barr   1793–1807
Barr, Flight and Barr   1807–13
Flight, Barr and Barr   1813–40
Chamberlain and Co.   1840–52
Kerr and Binns   1852–62
Royal Worcester Porcelain Co.   1862 – present day

Blue-and-white soapstone from 1751. Dinner services, dessert, tea and coffee services from 1763. Particularly recognizable mazarine blue and gold, sky blue, pea green, French green, sea green, purple, scarlet. Japanese in-

Pieces from an impressed Wedgwood creamware dessert service with cream-coloured body painted in rust, yellows and oranges, c. 1820. The service includes a comport (centre), two square dishes (example right) and 12 plates (example left).

fluence, in particular Imari pattern, modified colour palette, lattice gilding known as salmon scale, often on a blue ground, very recognizable. Much work commissioned during 1770s, 1780s by royalty and nobility.

Transfer-printing from 1757 as underpattern for artists, later with pastoral scenes of milkmaids, shepherds, romantic ruins, usually transfer-printed in black, deep red, lilac or pale purple till 1770, then blue and sepia, hand-finished with touches of gilding. Bone china from 1798 with wide range of impressive flatware, often with borders, rims of raised rococo decoration, enamelled or gilded. Fine soft-paste from 1811, translucent, fine clear surface, for matching dinner,

dessert and breakfast services. This range was known as 'Regent China' and continued in production until about 1820.

Bone china from that date frequently depicted views of castles, houses, each piece different in the set, with location printed on underside. Recognizable Worcester apple green dates from the second half of the eighteenth century, as well as resurgence of Japanese patterns, notably Imari, popular in 1830s. The firm has continued to make highly prized bone-china tableware until the present day, with many private commissions from the rich and noble; gilded, crested, particularly during Victorian and Edwardian periods.

Price Guide

Teapots (£12–£180)

Red stoneware, engine-turned, simple 18th century, £80–120. With applied relief, decorative handles, over £150.

Black basalte: Elijah Mayer 18th-century, £60–80. Early minimal decoration Wedgwood £60–80. Squared silver-shape, *c.* 1805, £70–100.

Early Staffordshire named potters (Astbury, Jackfield, Pratt, Wood), all out of price range.

Leeds, Liverpool late 18th-century, simple shape and decoration, £100–120 after good recent appreciation.

Smear-glazed Wedgwood stoneware £20–40.

Leeds and Liverpool 'bamboo' creamware £100–120. Wedgwood bamboo is now out of the price range.

Late 19th-century Wedgwood, classical with medallions £120–180.

Saltglaze: plain white 18th-century, tubby shapes £60–80.

'Pine-cone' pattern Worcester blue-and-white around £150–180.

Bone china: Early 19th-century printed and painted as little as £20 for florid gilded Rockingham-type to as much as £1,000 for rare Swansea. Taste and pocket best guide

here but good condition is essential. 'Novelty' teapots shaped like animals, houses, etc. now fetching high prices, even relatively poor-quality coarse Staffordshire around £100. Victorian lustre at a premium, also Mason's Ironstone and Herculaneum (Liverpool).

Early 19th-century Wedgwood 'Etruria' teapots from £70.

Huge kitchen and barge Staffordshire teapots now fetch £90.

'Cottage' pattern painted squat shapes around £12 with recent appreciation but made in vast quantities and not scarce.

Tea and Breakfast Services (£180–£500)

'Cabaret' sets for one or two (early morning tea services) late 19th, early 20th century, Coalport, Royal Crown Derby and others, £250–350. Larger sets, same period, comprising 12 small plates, 12 cups and saucers, sucrier and milk jug made by most leading bone china manufacturers, often without teapots which would have been silver, £250–450 depending on quality, decoration. If complete and in mint condition they are likely to be outside the price range.

Copeland 1830s breakfast/tea service of 12 teacups and saucers, 12 breakfast cups and saucers, 12 plates, milk jug, cake plate, teapot, £250–350 for 40-piece service.

Extraordinary value: late 19th-century breakfast services, Derby Crown Porcelain Company, not very high quality for collectors and with little value as singles, 12 cups, saucers, plates, teapot, jugs, bowls etc. can be found for £180–220.

Bloor Derby not considered high quality, similar service to Copeland, 60 pieces, £180–220. When rare with very fine decoration, single bone china cup and saucer fetches £30 but run-of-the-mill items little value in terms of investment.

Royal Crown Derby post-1890 tea service for 12 people, about the same at £180–220. Special collectable individual items with rich decoration fetch good prices at around £50–60 for single cup and saucer.

Royal Worcester famous 'Imari' pattern, mid-19th-century, incomplete £250–450.

Coalport tea service, six cups and saucers, teapot, milk jug, sucrier, around £150–250 with little recent appreciation.

Royal Worcester 1880s tea service for 12 totalling 40 pieces, £300–500. Designs made over long period, with replacements to service over the years, often worn with use, considered fairly low investment value but beautiful quality.

Coffee Pots (£25–£400)

Black basalte *c.* 1800 Wedgwood, £75–85. Unmarked pieces same period, same price. Earlier dates out of price range.

18th-century Worcester blue-and-white suprisingly reasonable at around £150–250.

Creamware, printed and painted, recently appreciating, now at £200–400 depending on quality, pottery, design.

Bone china: major manufacturers from 1830 to recent times £30–50 for standard shapes,

designs. Earlier dates less common than continental. English coffee pots usually made in silver and quality of bone china usually not very desirable with few exceptions. Thick coffee-house Mocha ware recently climbing from a few pounds to £25 and more.

Coffee Sets (£120–£300)

In England the custom of after-dinner coffee drinking was not widespread until the late 19th, early 20th centuries and so early coffee sets are rare and collectors' items. Late sets usually made without jugs and pots which would have been silver. Out of price range are Wedgwood bone china and characteristic pale blue/green with white relief. Edwardian fashion for presentation sets of coffee cups, saucers and spoons in satin-lined boxes produced enormous quantities of these rather ostentatious sets between 1900 and 1935 from all major potteries. Scarcely dishwasher-proof, with such heavy decoration, not suitable for too much regular use because insides of cups were frequently gilded, patterned, but most attractive, good potential investment value at around £120–180 complete sets with spoons. Birds, fruit, collectable themes rising slowly and steadily, the best already reaching £300.

Mugs (£15–£300)

Collectable, expensive. Not made in bone china until middle of 19th century.

Stoneware 18th-century Fulham mugs £200–300. Excellent Victorian copies cost almost as much.

Nineteenth-century Royal Doulton harvest beakers, £100–120.

Nottingham stoneware outside price range with little beakers already over £100.

Saltglaze well outside price range. Plain tavern mugs not less than £70.

Creamware: early transfer-printed, £60–80. Commemorative mugs outside price range.

Pearlware: recent fashion has pushed this outside price range. Simple tavern tankards *c.* 1800 £80–120.

Blue-and-white: many outside price range but 18th-century Worcester £100–150. 19th-century Staffordshire lustre decoration with mottoes £70–85. Nautical themes, Sunderland, Liverpool from £80. Early Staffordshire over £80. Victorian Staffordshire slightly less.

Davenport bone china 1850 onwards £30–60. Minton the same. Prices unchanged in recent years.

Coronation, commemorative bone china souvenir mugs, Victoria Jubilee, £45–65. Beakers around £25. 1900s Edward VII, George V, Edward VIII, £20–25, George VI £12–15.

Jugs (£20–£200)

Delft puzzle jugs and other jugs, outside price range.

Stoneware tavern jugs, 18th-century, £100–125. Famous 'bear' jugs *c.* 1760, now £350–450 even with some restoration.

Nineteenth century Royal Doulton harvest pitchers, £150–200.

Basalt 19th-century cream jugs £35–45.

Creamware: cream jugs with minimal decoration, Wedgwood and other potters, 1770–1800, around £20–40.

Pearlware: rising rapidly, with single sauceboats at £100–120.

Blue-and-white Liverpool cream jugs £55–75. 19th-century blue-and-white transfer-printed cream jugs £35–50. Other blue-and-white outside range.

Transfer-printed Staffordshire commemorative over limit. Large tavern jugs £55–75. With special themes (nautical etc) outside limit.

Welsh lustre small jugs £35–45. Early silver lustre decorated tavernware well over £100; small copper lustre cream jugs, 19th-century, £20–25.

Victorian, Edwardian washbasin and jug sets from £40. Jugs only £20–50 with good decoration. Bone china: late Victorian heavily painted commemorative jugs from £25, some attractive shapes, views, scenes, worth hunting for.

Worcester cabbage-leaf mask jugs from £150. Mason's Ironstone octagonal-shaped jugs, which were made in sets (smallest 3ins high), have been appreciating hugely – by several hundred per cent over the last few years – so that the smallest are now £50–70. Victorian Mocha coarse tavern ware is now around £45 and rarely found in good condition.

Serving Dishes (£10–£300)

Large dishes made before the 1800s were not necessarily intended for use with hot foods or hot water, and should be treated with circumspection. Many of them are not ovenproof and will not stand up to today's detergents and hot washing-up water. This said, they were made to be used: it is only the manner of use which has changed and providing they are treated with care can be used for cold buffets, cakes, fruit.

Most covered soup tureens, vegetable dishes, date from the 1820s and were part of huge complete services, together with

Worcester porcelain fluted cream jug, c. 1790, with painting typical of Davis, Flight period (1774–93). The design is influenced by silverware styles of the period.

smaller sauce tureens, side dishes and the full panoply of the 19th-century table. Unless they are French or German of earlier date, these dishes are seldom highly-priced and their investment value is dubious however attractive they are. Most originally had matching dishes on which they stood with little depressions for legs. They are considerably more valuable if they are still together. Highest price however should not be more than about £40–60 for reasonable quality pieces. Demand is low because they tend to be clumsy pieces in today's small dining rooms and only exceptional pieces are prized by collectors.

Delft single dishes with simple pseudo-oriental patterns from £70 depending on condition, and seldom under £100. Fetched £5 ten years ago.

Saltglaze stoneware. Plain white lattice work dishes under £50. Oval dishes also very reasonable from £20–45.

Late 18th-century Liverpool punchbowls, £210–300.

Blue-and-white: rare, collectable and outside price limit before 1800. Early 19th century Worcester covered serving dishes around £120–180, otherwise small sauce tureens and covered bowls in Staffordshire transfer-print around £40–60. Early Spode, Minton, transfer-printed, outside price range.

Pre-1800 Staffordshire unmarked meat dishes £10–50. From 1890 to 1900 more expensive at £35–60. Attractive early Liverpool 1770–90 relief moulded rims, scalloped rims, around £20–50. See under 'Dinner Services' for bone china.

Mason's Ironstone now heavily collected, huge mock Japanese gilded sets of meat dishes and serving dishes used to go for a song, now strictly for collectors.

Dinner Services
(£300–£1,000)

These are usually massive and comprise at least 60 pieces: 24 plates, 12 soup plates, 8-10 meat dishes, serving dishes, soup tureen, sauce tureens, vegetable dishes. This amount sounds daunting until the possibilities are realized. From a full set at around £750 two sets with considerably more pieces than an equivalent set of today's manufacture can be made. It is possible to split sets between two households and for the middle to lower range would by no means be considered a crime by purists and collectors. With this in mind, the initial outlay is more than reasonable for a dinner service that will at least hold its value if not increase, though investment value depends to a large extent on fashion.

Coalport 1820s dinner service of average decoration, incomplete, around £600. If particularly well-decorated, single plates are around £10 and upwards each, the same or more than when bought in a full service.

Davenport, same date, more expensive at £650–1,000 with fine examples going for as much as £50 for a single plate.

Incomplete early Royal Crown Derby, originally privately commissioned with armorial decoration, considerably more. Even incomplete they can be as much as £700 or more.

Minton 1870s standard services with sparse decoration: 12 dinner plates, 12 soups, 12 desserts, serving dishes, vegetable dishes, slightly smaller with 50 pieces to be found for around £550.

Royal Worcester and others: 1900s game services (decorated with birds, animals): 12 plates, serving dishes, sauce boats, more expensive at £500 or more. Smaller sets £300–500 with singles fetching from £10.

Well-known 'Imari' pattern Royal Worcester late 1900s mass-produced dinner services of 60 pieces at around £550–700 and appreciating rapidly.

Copeland services at second-hand value mainly. Not one of the 'great' houses for specially-commissioned work. On the other hand, Rockingham well out of reach.

Note: Full coats of arms add to the value; crests only or monograms tend to lessen the value.

Plates: Singles (£15–£75)

Two sizes only until mid-19th-century, roughly 9ins and 11ins described below as 'small' and 'large'. Soup plates begin in the late 18th century; covered bowls and porringers were the rule in some households until well into the 19th century. Side plates are a Victorian addition to the English table. Until after 1830 when machine-made mass-production standardized sizes, 'small' and 'large' are very variable.

Delft: Simple pseudo-oriental blue and white, small unexciting examples £35–50.

Creamware 1770–1800: unmarked pierced rim, small, around £20–30.

Leeds, Wedgwood small and large, up to £45 undecorated except for lattice, moulded rims.

Pearlware: Early Wedgwood 'botanical' dessert plates, around £50–65 and increasing rapidly. Davenport pearlware more heavily decorated desserts around £25–40.

Blue-and-white: Late Caughley, inferior quality, now over £75. Bristol and Worcester out of price range.

Monochrome transfer-printed early Spode, Minton, out of price range.

Unmarked pre-1800 Staffordshire blue small and large around £15–20.

Early series patterns, notably 'Beautiful America', now beyond limit.

Spode, Minton and others, 1800 onwards, around £15–35 both sizes.

Leeds 'Oriental', including early willow pattern, *c.* 1800, £25–35.

Victorian themes: ruins, overblown roses, flowers, 'series' from £25. Polychrome from £40–60 with birds always more than other subjects. *Note:* Polychrome heavily decorated 18th century 'cabinet ware' never intended for use. Plates, cups, saucers, etc. still very reasonable because of this, unless highly prized themes and collectable rarities. From £10–50 with earlier dates more expensive than Victorian, though recent vogue is

Supper dish set glazed in translucent blue with lion and fleeing Chinaman pattern and gilded lion finials as lid handles.

pushing up Victorian 'narrative' themes, scenes based on contemporary novels etc.

Bone china: 18th-century dessert plates unusable and some not resistant to hot water. If of no particular interest to collectors, cheap at £10–15 per plate but decorative value only.

Special named potteries: Rockingham, Derby, etc., out of range unless bought as part of dismantled service at around £10–20 per plate.

Cups and Saucers (£40–£120)

This is a highly complex field and very specialized: collecting harlequin sets of tea or coffee cups which will have some investment value requires special study. This is primarily a collectors' field as a glance in any antique shop which deals in porcelain will indicate. Many designs which typify named manufacturers have been made continuously for 100 years or more and a knowledge of marks is essential to know the date of any given piece. Cups and saucers in bone china from 'broken' tea services may be in worn condition or be of different dates, having been replaced at a later date. Transfer-printed ware is full of pitfalls; as much can be learned from the shape of the cup as from a maker's mark and here again, though at first glance the pattern may appear to match, closer inspection may reveal minute differences which mean a 'bad buy'. However, if it is the intention to become a serious collector, this is an extraordinarily rich field to study and providing you stay within a strict price limit, though you may make mistakes, you will still have some very pretty cups and saucers to use.

Late 18th-century Caughley and Worcester tea ware single fluted cups and saucers from £80–100, with blue-and-white highly collectable and out of price range.

Nineteenth-century Spode, Minton, from £80–120 for tea cups and saucers.

Bone china: singles from dismantled tea services, early 19th-century Worcester, Coalport, Derby, Minton with fine decoration, from £45.

Coffee-drinking in private houses was also limited to richer establishments until the late 18th century and some early coffee cups were shaped like miniature tankards and are known as 'cans'. Individual pieces, even without saucers, start at around £50, and any coffee cups before late Victorian are rare and not less than £65. Once they were mass-produced their value decreased, from a collector's point of view, and many single coffee cups from broken sets can be picked up for a few pounds, but are unlikely to appreciate.

Breakfast cups and large-sized cups were made in small numbers and Staffordshire named potteries now fetch £40 with steep appreciation in recent years.

'Bizarre' 1930s patterns now rising fast.

Care and Restoration

Care

Ceramics, like glass, are at greatest risk when being washed. Always wash one piece at a time, lift it out of the water carefully, put it on a drying rack or cloth and dry it immediately. It is not the washing that will harm a piece but careless handling.

Wash pottery and porcelain in hand-hot water with a little detergent. The more elaborately decorated the piece (particularly if it is gilded) the less detergent you should use. For terracotta use hot water and soda crystals. Leave terracotta to dry naturally, but dry glazed ware with a soft cloth, then rub it over with a little methylated spirit and when the spirit is dry polish with a soft cloth. This should be used for display pieces only, as methylated spirit does not enhance the taste of food!

Restoration

The biggest problem is breakage. If the piece is valuable (financially or sentimentally) or if the repair is complex, use a professional restorer. They can do an enormous amount, not just in sticking bits together but in filling and retouching, removing old rivets, dowelling, tinting adhesives and so on to produce a near-perfect result.

Straightforward breaks in pieces of modest value can be repaired quite easily with epoxy resins (either two-part or contact). It is essential that the surfaces to be joined be spotlessly clean and that no dribbles of adhesive be left – they are practically impossible to remove. Broken-off parts can be remodelled with plastic resins or ceramic pastes, but on the whole this will be a job for a restorer, who will know not only how to remodel, but how to repaint and glaze to disguise the repair.

If you are buying an old piece always check for rivets and signs of poor modelling of replaced parts. If the piece is cheap and attractive enough, you can have rivets removed and poorly remodelled parts taken off and done properly. If the piece looks sound, balance it if you can on three fingers and ping it with a nail of the other hand. An unrepaired piece will have a clear note, and so can a piece that has been repaired properly with epoxy resin. If the note is flat or dull look again for signs of repair.

Old pottery, whether glazed or not, can show a white deposit on the surface as a result of salts in the clay or paste working out to the surface. If the surface is flaky as well, take the piece to a restorer. If the surface is sound, half immerse the piece in distilled water. The water will gradually permeate the piece and soak out the salts. Change the water daily. After a few days, take a teaspoon of the soaking water, hold it over a flame and evaporate all the water. If the water is salt-free there will be no deposit on the spoon, but if salts are still leaching out of the piece there will be a mark of sediment on the spoon.

Further Reading

Mary & Geoffrey Payton, *The Observer's Book of Pottery & Porcelain*, London, 1977

Bernard Hughes, *Country Life Pocket Book of China*, London, 1956

Geoffrey Godden, *Encyclopaedia of British Pottery & Porcelain*, London, 1966

— *The Handbook of British Pottery & Porcelain Marks*, London, 1968

G. Bembrose, *Nineteenth Century English Pottery and Porcelain*, London, 1952

A. W. Coysh, *Blue and White Transferware 1780–1840, London* 1974

Donald Towner, *English Cream-Coloured Earthenware*, London, 1957

F. H. Garner & Michael Archer, *English Delftware*, London, 1972

Rugs
Up to £1,500

Kashan made in the 1920s for the European market. Note the Herati pattern in the border.

Introduction

Rugs old and new

By comparison with modern fitted carpet old rugs are not an outrageous self-indulgence. Old rugs will cost more, square metre for square metre, but fitted carpet has the hidden costs of fitting and so on. Also, a rug can be turned and turned, to give it even wear and make it last longer; a fitted carpet that has worn badly in just one place will need patching or replacement. A well made and reasonably cared for old rug can have a great deal of life in it, and remain attractive throughout.

We refer deliberately to 'old' rugs rather than to 'antique rugs'. A genuine antique rug – 100 years old or more – is unusual; it will almost certainly be well outside our price range and will be a collector's piece. The majority of rugs in dealers' shops will be a mixture of old rugs – perhaps 30 or 50 years – and rugs of new or nearly new manufacture. Certain dealers of course will stock only genuine antiques or rugs that are at least very old.

The value of a rug depends on a mix of factors: age; size; condition; materials used; whether it is hand- or machine-made; and provenance – some traditional rug-producing areas no longer manufacture or no longer export their goods, and the resulting scarcity puts up the value of those rugs that are on the market.

We have adopted a price ceiling of £1,500 and have given detailed descriptions of rugs within that range. Some rugs that are well beyond the price range are mentioned because their names will crop up in dealers' shops and in salerooms. Modern production under traditional names is mentioned from time to time, partly to point out the general decline in quality and partly to indicate which designs and types are widely reproduced.

Where do they come from?

There are five groups of prime importance (see map p. 109). 1 Persian; 2 Turkish; 3 Caucasian; 4 Afghan; 5 Turkoman. In addition we have included China and India, which are of lesser importance to collectors, as well as Pakistan, Tibet and the Balkans. Each has its distinctive traditions and patterns, construction, materials, colours, design, which all go to make up the 'language' of rugs. Although complex, this vocabulary is fascinating and its rudiments need to be mastered if you are thinking of buying.

There are three basic types of rug (for the sake of simplicity the word 'rug' is used throughout, although technically speaking a rug becomes a carpet when it is over 5 × 8 feet —1.5 × 2.4 metres):

1 *Nomad or tribal* There are two types within this group, irrespective of which area they come from. The mountain or pastoral nomads with their rich pastureland produce lustrous wool which makes thick long-pile rugs affording good insulation in the extreme cold of the mountains. Desert animals, on the other hand, on their more arid land produce dry, brittle wool and the rugs tend to have short, tight pile woven on thick backing to compensate for the relatively poor quality of the wool. All tribal nomadic rugs tend to be small as the looms have to be transported with the tribe. The colour range is also fairly

limited by available natural dyes.

2 *Village* rugs have a shorter pile than most mountain nomadic rugs, which allows more detailed design (longer pile tends to favour simpler, more geometric patterns). They can be larger because rugs are woven on fixed looms, and the range may include sets of room rugs as well as runners of considerable length.

3 *City or town* rugs are characterized by a very fine, dense, short pile resulting in rich design and colour and very fine knotting.

In Turkey and some parts of the Caucasus, carpet–producing centres are better–known for the purpose of their rugs, i.e. prayer rugs, room rugs, runners and room sets and where this is the case they are classified in this way under the sub-heading 'Type', under their place of origin.

Structure and Materials

The diagram shows the three principal types of knot which are one of the main indicators of authenticity. Gently fold the rug back in a line parallel to the weft. If the ends of the knot appear together and the knotting thread covers both warp threads then the knot is the Turkish (T) or Ghiordes. If a warp thread can be seen between two upright ends of the knot then it is Persian (P) or Sehna. If the knot is wound round three, four or more warp threads it is the Djufti (Dj). A Djufti knot will allow a thread to be pulled away easily from the groundweave because it is so loosely tied. It will wear quickly because of the lack of density of the pile. Machine-made carpets and rugs are easy to identify for they have no knots, the pile being held in by glue or rubber backing.

The pattern of the rug should be clearly visible on the back. Handmade rugs are knotted with the wool being taken round and over the warp thread and then back again to the front. Machine-made rugs will not normally show the pattern on the back.

Rugs are made on horizontal and on vertical looms, and are made up of the warp, weft, side cords and overcasting. Jute, animal hair, cotton and wool are all used for the warp

Knots

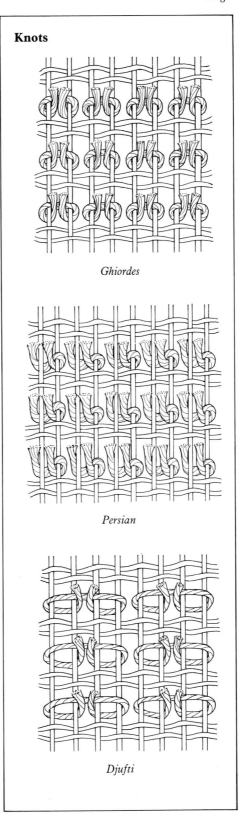

Ghiordes

Persian

Djufti

and weft. Wool tufts knotted individually form the pile, as well as silk, which does not come into this price guide because of its very high cost.

Kelims (see page 123) are a type of woven cloth rather than a carpet, and indeed were intended for use as hangings.

Dyes

One of the most contentious subjects in the world of rugs and carpets is that of dyes. Many dealers, buyers and collectors will turn up their noses at any rug whose wool has been dyed with anything other than natural vegetable dyes. To a certain extent this is an excellent rule, but it does not hold good entirely. There are two kinds of synthetic dye: aniline and chromatic. It is the aniline dyes which provoke disparagement because they are not colourfast or lightfast and fade quickly to a drab shadow of their original. Aniline dyes were used indiscriminately in harsh colours for about 70 years from 1880 to 1950 with the result that there is a sad trail of beautifully-knotted and woven rugs and carpets with some colours almost bleached out where these dyes were used. Chromatic dyes, first used in the 1920s and 30s, have a good range of subtle colours, fast to light and water, and today, particularly in Turkey, many rug-weavers use a mixture of wools, some dyed with natural dyes and some with chromatic.

A quick though by no means entirely reliable test to discover whether aniline dye has been used is to spit on a clean white handkerchief and rub it fairly briskly over each colour in turn. If none of the colours show up on your handkerchief, the carpet is almost certainly not guilty. If there is a suspiciously bright stain, one of three things has happened: aniline dye has been used; the wool has been dyed and insufficiently rinsed so that it is not completely 'fixed' and may either run or fade drastically; or if the rug is over 40 years old it may have been 'painted' to restore its faded colours. Many rugs woven with aniline-dyed wool have been given this treatment.

How to Buy

Rugs and carpets need examination before you decide to buy. The rug should be laid on the floor to make sure that it lies flat. Many dealers hang rugs from batons or frames, and you should insist that they be taken down. The weight of a hanging carpet will conceal any lumps and humps caused by years of rolling or folding, ruckling, or faults in warp, weft and weaving. Again it should be stressed that the salerooms are no place for a novice, particularly in this field. Even on viewing day it is often difficult to lay out a rug or carpet properly, and it is difficult to judge one rug's effect among many others. Most reputable dealers will allow you to take a rug home on approval.

The value of a rug or carpet lies in the degree to which it is handmade. A rug can be hand-knotted, but if the yarn has been machine-spun or the dyes are uniform as a result of controlled vat-dyeing the appeal and value will be less than those of a piece in which every stage has been carried out without benefit of machines. Hand-spun yarn and domestically dyed wool add not only to the value but to the extraordinary depth of colour and design which gives so much lasting pleasure.

It comes as a surprise to many people embarking on buying old rugs to find that often the pile is worn down so that it looks more like a thick flat stitched fabric. At the first viewing, examine the rug carefully and note the overall condition. Remember that if you buy in the salerooms, mistakes such as buying an original which on closer inspection turns out to be a copy cannot be rectified. If buying from a dealer make sure you have a full description on the receipt and be certain to keep it. It is your insurance – if, on getting home you find you have made a mistake with size or colour the dealer should take it back for the price you paid. The potential buyer of an oriental rug or carpet may be persuaded to buy something which is not what it seems; the traditions of the bazaar are nowhere more persuasively practised. At least it is as well to go armed with the right questions, to be confident enough to ask them and to insist on clear answers.

Care and Restoration

Cleaning

A vacuum cleaner is a mixed blessing for good rugs and carpets. It will only remove surface dust and dirt and, if allowed to run over the fringes, will slowly damage them irreparably. The best method is to hang the rug over a line and to beat it gently with a bamboo or garden cane to dislodge the grit which has worked its way into the fabric and which can eventually cut it like a knife. Care must be taken to avoid picking the rug up by one end in the case of smaller pieces in order to shake them, as the weight of the rug may pull at the places where it is gripped. If it is not possible to beat your rugs, then once every two or three months turn them over and vacuum the back as well as the front. If the vacuum cleaner beats at the same time, this will help to dislodge grit on to the floor where it can be swept up. Gentle rubbing with a cloth dipped in a very weak solution of ammonia and warm water – about a tablespoonful to a gallon – will help to restore the brilliance of the colour. On no account should the rug be allowed to get more than very slightly damp. If proprietory brands of carpet cleaner are used for more extreme cases of dullness and dirt, try a small section of the back with the solution first to make sure your colours are fast and will not run. Some brands of carpet cleaner are only suitable for modern machine-made carpets and advice should be sought before embarking on cleaning rugs with them.

Stains. In every case, speed is of the essence, since once a stain has dried into the fabric it is often extremely difficult to remove. Fresh ink should be mopped with a wet cloth, turning to a fresh piece with each dab in order to dilute the ink and avoid spreading the stain. Wine stains should be well diluted with soda water and then mopped quickly, again turning the cloth each time. Salt, which is often the remedy for spilt wine on table linen, should not be used because it has a bleaching action. Pets' urine (and children's) will mark rugs badly, removing or discolouring dyes by its acidity. The quickest remedy and the most effective is to sprinkle the whole area liberally with an antacid or bismuth stomach powder which will neutralize the chemical action by alkalinity. Rub it in very gently with the fingertips, wait until it is dry and then brush off with a soft handbrush. Grease stains will respond to a light brushing with talcum powder which should be left for at least 24 hours before gently wiping it off. Alternately, a layer of thick brown paper, the coarse furry kind, can be laid over the grease spot and a hot iron passed quickly over it. The heat will melt the grease and the brown paper will absorb it as it melts and lift it out of the pile, but this should be done with considerable care. Dry cleaning grease solvents such as benzene and ether should first be tried on a corner of the carpet before using to remove stains. In all cases, remember that each colour is composed of a different dye and treatment should be tried on a penny-sized patch of the same colour before attempting to remove the stain.

Care

If you are storing your rugs or carpets, they should never be folded but always rolled, if possible round a cardboard cylinder or a roll of cloth stiffened with a broom handle. Ideally, lay an old sheet over the rug before rolling it so that it protects the pile from the backing. Brush the rug well before storing, and spray the old sheet with an anti-moth preparation to protect it from attack.

If moth, silverfish or carpet beetles do get into a carpet during storage or use, the traditional cure is to take it to a carpet dealer and ask him to 'beat and bake'. Baking in an oven kills the larvae and beating removes them. A home cure for smaller rugs is to put them in a freezer for about four days in the spring when the eggs are hatching and then beat.

Strong sunlight eventually fades even the most colourfast dyes. If your rug is in pride of place in a living room with large windows, turn the rug as often as you can to ensure even exposure. Better still, avoid areas of strong sunlight altogether. Runners are an ideal shape and length for passages, but they

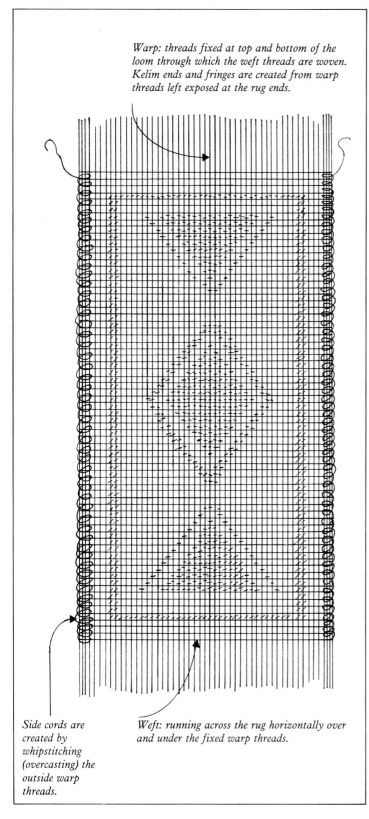

Warp: threads fixed at top and bottom of the loom through which the weft threads are woven. Kelim ends and fringes are created from warp threads left exposed at the rug ends.

Side cords are created by whipstitching (overcasting) the outside warp threads.

Weft: running across the rug horizontally over and under the fixed warp threads.

will wear badly, as will all rugs where the wear is constantly in the same place. If your floor has an uneven surface use an underlay. Stitch a strip of the same underlay at either end of rugs which are lying directly on a smooth floor to prevent them from ruckling up and wearing thin on the folds. Turn rugs, runners and carpets regularly so that the wear is on different parts near doors, etc. Small cups can be purchased from most iron-mongers in which to stand legs of heavy furniture such as tables and sideboards. If you cannot track these down, use pads of felt, particularly under castors or metal feet.

Repair

The fringes are the most vulnerable part of a rug. If there are signs of disintegration, act quickly and with a large blunt needle either oversew or blanket-stitch between each clump of warp threads using carpet twine or thick button thread. Side cords may pull away from the edges, and as long as they are only the additional decorative edges, the matter is not serious. Repair them by oversewing with several strands of embroidery wool matched as closely as possible to the original colour and a thick blunt needle or curved carpet needle which can be bought at most haberdashers' departments. If a careless person has dropped a cigarette or a small coal has burnt a hole in your rug, it is possible for the worst of the damage to be concealed, but the art of knotting is difficult and expert advice should be sought if the damage is bad. A small hole should be carefully ringed with stitching to prevent the damage spreading, and then darned by taking your blunt-ended needle well into the warp and weft threads with loose threads so that you do not make the damage worse by pulling the fabric.

Hanging rugs

If you do not wish to expose your rug to heavy wear, hang it like a tapestry from the wall. Fix a baton to the wall on to which tack a length of Velcro. Stitch a matching length of Velcro to the rug below the fringe and press the two surfaces together. If this proves difficult, using small stitches sew webbing to the top and bottom of the rug, kelim or hanging. Slide a bamboo rod or thin pole between the rug and the webbing, and hang it on a couple of hooks in the wall. The weight is thus distributed evenly and the carpet will not pull out of shape.

Kelims should really be hung as, with the exception of Soumaks, they were not intended to be used on floors; if you do use them as rugs, always use underlay on a bare floor.

Sources, Styles and Prices_____

Persia

One of the most prolific of all carpet-producing areas, Persia has been supplying the European market for over 200 years. From here came the fabulous silk Persian rugs made for the courts of kings and emperors, with rich, velvety pile woven into patterns in imitation of gardens, as well as the mosque carpets with hanging lamps and central medallions and the long runners which flanked them. Every motif woven into a carpet has a symbolic meaning: the vase of cut flowers, reminding man of his ephemeral existence; the tree of life; the cyprus and weeping willow; the garden of Paradise; the Herati pattern, said to symbolize the world surrounded by the four elements, looking like a rosette encircled with leaves (see p. 128). From Persia too comes the palmette, as well as the Serabend or Saraband, which in its continuous convoluted form makes the Paisley pattern. Persia is the home of many tribal nomads who weave small rugs with fresh, naive designs, many of them traditional, with their own symbolism of desert and plain, mountain and high pastureland. Designs, shapes and symbols occur and vanish, only to reappear in a different form hundreds of miles away.

Afshar
Type: Desert nomad.
Construction: Knot: T or P. Warp: wool or cotton. Weft: cotton. Double or treble side cord, multicoloured overcast wool.
Colours: Typically nomad dark red or indigo blue. Natural wool, white, cream.

Design: 'Boteh' resembling Caucasian pecking bird, lozenges, two or three angular medallions with stylized floral grounds – animals, little figures, 'akstafa' or stylized cockerel.
Price: Inflated prices due to fashion for ethnic work. Long-term investment value offset by their relatively short lifespan due to poor quality of desert wool. Nomad Afshar 6ft 6ins × 4ft 6ins, £700–1,000; same size village-made rather less: £600–900.

Ardebil
Famous 'Ardebil' carpet dated *c.* 1540 now in Victoria & Albert Museum shows clearly origins of antique Tabriz medallion design and rich blue ground colour. Today Ardebil is particularly known for runners made in villages surrounding towns.
Type: Town, village.
Construction: Knot: T. Warp: cotton or wool. Weft: cotton. Single side cord overcast cotton.
Colours: Deep reds, blues, traditional Persian palette. Cream field characteristic.
Design: More angular, almost more Caucasian than Persian, though more rigid and formal than true Caucasians. Coarse wool. Many carpets of poorer quality, rougher work from outlying districts sold through Tabriz, particularly 'Ardebil runners', made in villages, often reaching considerable lengths, sold as stair-carpets to Europe, America.
Price: Good rugs outside price range. Care should be taken if offered one of this name under £1,000; it is likely to be a coarse Tabriz copy. Caucasian-type room rugs made in the

district may be worth considering though, in their eagerness to simulate genuine Caucasians, the blacks and browns have been chemically corroded to make them look older and purchases should be made with this in mind. They are not as old as they look. 6ft 6ins × 3ft 10ins for around £560.

Birdjend (Birchend, Birjand, Birchand)
Type: Village.
Construction: Knot: P, T and Dj. Warp: cotton. Weft: cotton. Single cord overcast wool.
Colours: More vivid, but same dark plums, greens, blues as Meshed (see page 111).
Design: Thicker pile, fresher design, though more formal than nomad. Geometrical patterns, stylized flowers, Herati pattern, often covering whole ground.
Price: Hand-knotted prayer rugs 6ft 1in × 4ft 2ins, about £1,000.

Fars (also known as Gabeh, Gaba)
Type: Village.
Construction: Knot: T. Warp: wool. Weft: wool. Thick single cord, overcast brown or cream.
Colours: Undyed, untreated wool, natural colours, cream to dark brown.
Design: Simple geometrics, diamond-shaped medallions, dark on light ground or vice versa. Two main qualities: those made in foothills of Khorassan mountains finer, often with little red embellishments; poorer quality from district around Shiraz, often with similar stylized birds, animals, figures to Afshar. Can be confused at first sight with Northern Persian and Caucasian rugs.
Price: Khorassan around £450 for 6ft × 4ft. Poorer quality from Shiraz should not be much above £200 for same size. Not particularly special, but considering political situation and possible future rarity of such work, investment value may be quite good. Too new on the market for many precedents.

Fereghan (Ferahan)
Type: Town, village.
Construction: Knot: P. Warp: cotton. Weft: cotton. Single cord overcast wool. Cotton ribbed kelim ends.

Colour: Typical celadon green border, pale lustrous colours.
Design: The best work of this district of plains villages shows all-over floral patterns like rich pasturelands. Unusual feature is that distinctive celadon green often corrodes because it is copper-based.
Price: Much prized in the Edwardian country house, and increased in value by over 250% between 1951 and 1961 when pale colours were very fashionable. The rise over next ten years was only 150%, and today's more vivid modern colour schemes tend to make these rugs look a little drab. Large room rugs can be found for around £1,000. Increased demand for runners has lowered standards in this, one of the largest carpet-exporting districts of Iran today.

Hamadan
One of Iran's largest carpet-making centres with thousands of fixed looms turning out almost every possible mixture of design. Loose knotting, heavy-handed use of chemical dyes partially disguised by long thin pile.
Type: Town, village.
Construction: Knot: T. Warp: cotton. Weft: cotton. Single cord wool overcast.
Colours: Traditionally natural camel-coloured ground. Now wide and indiscriminate palette.
Design: Once traditional designs of zigzag diamond medallions on natural camel ground with broad camel-coloured edging, easily recognizable. Today, unsuitable floral designs, crude because of coarse knotting, hybrid 'boteh' designs which are flat and dead. Recent attempts to improve both quality and design have produced Malayer, Sehna-Hamadan, with many copies of Caucasian patterns.
Price: Very wide differences in quality, so great care should be taken when confronted with this name. Good quality rugs in traditional patterns can be found for as little as £300 for 6ft 6ins × 4ft 6ins but the name alone is no guarantee. There is a large output of Caucasian-type rugs which sell for high prices. Hamadans with Caucasian designs, known as Hamadan Kurds, may be as much

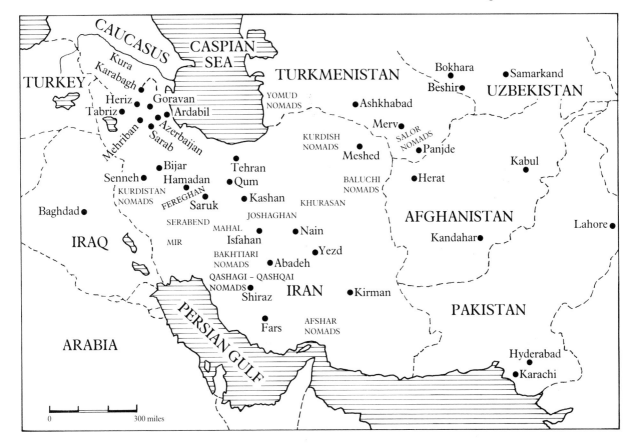

as £900 for a rug measuring 8ft × 4ft; 6ft 6ins × 4ft 6ins start at £400. More runners are made in the Hamadan area than anywhere else, and again, vary in quality from poor to very good. Prices for a 10ft × 3ft vary from about £400 to about £800.

woven in Nain which has no long tradition of weaving.
Price: Good value for one of the finest modern carpets made to traditional standards. New Isfahan or Nain rug 6ft 6ins × 4ft 6ins £1,000 upwards.

Isfahan (Isphahan)

Old carpets knotted with Turkish, recent ones with Persian knot. Noted for very high knot-density, but the quality of the wool is often inferior.
Type: City.
Construction: Knot: P. Warp: Cotton or silk. Weft: cotton or silk. Single cord wool or silk overcast.
Design: As befits the one-time site of Persian Court carpet manufactory, designs are exquisite. On short velvety pile, they derive from tooled leather of Koran covers with ivory-cream ground and all-over Herati stemmed pattern. Today these designs are also

Kermanshah

Type: Manufactory.
Construction: Knot: T or P. Warp: cotton. Weft: cotton. Single cord wool overcast.
Colours: Wide range but dull.
Design: Derivative, copies of traditional patterns, an unvarying flat texture even when handknotted. Coarse versions of traditional Hamadan, Kirman, Sehna. Floral-patterned European-style carpets.
Price: As with Hamadan, Mir Serabend and Malayer, derivative designs mean they are less expensive. If you find them attractive they could turn out to be a reasonable investment. 6ft 6ins × 4ft 6ins from £600.

Kurd

Type: Mountain nomad.
Construction: Knot: T. Warp: wool. Weft: blue wool. Multiple sidecord, coloured wool overcast, often blue.
Colours: Dark, vibrant, lustrous due to high-quality wool. Dyes are often chemical but harsh colours will fade to pleasant shades.
Design: Simple geometrics, very distinctive. Kurdish rugs particularly recognizable by erratic warp tension resulting in lumpy carpets which will not lie flat and wear unevenly. Saddle bags, small rugs, common output of tribes.
Price: Beware copies made in Mossul. Look for small pieces which are more likely to be genuine. Typical are small marriage rugs, made as wedding presents for brides: under £100 for 2ft × 1ft 6ins.

Mahal (Sultanabad)

Type: Town, manufactory.
Construction: Knot: T or P. Warp: cotton. Weft: blue cotton. Single cord overcast wool or cotton. Characterized by large knots and soft pile. The good ones can be very silky.
Design: Pressure of demand forced too many changes on traditional industry resulting in speedy deterioration; dead, meaningless patterns. Some improvement recently and Saruk-Mahal made to better standards.
Price: Saruk-Mahal worth considering, or Mahal rugs, carpets over 50 years old at around £1,000 for 11ft × 8ft. Recent manufacture a poor investment.

Malayer (Mazlaghan)

Type: Village (modern).
Construction: Knot: T. Warp: camel or goat hair and cotton. Weft: the same. Single cord wool or, if fine quality, camel overcast.
Colours: Traditional Hamadan-type camel-coloured ground with blue borders. Red grounds with dark red borders.
Design: More tribal version of 'boteh' than manufactured carpets, stylized Herati pattern on red ground with dark red border, rosettes. Characteristic zigzag lines along the length of the field. Sadly these good quality carpets are much in demand and already are becoming stereotyped with repetition.
Price: May be found of smallish room rug size for less than £1,000 but do not look for spectacular appreciation.

Meshed

Type: City.
Construction: Knot: P, T, Dj. Warp: cotton. Weft: cotton. Single cord overcast wool.
Colours: Plum, purple-rose, dark greens.
Design: Mainly medallion designs on covered ground, also all-over Herati pattern with never-ending repeat. Palmette often as border design. Djufti knot used, leading to much poorer, less dense work. Turkish knots also used in recent years. East Persian rugs have more guard stripes and broader borders than other regions. Meshed Belouch (see page 120) rugs also sold through Meshed. Prayer rugs with flowery hunting scenes very occasionally found.
Price: Fair quality Persian designs around 50 years old, 11ft × 8ft start at about £1,000. Smaller rugs, 6ft 6ins × 4ft 6ins, from £500.

Mossul

Iraqi trading centre for Kurdish tribal rugs. Recently looms set up here to mass-produce rugs strongly resembling Baktiari work. Mossul carpets bear most of the identifying marks of factory-produced work. Worst Baktiari traits copied, including use of harsh bleached whites, bright unsubtle colours, as well as traditional dull brownish red. Mossul copies use Persian knot.
Price: Today's production of pseudo-Baktiari work is harsh in colour and quality. A surprising development is recent arrival of machine-made 'Mossul' rugs from Brussels. The colours are less crude, wool slightly better quality, but more stereotyped and muted than copies of tribal work from Mossul. £150–250 for a 4ft × 3ft rug from either source.

Qashqai (Kashkai, Kashkay)

Type: Desert village, nomad.
Construction: Knot: T. Warp: wool. Weft:

OPPOSITE Malayer rug, c. 1900, of small room rug size with stylized Herati pattern in the border.

wool. Double, triple side cord multicoloured overcast wool.

Colours: Typically desert nomad spectrum, sombre reds, greens, blues, indigo, natural.

Design: Exuberant to point of hysteria. 500 or even more animals, birds, in single centre ground, as well as 'boteh' borders, stylized tree-of-life patterns. Recent settlement of tribes by Iranian government has led to decline in spontaneous design, sad loss of embroidered kelim ends to rugs.

Price: Since much-publicized TV coverage of these tribes, prices have rocketed. Village Qashqai, 7ft × 5ft, £700. Twenty to 30-year-old rugs have real character. Brittle wool limits their long-term potential, however. Mock Qashqais now made in pale colours and soft wool in Pakistan are attractive and well made, but expensive at £1,500 for 11ft × 8ft.

Qum (Kum)

Type: Town, manufactory.

Construction: Knot: P. Warp: cotton. Weft: cotton. Single cord overcast wool, often red.

Colour: Lustrous, varied, white and ivory most common field colours.

Design: Serabend pattern in pyjama stripes on natural ground, also known as 'cane pattern'. 'Boteh' pattern shows clearly how Paisley pattern evolved. Short pile, lustrous wool. Also delicately patterned medallion rugs, copies made since the 1930s of antique Persian hunting carpets.

Price: Quality of wool, workmanship has always been high, hence much in demand. In good condition, elongated room rugs of about 7ft × 4ft 6ins over 30 years old will not be less than £1,000.

Saruk (Sarouk, Sarug)

Type: City, town.

Construction: Knot: P. Warp: cotton. Weft: cotton. Single cord overcast wool.

Colours: Rich red, blue for grounds.

Design: Koran cover, large medallions, Herati pattern in simplified flowing version much in evidence in borders. Rich and spontaneous decoration. So finely knotted and dense, it is not unusual to find old Saruk

carpets cracked through stiffness of texture. Inferior designs exported, especially to America.

Price: These more traditional carpets have not appreciated as much as other more popularly designed carpets of other districts. Room rugs of 7ft 6ins × 4ft 5ins were £1,500 ten years ago. Today they are still to be found in good condition for £1,800. Smaller rugs are just within the price limit.

Serabend

Type: Town, village.

Construction: Knot: T, or recently P. Warp: cotton. Weft: cotton. Single cord often overcast madder-red wool.

Colours: Blue, red, ivory grounds.

Design: Almost exclusively 'boteh', resulting in this design being named 'Serabend' or 'Saraband'. Crests or feathers of 'boteh' usually change from left to right in alternate rows. Used in every size from large to very small version known as 'flea pattern'.

Price: Rugs £300 up to £1,000; carpets now from £800 to £1,500. Pakistan copies, often natural ground or washed-out reddish pink good value at £150–200 for a runner measuring about 8ft 6ins × 2ft 3ins but do not expect them to wear too well as the wool is soft. Machine-made copies of same designs from Brussels may be better buy in terms of quality at £225 for similar size.

Shiraz

Type: Desert nomad (see Afshar, Qashqai).

Construction: Knot: T or P. Warp: cotton or wool. Weft: wool. Double, triple side cord, multicoloured overcast wool.

Colours: Sombre, typically nomad.

Price: Nomad work selling through Shiraz: small rugs 5ft 6ins × 3ft 6ins start at £350 and go up to £700. Persian designs from village looms, 6ft 6ins × 4ft 6ins, range between £500 and £1,000.

Tabriz

Type: City, town, manufactory.

Construction: Knot: T. Warp: cotton. Weft: cotton. Double flat side cord wool or cotton overcast.

Colours: Traditional deep red, deep blue ground.

Design: Traditional antique Tabriz carpets have all-over patterns of flowers, never-ending foliate trails overlaid with rich, dark medallions. Local wool can be poor quality. resulting in tired colouring without depth or brilliance. Today, about 15 per cent of the output is of high quality, but if an attractive design appeals, watch out for irregular cotton wefts, flat matt pile – indicators of low standards of materials and manufacture.

Price: Recent production not likely to be an investment unless outside price range. Those from the first half of the century from £1,600 for 11 × 8ft to £2,250 for 13 × 9ft 6ins. 6ft 6ins × 4ft 6ins start at £700.

Turkey, Anatolia

Turkish rugs are less sophisticated than Persian, their designs less elaborate. By far the greatest quantity of rugs imported into England during the Victorian and Edwardian eras came from Turkey. 'Turkey rug' conjures up old-fashioned standard patterns in red and blue, with thick pile, large medallions, rich floral patterns. Turkish carpets are woven on a wool groundweave and are more pliable than Persian ones which are more tightly woven on unyielding cotton groundweave. They almost always have geometric, abstract designs, because the Moslem religion forbids the depiction of living creatures in lifelike manner. There is a very high output of prayer rugs of all kinds, each one basically consisting of a prayer arch (mihrab) in the centre surrounded by decorative border, with corner-pieces which are often elaborate. Saphs or family prayer rugs with several mihrabs are also widely made in many regions of Turkey. However, it must be remembered that many fine Persian carpets came through Turkey on their way to Turkish ports, and many of the early Turkish carpet-producing centres based their designs on rich and rare rugs from Persia.

Bergamo (Bergama)

No carpets made in town itself, but in sur-rounding countryside.

Type: Room, prayer rugs.

Construction: Knot: T. Warp: cotton or coarse wool and hair. Weft: the same. Double flat side cords overcast blue wool. Woven kelim end with diagonal central pattern. Low knot density.

Colours: Typical dark reds, blues, some yellow.

Design: Geometric, not unlike traditional designs from Caucasian Kazak-Gendje area. Unusually, red dye corrodes. In general, work sold from Bergamo today is fairly undistinguished though of reasonable if coarse quality, redeemed by handsome woven kelim ends.

Price: These attractive geometric rugs have escaped current boost to prices of anything with a Caucasian look. Prices have remained steady over past two decades at around £450 for 6ft 3ins × 4ft 3ins. Investment potential does not look good on past evidence.

Ghiordes

Once-flourishing centre for very recognizable prayer rugs, today makes sad, poor-quality copies of famous traditional design.

Type: Prayer, room rugs.

Construction: Knot: T. Warp: wool. Weft: red wool. Double flat side cords red wool overcast.

Colours: Reds, yellows, blues and pale green.

Design: Typical larger Ghiordes rugs have giant stylized carnations and geometric leaves. Traditional Ghiordes prayer rugs have columned prayer niche, usually on natural ground, tending to be small because of encroaching decorative borders, corner-pieces.

Price: Proper antique Ghiordes rugs command a high price – well outside the price range. Old, but not antique, Ghiordes can be found at between £500 and £1,000 for 6ft 6ins × 4ft 6ins. Copies from Konya are about £400 and are of good quality. Modern Ghiordes-looking rugs are around from Romania and Bulgaria – beware.

Kars

Near Russian border, trading centre for

nomad rugs more Caucasian than Turkish.

Type: Nomad.

Construction: Knot: T. Warp: Blue wool. Weft: wool. Single cord wool overcast.

Colours: Bright, primary – use of both vegetable and synthetic dyes.

Design: Bold geometrics, lozenges, zigzags, hooks. Quality of wool and knotting varies considerably from tribe to tribe.

Price: The eye should be best guide for preference, the price should not exceed £300–400 for about 5ft 6ins × 3ft 6ins.

Kayseri

Type: Large room rugs, short-piled wool, made to order, prayer rugs.

Construction: Knot: T or P. Warp: cotton or silk. Weft: cotton or silk. Fine side cords, cotton or silk overcast.

Colours: Wide palette, often pale, with pale pistachio or celadon green very typical.

Design: Many niched prayer rugs or 'saphs' made here for export as well as traditional ones for home market. Old designs, patterns still used, and both Persian and Anatolian designs copied. Kayseri carpets have no particular style of their own.

Price: Well outside price range (£1,800) but artificial silk, rayon and mercerized cotton 'flosh' Kayseri can be attractive and good value at £300 or less for 5ft 6ins × 3ft 3ins but doubtful investment value.

Kirshehir

Type: Room rugs, prayer rugs.

Construction: Knot: T. Warp: wool. Weft: wool, often red or greenish-yellow. Double side cord overcast greenish-yellow wool.

Colours: Yellow, olive-green grounds most typical among wide spectrum.

Design: Rich floral carpets much influenced by European designs with rococo swirls on white ground. Prayer rugs, saphs and cemetery rugs with sketchy mihrabs overlaid on yellow, olive-green grounds. General effect a little drab compared with other districts.

Price: Prayer rugs only within price range, with less appreciation in last decade than

previous ones. Perfect condition around £550. 4ft × 2ft good value at £200–300.

Konya

Type: Room rugs, prayer rugs, village.

Construction: Knot: T. Warp: wool. Weft: red wool. Double cord overcast wool.

Colours: Reds, yellows, blues and pale greens.

Design: Today Konya reproduces 'Ghiordes' and 'Ladik' prayer rugs. Work is good, much of it still made by peasants in outlying villages using traditional red-dyed weft, or undyed brown wool or goat hair.

Price: Good quality copies of Ghiordes and Ladik (beyond our price range) prayer rugs, but copies all the same: £350 up to £600.

Kula

Type: Prayer rugs, room rugs.

Construction: Knot: T. Warp: wool. Weft: thick wool. Double flat side cord wool overcast.

Colours: Apricot most distinctive in wide palette.

Design: Tends to be hotch-potch of features from other districts. Traditional Mudjur tiled border, central floral pillar or column which is weak version of three-column Ladik.

Price: Antique distinctive prayer rugs well outside price range. Fifty to 60-year-old pieces at about £400-600. Copies of Mudjur and Ladik rather cheaper.

Melas (Milas)

Type: Prayer rugs.

Construction: Knot: T. Warp: wool. Weft: red wool. Double flat side cord overcast red wool.

Colours: More yellowish than other Anatolian prayer rugs, with distinctive rust-red often predominating.

Design: Instantly recognizable by waisted prayer niche often with red, yellow centre. Saw-edged leaf pattern often used in border.

Price: Outside price range for antique prayer rugs. However, good-quality rugs for overseas buyers are also made. 6ft 6ins × 4ft 6ins £600–900. Danger that Melas will

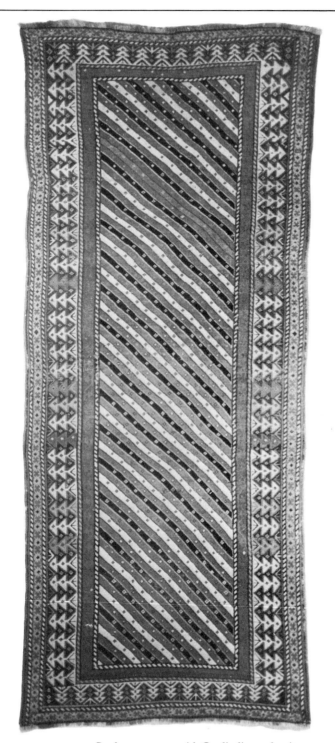

Daghestan runner with Gendje diagonal stripes, multi-coloured ground design. Today Daghestan has been absorbed by the Soviet-controlled Derbend manufactory, with a consequent loss of vivacity.

fall prey to imitation because of distinctive design and suffer consequent depreciation.

Mudjur

Type: Prayer rugs.

Construction: Knot: T. Warp: wool. Weft: red wool. Double cord overcast wool.

Colours: Unusually bright, rich colour range, in particular distinctive red ground for prayer niche.

Design: Traditional prayer rugs had subdued, tiled-effect borders and stepped prayer niches with red grounds instead of usual Anatolian blue. Today this design still being made, but many copies elsewhere. Particularly wide borders are characteristic.

Price: Mudjurs cost between £500 and £600 for 6ft 6ins × 4ft 6ins. There are many copies around, in particular from Kula, which are also colourful and decorative.

Panderma (Banderma)

Misleadingly, fine 'silk Pandermas' are not made here but in Kayseri.

Type: Saphs, prayer rugs, room rugs and export goods.

Construction: Knot: T. Warp: silk, rayon or mercerized cotton. Weft: the same. Double or single flat side cord silky overcast.

Colours: Wide range, including pastel colours for silks.

Design: Copies of ancient Turkish and Persian antique designs most skilfully made, often artificially aged by rubbing with brick to bruise pile and make it soft and silky. May often be identified by cotton overcast instead of silk. Source of multiple-niched prayer rugs in pale-coloured silky materials, recently popular in Europe and America to hang on bare walls. Rayon as well as silk is used in pile to give silky soft appearance.

Price: Mixed wool and cotton pile and their soft, unfashionable slatey colouring may be the reason for low appreciation over last decade. Recently-made Panderma 5ft 8ins × 4ft 3ins, around £600, same price as 10 years ago. Saphs high at £400–600 with little resale value at present.

Sparta

British Oriental Carpet Company set up at Smyrna at turn of century to produce Sparta carpets. Tremendous output. Sparta carpets could be ordered by the yard, of any pattern or size – durable and hard wearing.

Type: Room rugs and export goods.

Construction: Knot: P. Warp: cotton. Weft: cotton. Heavy double side cord often overcast cotton.

Colours: Typical slatey blues and blue-tinged reds, but muddy and dull.

Design: Carpets from this district used to be known as 'Smyrna' carpets because of their port of export. Some quite reasonable copies of old designs still made in the local gaol using traditional methods and materials.

Price: Rugs made in local gaol are only ones with investment potential and even then appreciation has not been that high over last two years. Too much 'carpeting' as opposed to 'carpets' has been made here for any great investment value. Condition and comparable price for new carpets should be your guide to second-hand Sparta carpets.

Ushak

Type: European shapes, sizes, room rugs, carpets.

Construction: Knot: T. Warp: green wool. Weft: wool. Double flat side cord overcast wool. Not particularly durable due to widespread use of mercerized cotton for groundweave, also sometimes mixed with wool for pile.

Colours: Deep reds, blues typical ground colour.

Design: Persian-based, but dark blues and reds are harsh and shallow, often due to chemical dyes.

Price: Early Ushaks have soared to millionaire prices, but modern copies do not bear much relation and are made in most carpet-making centres. Not particularly fashionable in design at present, and not particularly durable. They compare well for price alone with brand new tufted carpets as alternative floor covering in second-hand condition and were almost standard Victorian dining-room carpets. 'Turkey' rugs made in 1920s are sound value at £400–500 for 11ft × 8ft in good condition.

Yajebadir

Type: Room, prayer rugs.

Construction: Knot: T. Warp: cotton or coarse wool and hair. Weft: the same. Double flat side cords, overcast blue wool.

Colours: Dark-blue grounds, reds and whites.

Design: Similar in many way to antique Bergamo rugs in concept and colour. Geometric patterns, motifs, knotted in good-quality lustrous wool.

Price: Probably due to appreciate; 20 to 40 years old, 6ft × 4ft should be around £400.

Yuruk

Type: Pastoral nomad, prayer rugs.

Construction: Knot: T. Warp: wool. Weft: wool, often brightly coloured. Triple or quadruple cord weft-coloured wool overcast.

Colours: Very vivid but limited palette as with most nomad work.

Design: Two important factors distinguish work of Yuruk: long pile and simple patterns, usually geometric, with hooked or zigzag outlines. Often extra strands of long hair woven into pile, or a glass bead, believed to ward off evil eye.

Price: Genuine Yuruk about £100 for small prayer rugs.

Caucasian

Although Caucasian rugs and carpets have recently gained tremendous popularity in the West, it should be remembered that at the beginning of this century it appeared as though half the total population of the Caucasus was knotting carpets for the Russians and for export. They were not considered of any great importance to the European rug collector.

The centre of carpet-making in the Caucasus was the wild districts of mountain and plain on the Eastern side which shelves down to the Caspian Sea. The western side of the Caucasus has always been an area of settled people and rich crop-growing communities. Cotton has long been grown in

Shirvan, and in both Shirvan and the Karabagh districts silk has been cultivated for centuries. In the 18th century the Caucasus was divided into Khanates, and their names used to identify the carpet producing centres.

A common feature of Caucasian rugmakers is a childlike delight in bold primary colours and simple shapes. Every pattern, flower, leaf, animal and human is reduced to a geometrical shape.

Caucasian rugs and carpets are worth a little judicious speculation even when not in prime condition. This is because genuine work from these districts has ceased altogether and restorers of old rugs and carpets will pay a reasonable price for those which are not past redemption. That said, do not plunge into this field without considerable experience, nor without thoroughly comparing the many copies being offered. Caucasian carpets were not considered in the same league as Turkish or Persian, and right up to the 1950s the highest prices paid were in the region of £35–50. It is still possible to pick up a poor-condition Caucasian from a contents-of-house sale for under £500. Good-condition Caucasians have appreciated by over 300% in the last decade and are seldom to be found for under £3,000. Even then, as long-term investment they will continue to appreciate because they will never be made again and cannot be copied successfully. Look at the Soviet-made work and compare it with a genuine piece and you will understand the value of Caucasians made before World War II. Some of these are still seeping on to the European market from Israel, in mint condition with their woven, knotted kelim ends still intact.

Baku (Azerbaijan)

Recent attempts to resuscitate traditional designs, resulting in forlorn shadows of once-bright geometric, 'boteh', Persian-influenced designs of old production.

Type: Manufactory.

Construction: Knot: T. Warp: wool. Weft: wool. Double flat side cords overcast wool.

Colours: Washed-out indigos, pale greens and blues, dull colouring looking faded even when new.

Design: Persian-influenced, 'boteh' similar to Persian 'feather serabend' and striped medallions with fine outline, usually on dark-blue grounds. From Baku are sold carpets with similarity to Turkomans and other octagonal lozenge patterns, not to be confused with genuine nomad work.

Price: Turkoman-type patterns made in manufactories without lustre, fluidity. Do not confuse deliberately faded colouring with genuine old Turkoman. Prices should be in the region of £250–500 and not a bargain for quality.

Derbend (Derbent)

Recent Soviet control of production has resulted in poorer quality.

Type: Village, nomad.

Construction: Knot: T. Warp: undyed wool. Weft: cotton. Double side cord overcast dark brown wool.

Colours: More muted palette than those of other districts.

Design: Many motifs borrowed from neighbouring Kuba, adapted and mixed with some Shirvan motifs. Not uncommon to find 'running dog' borders, small tribal symbols mixed into town versions of more formal stepped polygon designs. Large Derbends are common, reaching sizes of 19ft × 7ft.

Price: £800 for 7ft × 4ft.

Genje (Kazak Gendje)

Type: Village, nomad.

Construction: Knot: T. Warp: undyed wool. Weft: natural reddish-brown wool. Double and triple side cord overcast red, brown or multicoloured wool. Village-made distinguished from nomad by shorter pile.

Colours: Unusually subdued for Caucasian.

Design: The 'crab' border is quite common, more controlled geometric designs from villages. Room sets or 'dast khali gebe' were made in this more settled area. Some carpets have tiled or diagonally striped ground.

Price: 7ft 6ins × 4ft 6ins £900–1,000. Soviet-made small room rugs, 7ft × 4ft, industrially manufactured with lifeless design, around

£500. Copies from Turkey are slightly more expensive at £620–650. Prayer rugs from borders of Anatolia and Bordjalou sometimes labelled Kazak but are the work of mountain nomads and fetch similar prices to Turkish mountain nomad work. No prayer rugs are made in Soviet Russia today.

Karabagh

Area now mainly in Soviet province of Armenia. Wide use of chemical dyes in modern production.

Type: Formerly village, now manufactory.

Construction: Knot: T. Warp: undyed brown wool. Weft: dyed red wool or cotton. Double flat side cord overcast reddish wool.

Colours: Cochineal reds and vermilions, rich to the point of violence, combined with the widespread use of black.

Design: Bold geometric shapes and immense stylized flowers sometimes know as 'Sunburst Kazaks' or 'Eagle Kazaks'. Crab border is common, also Chinese-influenced 'cloudband' motif in border. The swastika also found in more fluid form, as well as interlocking T-border stemming from farthest eastern territories of Central Asia. Many very floral pieces with large cabbage roses.

Price: Old Karabaghs 6ft 6ins × 4ft 6ins from £500 to £1,000. 'Carpet of roses' still produced but lacking exuberance of older versions: 6ft 6ins × 4ft 6ins: £1,000.

Sejur (Seichur)

Type: Room rugs, larger sized than usual.

Construction: Knot: T. Warp: thick natural wool. Weft: white cotton. Single or double side cord overcast blue wool or cotton. Fine net-like knotted blue cotton kelim ends.

Colours: Clear soft tones of red, blue and yellow, with unusually flat browns.

Design: Giant sunburst or cross-shaped medallions and huge diagonal crosses. 'Running dog' border with more sinuous, less angular shape. Rugs from this province often called 'Kuba Sejur'.

Price: around £500 for 7ft × 4ft.

Shirvan (Erivan)

Although Shirvans have been exported main-

Shirvan runner, c. 1880, with indigo field, four medallions, an ivory lovebird border and three guard stripes.

ly since 1850 (and indeed produced since the 16th century), since the 1920s huge carpet manufactories have produced thousands of carpets every year.

Type: Village, manufactory.

Construction: Knot: T. Warp: thick natural wool, or cotton. Weft: undyed cotton. Single or double side cord overcast dyed blue or brick-red cotton. White plaited cotton kelim ends.

Colours: Traditionally vibrant, now flat.

Design: 'Perepedil' has uniform ram's horn motifs. 'Snake Caucasian' is a lifeless interpretation, copied in Ardebil, of 'Cloudband Kazak'. 'Karashli' is a modern Soviet-produced design using traditional forked leaves, and scrolls.

Price: Reasonably priced at £800–1,000 for older rug 7ft × 4ft.

Shusha

One-time capital city of Karabagh Khanate. Small city manufactories producing more formal, disciplined versions of exuberant Karabagh designs.

Type: Room rugs.

Construction: Knot: T. Warp: natural wool. Weft: cotton. Single or double side cord often overcast coloured wool or cotton.

Colours: More judicious use of flaming cochineal reds, bright, luminous but disciplined.

Design: Finely knotted, short pile, silky wool with more intricate patterns with Persian, European influence. Fixed looms allow stricter control, larger sizes.

Price: around £1,000 for new 6ft 4ins × 4ft 7ins.

Turkoman (Turkestan, Afghan, Bokhara)

Turkoman rugs and carpets, tent trappings and camel trappings are easily identifiable as a group and impossible to subdivide without considerable study. Colouring is distinctive: brown shading to dark red and plum, often with a faint blue overtone. Unlike any other Oriental rug, Turkoman work keeps the same ground colour in the border as in the central field. The Persian knot is used and the work is short-piled and incredibly fine and dense, for rugs and trappings must withstand the constant abrasive action of sand and be closely-woven enough to prevent the sand from penetrating, even in desert storms.

East of the Caspian Sea, the Turkoman 'gul' is to each tribe of Central Asia what heraldry is to the West. Each has its own particular 'gul' with which it marks all its possessions: horses, tents, bags – even women.

Afghan

Common ancestry with Turkoman work, though 'guls' are larger, symmetrical octagon, sometimes known as 'elephant's foot'.

Type: Carpets, prayer rugs. Tribal mountain nomad hatchli, tent trappings, bag faces, camel trappings.

Construction: Knot: T or P. Warp: brownish wool or goat hair. Weft: undyed wool. One to three flat side cords overcast dark goat hair. Long red kelim ends, occasionally with diagonal striped pattern.

Colours: Similar to Turkoman but reds are more scarlet, browns more chestnut.

Design: Afghan hatchlis are less rigid, panels and cross-pieces often broken with stylized tree of life, decorated with miniature border patterns.

Price: Good genuine Afghan 'gul' room rug 11ft × 8ft can still be found for £800–1,000 with recent high appreciation. Quarquin cheapest (around £750 for 13ft 6ins × 8ft 6ins), Pendiq medium quality, Davlatobad best. Recent changes in the political situation may reduce genuine production drastically, with consequent rise in likely investment value. Tent and camel trappings, bag-faces, seeping on to market from displaced tribes: £100 upwards, with totally modern added decoration of bullet cases and beercan ringpulls as sad but authentic record of current events. Mass produced 'Red Afghan' runners from Pakistan are around £350 for 11ft 6ins × 2ft 3ins. See also Golden Afghans, p. 122.

Belouch (Belouchi, Balouchi)

Type: Prayer rugs, room rugs, tent trappings,

camel trappings.

Construction: Knot: P. Warp: natural wool and goat or camel hair and, more recently, cotton. Weft: the same. Two or three side cords, overcast two-colour check pattern.

Colours: Subdued, sombre browns and natural beige, smoky blue-reds, occasional use of bleached white.

Design: Combination of Caucasian and Afghan smaller motifs, including hooked lozenges and 'running dog' borders. Uneasy marriage of Caucasian 'botehs' with Herati pattern in the border. Little animals and birds are often incorporated as well as the 'akstafa' cockerel met with in other nomad work. Prayer rugs may have hand shapes each side of the niche.

Price: Belouch rugs are made on both sides of the Iranian-Afghan border and differ considerably. Iranian rugs sold in Meshed and known as Meshed Belouch: 6ft × 3ft: £400–600. Those made in Afghanistan are sold in the town of Herat and are known as Herat Belouch. These tend to be smaller; 5ft × 3ft can be anywhere from £100 to £1,000. 'Belouchi' rugs with mercerized cotton or rayon pile are produced in Soviet manufactories. They sell for about £200.

Beshir (Yagbeshir, Kabul)

Settled in communities longer than any other Turkoman tribe, possibly with different ethnic origins. The Turkish knot is used as well as the Persian. Sold through Kabul as well as other trading towns.

Type: Prayer rugs, hatchli, room rugs.

Construction: Knot: T and P. Warp: coarse wool or goat hair. Weft: the same. Four side cords overcast black-brown goat hair or double cord overcast red and brown.

Colours: The exception to Turkoman work, with very rare blue ground, packed with red motifs, the results looking almost purple, or red-on-red, with judicious use of yellow. Narrow bands of alternating colours are distinctive in the borders.

Design: The 'gul' is subordinate, and many designs come from recognizably Chinese motifs, such as the cloudband, as well as the Herati pattern. Small 'guls' may be incor-

porated into stylized flower-shapes, or in borders which are unusually wide.

Price: Attractive old Beshir rugs can be had for between £400 and £1,000, 6ft 6ins × 4ft 6ins. Recent production of similar size sell at the lower end of this price range.

Bokhara (Bukhara)

Old misnomer for Turkoman rugs sold through the bazaar of Bokhara. The practice of dyeing brown wool with indigo to make black once earned them the misleading name of 'blue Bokharas'. Today the vague category of 'Bokhara' is to be viewed with suspicion, as the name itself has been largely discredited by specialist Turkoman dealers.

Price: Old Bokharas of genuine tribal origins can be found for £300–£700 for 5ft 6ins × 3ft 6ins and £500–1,000 for 6ft 6ins × 4ft 6ins. There are however copies from many sources – Meshed, Hereke, Sivas, Russia, Rumania and large quantities from Pakistan. Modern Soviet Bokharas with part silk content – a sure sign of manufactory work – sell for £900–1,000. Small copies of quite good quality from other sources: about £200.

Ersari (Kizil Ayak)

Originally made all the so-called Afghans. Their territory ranges as far as the Caspian Sea to the Afghan border and they are more truly Turkoman than the Beshir.

Type: Hatchli, bag faces, room rugs, trappings.

Construction: Knot: P (sometimes single row of T before kelim ends). Warp: undyed dark goat hair. Weft: the same. Single or double side cord overcast undyed goat hair. Cotton is never used.

Colours: Yellows and greens as well as plums and browns of Turkoman palette.

Design: The 'gul' is often arranged in trellis or diamond pattern; some Ersari work is typical of mountain nomads in its liberal sprinkling of flowers, leaves, in random fashion over the ground colour.

Price: Genuine Ersari work scarce, fetching higher prices than Beshir. Recent good reproductions of old designs from Afghanistan, chemically washed to pale smokey pink, reasonably priced at around £250–500 for room rug but of doubtful investment value.

Golden Afghans (Washed Afghans)
Originally occurred in 1920s by accident when harsh red dyes were chemically washed to tone down colour. French interior design and fashion made these 'washed Afghans' extremely popular and they have been made in quantity ever since. Recently 'made golds' have come on the market, made from wool specially dyed to the same palette, but which will hold their colour and last longer than chemically washed products. 'Washed golds' can be detected by red at the roots of tufts.
Type: Same range as Afghans.
Construction: Knot: T or P. Warp: coarse goat or camel. Weft: the same. One to four flat side cords overcast wool or camel hair.
Colours: Pale beige-golds, faded reds.
Design: Identical to Afghans.
Price: Chemical washing lessens the life of the wool and the colours are currently out of favour, so Golden Afghans tend to be on the cheap side: £300–500 for 6ft 6ins × 4ft 6ins and £300–700 for 10 × 7. 'Made golds' may or may not appreciate from current £450 for 5ft × 6ft.

China

In the 1920s there was a surge in popularity for 'chinoiserie' and a consequent increase in Chinese carpet imports into Europe and America. As demand increased the previously high standard seen in excellent hand-knotting, subtle pale colours, often with flowers, and patterns embossed by clipping the pile, declined, leading to low-grade 'boudoir' carpets. Today there are huge carpet industries in Sinkiang, Peking and Tientsin, mass-producing carpets of every size and design. Patterns are derivative, owing more to French Savonnerie and Aubusson designs, though Chinese symbols in standardized forms are often incorporated.
Type: Mass-produced, any size or shape.
Construction: Knot: P. Warp: machine-spun cotton. Weft: the same. Single cord overcast cotton. Low knot density.

Design: Embossed, clipped pile, circular, half-moon, and many copies of European, Caucasian, Persian, made in unconvincing colours. Symbols incorporated into designs include the cloud, the dragon, the lotus, the fish and the flower vase.
Price: 1920s 6ft 6ins × 4ft 6ins £300–1,000 for top quality; otherwise second-hand value.

Tibet

Sold through China, hand-knotted by mountain people, and though colours are more crude than Caucasians they are less tame than many other derivative rugs, though the quality of wool is coarse, knotting looser.
Price: Caucasian-type, a far better bet than many other copies at £450–550 for 8ft × 5ft. Must not be confused with factory-made Chinese Caucasians, which have little resemblance to originals.

Pakistan

Thriving carpet industry established in last 30 years, making Turkoman-type rugs with quick economical 'Djufti' knot. Also 'Red Afghans' and 'Pakistan Bokharas', Turkomans. Some genuine Belouch work sold through Pakistan to West.
Type: Runners in Turkoman patterns, room rugs, prayer rugs.
Construction: Knot: P or Dj. Warp: cotton. Weft: mercerized cotton, rayon. Single cord overcast silk, mercerized cotton. Often very high knot density.
Colours: In Turkoman copies the reds are too cherry, blues too dull.
Design: Derivative, some well-made to high standards of knotting, but wool too soft, pile flattens quickly.
Price: Danger area. All qualities from top quality Pakistan 'Bokhara', tightly knotted, excellent quality workmanship, to lower quality 'Djufti' knots, even machine-made tufteds. Addition of Australian wool gives soft finish, chrome dyes used, but mostly colourfast. Purists, specialists, tend to dismiss all Pakistan work but some good dealers with sound knowledge of this work will guide you

to the best. Prices for 'Bokharas' about £230 for 6ft × 4ft handmade. Recent production of identical copies of Persian rugs with Kashan designs, the best hard to tell from originals. Half the price of Persian, but still outside our limit.

India

Originally 'Indo-Isfahans' were excellent, of high quality, good craftsmanship. Mirzapur, largest carpet-producing centre, produced enormous quantities of carpet in 1920s with consequent decline in quality; miserable Persian-derivative designs. Since 1950 quality has risen, wool imported from Australia has improved texture, pile. Today Amritsar produces carpets, rugs, textiles in staggering quantities, variable qualities, nothing of aesthetic interest.

Price: Apart from small rugs made in Agra gaol which are now collectors' pieces and well over £1,000, prices should be calculated against same area-covering for European equivalents. Little hope of investment value even of best quality, because of gigantic output from Mirzapur, Amritsar.

The Balkans

Historic tradition of carpet- and rug-making throughout the Balkans since occupation under Ottoman Empire.

Rumania

Today Rumania has enormous carpet industry, copying almost every known design, using Turkish knot and coarse cotton groundweave.

Construction: Knot: T or recently P. Warp: hemp or cotton. Weft: coarse cotton. Single heavy side cord overcast thick wool.

Price: Reasonable copies of Caucasians, but on coarse cotton groundweave, harsher, more uniform colouring, around £230–250 for 6ft 6ins × 4ft 6ins. Persian-type room rugs more genuine. Many Iranian emigrants using traditional patterns, European colour palette, identifiable with experience. 6ft 6ins × 4ft 6ins, Persian-type, around £360.

Bulgaria

As for Rumania, also with addition of emigrant carpet weavers from Iran using genuine Persian patterns, unhappily with European palette. Copies of Turkoman, Caucasian, with strange dead look of misunderstood symbols, antique designs.

Construction: Knot: P and T. Warp: hemp or goat hair. Weft: cotton or cotton and wool mixed. Single side cord overcast thick coarse wool or cotton.

Price: Fine pre-1939 Kirmans very hard to tell from real Persian Kirmans and outside the price limit. Modern copies of Caucasian and Turkoman rugs better than those from Pakistan – Bulgarian mock Caucasian 6ft 6ins × 4ft 6ins about £250.

Kelims

This is a general name given to flat-weave woollen textiles which are more like coarse cloth than a carpet. Indeed, except by desert nomad tribes, they were never used as floor-coverings, but instead served as coverings for chests and boxes, tent hangings and wall-hangings. Kelims in general were considered of such little account until recently that thirty years ago shipments of carpets were wrapped in kelims and no charge was made for them, nor for their Indian equivalent – the cotton 'dari'. In rug markets in Turkey and Persia, kelims were sold by the kilo. Only the Soumak flat-weave is really suitable for floor

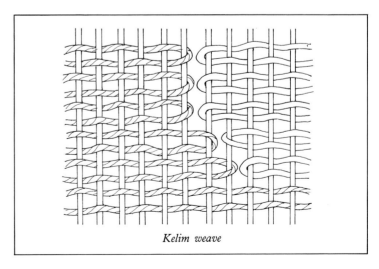

Kelim weave

use because it is thicker, though its embroidered face wears less well.

Anatolian kelims

The finest of these is the Karaman or Karamanli which comes from the region around Konya. The weft thread of each colour is woven to and fro in its own part of the pattern and no weft runs the entire width of the piece. Thus small slits separate each part of the pattern, usually staggered so that the slit is as small as possible. Anatolian kelims are reversible. The weft is usually dyed red.

Sehna

Finest of all kelims, woven by the Kurds on very fine warps, sometimes of silk. The best known pattern is the Fereghan or Sehna, but there are others with roses packed tightly overall. Kurdistan kelims are never large because of the delicacy of their construction. It is said that the women of the tribe wrapped themselves in Sehna kelims in the bath houses – hence these kelims' particular elegance.

The Balkans

Bright and decorative kelims are traditionally made all over the Balkans, but almost all are modern, with little value.

Caucasian

Flat-weaves from this area are made differently from Anatolian and Iranian kelim-weave. Instead of the under-and-over technique, the weft thread is taken in a loose over-and-over stitch like a herringbone. New colours are introduced and worked in, and the ends are left loose at the back to make them warmer and thicker. This technique, known as Soumak, is also found in parts of the Balkans, but takes its name from a town in the Eastern Caucasus. Particularly fine are the Kuba-Soumaks. They are also made in Shirvan, Daghestan and Derbend, many of them with the familiar hooked lozenge motif.

Sileh

Sileh kelims are woven with a refined version of the Soumak weave, so that the back looks more like a knotted carpet back, except where the threads are carried over to the next part of the pattern with the same colour. Sileh kelims come from the Southern Caucasus, notably Karabagh, Kazak and Baku. The most beautiful are the 'Dragon' kelims with huge scrolled S and Z shapes. White cotton is always used in Sileh kelims for the white parts of the pattern. They are woven in narrow (12–14inch) strips. For wider pieces, two or more strips are sewn together with the pattern matched.

Verneh

Large curtain-like hangings, native to Karabagh and Kazak, recognizable for their brick-red, yellow-brown, dark yellow or brown-black groundweave. These hangings are also known as 'shadda'.

Azerbaijan or Bidjar

Like other nomad work, these kelims often include little stylized birds, animals, humans.

Shiraz

Some of the brightest and boldest of all, with great lozenge shapes and zigzag motifs.

Kis-kelims

Kis-kelims formed part of a girl's dowry and were suitably large and grand, often with silver or metallic foil threads woven into them.

Price: Fine kis-kelims with much detail may cost as much as £500 or more, but there are excellent ones with some age to be found in large sizes for about £125. Sehna, Shiraz and particularly Caucasian kelims have so far established investment value. Owing to their fragility there is a scarcity value as well as an aesthetic one. Some more sombre-coloured Sehnas are to be found at around £250, but paler colours – rose, ivory, pale yellow and pale green – in good condition can go from £500 to well over £1,000 for 6ft 6ins × 4ft 6ins.

With the general rise in price and value of so much nomad work, specialist dealers have recently been acquiring kelims of such excellence that they should be valued on the

OPPOSITE Turkish *prayer kelim with narrow mihrab filled with tree-of-life motif.*

same scale as rugs from the tribes from which they originate. These fine pieces of work should never be put on the floor, and should be hung properly if they are not to be pulled out of shape.

Kelims of recent make from the Balkans and Turkey are bright and colourful, but should not be more than £125 for a reasonable size. Owing to the ethnic trend, there are shops, usually not regular dealers in textiles and carpets, who sell them at a much higher price than is justifiable.

Rug Terms

Abrach An uneven line across a rug where the colour of dye changes slightly due to new hanks of wool being used from different dyeing. Once a sign of authentic age and hand-dyeing, now frequently deliberately incorporated to mislead. Artificial abraches can be recognized because they run evenly across a row of knotting. With genuine work the change is uneven and the same variation of colour will appear in other parts of the carpet.

Akstafa A stylized bird pattern.

Aniline dye A chemical dye which replaced vegetable dyes in the 1880s much to the detriment of many carpet-making centres. It is not lightfast or colourfast – most easily seen from the back of the rug where it has not faded.

Aubusson A French carpet-making centre with a distinctive pattern and colour.

Backing General term for the weave on to which the pile is knotted.

Bag face The patterned, knotted front of a nomad saddle bag or other bag. The backs of these pieces are plain.

Baktiari Nomad tribe living mainly on border mountains between Iran and Turkey. A name often inaccurately applied to indeterminate nomad work from the area.

Belouch, Beluchi Nomadic tribes living on the Pakistan/Iran/Afghanistan borders.

Bleached white Most nomad work and genuine handmade rugs use the natural wool for white – bleached white is often a sign of more commercial manufacture.

Bokhara Misnomer for Turkoman tribal work, originally so-called because it was sold through the trading centre of Bokhara.

Border The 'frame' or border pattern surrounding the central motif. Characteristic of place of origin.

Boteh A tribal and Caucasian pattern, shaped like an inverted comma, ranging from a fluid shape to an angular one, which is often known as the 'pecking bird'. The basis of the Paisley design.

Caucasian Rugs and carpets made in the Caucasus with such distinctive colours and patterns that the term 'Caucasian' also denotes these as well as the place of origin. Since Soviet control of this area, true Caucasians are no longer made.

Celadon Pale green often made with a copper-based dye which may corrode the wool.

Cemetery rug Graveyard rugs: common to many districts, used for funerals, usually incorporating a cypress tree or a weeping willow, with one or two houses, the whole being repeated several times.

Chemical wash Rugs with too-hard colours washed in a chemical solution to soften them.

Chromatic dye As distinct from the crude aniline dyes, chemical dyes with far more subtlety of colour, lightfast and colourfast, introduced in the 1920s.

Cloudband Design probably originating from China, found in Persian and Caucasian work, sometimes also known as 'ram's horn'.

Cochineal Red dye originating from China where it was made from the carapace of a beetle. More brilliant and rose-coloured than other red dyes.

Corrode, corrosion Some dyes have a natural chemical content which in time eats away the wool pile of a rug. Most commonly a black or dark brown, but also copper-based celadon and some other dyes.

'Crab' border A Caucasian version of the **Herati** pattern resembling a crab. Found in work from districts near Black Sea.

Dari Indian cotton drugget or flat-weave.

Dast khali gebe A set of rugs for a room, also known as a **room set.**

Djufti knot A rather loose knot, most common in Pakistan work. See **Knots.**

Elephant's foot Often used to describe the Turkoman 'gul' pattern.

Embossed Pile clipped to make patterns in relief.

Engsi Nomad tent-flap or opening.

Everlasting knot Chinese motif often found in Eastern Turkoman and Turkmenistan nomad work.

Fereghan pattern A flowing version of the Herati pattern developed by the Fereghan and Sehna carpet makers.

Field Background colour. See **Ground.**

Flosh Cotton mercerized to look like silk.

Foliate Composed of leaf-patterns.

Ghiordes knot Turkish knot, found mainly in Turkey and the Caucasus, with notable exceptions among nomads and displaced carpet weavers. See **Knots.**

Golden Afghan Afghan rugs which have been chemically washed to give them a golden appearance.

Ground The background colour of the central part of a rug.

Ground-weave The warp and weft.

Guard stripe Thin stripes separating borders from each other, or from the main part of the design.

Gul An eight-sided motif used in a similar way to heraldic shields by the Turkoman tribes.

Hatchli A nomad tent flap or opening with a design resembling a simple wooden door, with the cross-pieces giving them the name 'hatchli', and a broad band at the bottom forming a skirt, often a kelim-weave with a thick fringe. Hatchlis also doubled as prayer mats, and some have simple niche-shapes at the top. Hatchlis are symmetrical from side to side, but asymmetrical from top to bottom.

Herati pattern A classic pattern appearing in many variations, such as the 'crab' and the 'lion's mask'. Basically composed of a rosette encircled by four curved leaves, it is also found as a continuous pattern in the central field as well as in borders.

Hook motif A rectangular hook shape characteristic of many Caucasian designs. In borders it is known as 'running dog'.

Jap silk Poor quality 'seconds' of silk from silk cocoons.

Kelim   A flat-weave used for tent hangings and coverings, made in most carpet-producing areas.

Kelim ends   The ends of a carpet which have been flat-woven to form a broad band between the pile and the fringe.

Kis-kelim   Flat-weave tent hangings of more grand design which formed part of a girl's dowry. Often with metallic threads interwoven in the fabric.

Knots   Persian or Senneh, Turkish or Ghiordes, and Djufti. See p. 103.

Knotted   Confusingly carpets are usually described as 'woven' but the pile is knotted into the groundweave.

Lanceolate   Shaped like a spearhead, leaves tapering at each end.

Leaf scroll   Curled leaf motif forming scroll.

Lion's mask   Another version of the Herati pattern.

Lozenge   Diamond-shaped.

Machine-made   Carpets made on machines are not knotted but tufted – the pile is simply looped round the weft thread without being secured.

Machine-spun   Wool spun by machine lacks the depth and unevenness of hand spun wool and does not bush out to form a thick pile but remains in its individual yarn form.

Madder   Red dye made from madder root, most typical in Turkoman and tribal work, distinguished by a faint blue overtone which originally gave its name to 'Blue Bokharas'.

'Made gold'   Rugs made of wool dyed to the same shade as Golden Afghans, as opposed to being chemically-washed to soft colouring.

Manufactory   Not to be confused with 'manufactured'. Small or large carpet-making centres where knotted carpets are made in quantity by hand.

Medallion   Circular central motif.

Mihrab   Prayer niche.

Mordant   Literally 'eating'. Those dyes which corrode the woollen pile.

Motif   Design.

Motifs

Herati

palmette

Turkoman gul

boteh or sarabend

running dog

Natural dye Those dyes made from natural and vegetable extractions and not from chemicals.

Niche Arch-shaped design at the top of a prayer rug and enclosing the main part of the rug.

Overcast Whip stitch usually in wool, which covers the side cords of a rug.

Painted Literally means painted with paint or dye where the original colour has faded.

Palmette One of many patterns originating from Shah Abbas' workshops in Iran in the 16th and 17th centuries. Palmettes are based on flower shapes.

Pastoral Nomad tribes inhabiting the foothills as opposed to the mountainous territory.

Pecking bird Angular Caucasian version of the boteh pattern.

Persian knot Senneh knot, predominating in Iran, Central Asia, Pakistan, Turkmenistan, Afghanistan and used by many scattered nomad tribes. See **Knots.**

Pile The surface of a knotted rug formed by closely-packed individual tufts knotted on to the groundweave.

Pistachio A particular pale olive green dye.

Prayer niche The church-window shape in the centre of a prayer rug, arched at the top. Proper name: mihrab.

Prayer rug Traditionally made for Moslems, the arch of the mihrab or prayer niche must always point towards Mecca when in use.

Ram's horn Curled motif like a Greek Ionic capital, roughly similar to a cloudband.

Room rug A rug usually measuring about 15–18ft by 6ft and made as part of a room set. Now describes any rug larger than about 5ft × 8ft.

Room set See **Dast khali gebe.** A set of rugs comprising a central rug 15–18ft × 6ft; a principal rug set like a T across the top of the central rug and measuring about 10 × 5ft 6ins. These two main rugs are flanked by two runners measuring about 17 × 3ft.

Rosette Stylized flower pattern.

Runner Long thin rug, originally forming part of a room set, measuring about 15–18ft by 3ft.

Running dog Repeated hook motif resembling heads of animals used as a border pattern.

Saph Prayer rug with many mihrabs, for family prayer.

Serabend, Saraband Design motif also known as the pine or leaf pattern, shaped like an inverted comma or tear-shaped boteh repeated all over the ground, from which the Paisley pattern was derived.

Savonnerie French carpet manufactory with distinctive pattern and colour.

Saw-edged leaf Serrated edged angular leaf.

Sehna knot see **Persian knot.**

Shadda Large pieces of flatweave tent hangings native to parts of the Caucasus.

Shirazi The overcasting to the side cords on silk rugs.

Shah Abbas 16th–17th century ruler of Iran whose workshops originated many of the now-traditional patterns of Persian carpets.

Side cord The thick cords on either side of

a rug round which the weft is woven. Many rugs have more than one side-cord to add strength and these are often overcast in coloured wools as a decorative finish.

Sileh kelim   Flatweave hangings woven in narrow strips and sewn together. The most famous are the 'dragon' Silehs with huge scrolled S-shapes over several narrow widths.

Smyrna   Name given to many Turkish carpets at the end of the last century which were shipped through the port of Smyrna.

Soumak   A much more sturdy form of flatweave with a thick undersurface where the weft threads are left loose – a technique which makes them the only kelims or flat weaves at all suitable for floor coverings.

Stem wave   Boteh design linked by a waving line.

Trappings   Decorative bands, camel harness, etc.

Turkoman   A group of desert nomads whose territory extends from the Caspian Sea across the deserts of Central Asia. These tribes are not Turkish. The name derives from the Turkic language.

Turkic   Not to be confused with Turkish or Turkey – generic term for nomad tribes speaking the Turkic language.

Turkish knot   see **Ghiordes knot.**

Vat-dyed   Wool or yarn dyed in huge batches without variation of colour.

Verneh   Large curtainlike tent hangings, also known as 'shadda'.

Warp   The lengthwise threads of groundweave which are attached to the loom at the top and bottom.

Warp threads   The ends of the carpet, often fringed plaited or knotted.

Washed Afghan   see **Golden Afghan.**

Washed gold   Chemically washed Golden Afghans as distinct from 'made golds'.

Weft   The threads woven crosswise between each row of knots which are on the warp threads.

Wineglass pattern   Alternating wineglass shape inverted and upright, often used in a border.

Further Reading

Ian Bennett, *The Country Life Book of Rugs & Carpets of the World,* London, 1979

Jack Franses, *European & Oriental Rugs,* London, 1973

Reinhard G. Hubel, *The Book of Carpets,* London, 1971

J. Housego, *Tribal Rugs,* London, 1978

Georges Izmidlian, *Oriental Rugs & Carpets Today,* Newton Abbot, 2nd edition, 1983.

Yanni Petsopoulos, *Kilims,* London, 1979

Caroline Bosly, *Rugs to Riches,* London, 1981

English Silver
Up to £1,500 for single pieces

Pear-shaped cream jug with scalloped rim and double scroll handle on three splayed feet, 1796.

Introduction

People often think that silver can only be for the rich. This is not true. Admittedly, it is not for the poor, but everyone in between can collect worthwhile silver as long as it is done with patience.

Georgian coffee pots at several thousand pounds are, on the whole, out of the question. Sets of cutlery, however, can be bought whole for under a thousand pounds or pieced together over the years without ever spending as much as a hundred pounds at any one time. There are in addition thousands of small single pieces available, some of them at quite modest prices. Silver to use is still accessible, and it is still possible to form a collection which is of interest and value.

Silver wisely bought has proved a spectacularly successful investment over the last decade; it would be most unwise to imagine that this success will be repeated. On the other hand, silver is likely to remain precious for the foreseeable future, so sensible buying for the pleasure of using and owning it now is unlikely to be disappointing as an investment in the long run.

Sterling Silver

A sterling hallmark: from left – the maker's mark; the sterling lion passant; the George III London leopard; the date letter (1808) and the monarch's head.

English silver or 'sterling silver' is an alloy of pure silver and a small amount of copper without which it would be too soft and too malleable to work. Precious metals are weighed in Troy weight which differs from standard avoirdupois and is measured in ounces and pennyweights or 'dwts'. A troy ounce (20 dwts) is 0.9115 of an avoirdupois ounce.

The standard proportion of pure silver to alloy which constitutes sterling silver is 11oz 2dwts pure metal to 18dwts alloy. Scottish silver up to 1836 contained minutely more alloy.

Silver can be adulterated with an almost equivalent weight of base metal before the alloy can be visibly detected – hence the practice of hallmarking and assaying, which was first enforced by an Act of Edward I in 1300 when the King's Mark or leopard's head was first stamped on silver which had been assayed. The leopard's head later became the hallmark of the London Assay Office, and the lion passant or walking lion was universally adopted in England as the assay mark for all sterling silver. It is now illegal to describe as silver any piece not properly marked.

Apart from a brief period from 1697–1720 when a higher 'Britannia' silver standard was in force, full sterling hallmarks since 1543 have consisted of the sterling silver lion passant, a single letter of the alphabet to denote the year, the mark of the assay office, between 1784 and 1890 the head of the monarch to whom duty was paid, and the initials or symbol of the silversmith who made the piece. Silver made during the period of the Britannia standard contains a higher proportion of pure metal and is therefore more costly. The Britannia standard is still used occasionally, with its own marks. In 1790 certain articles of less than 5dwt of silver were exempted from payment of duty and consequently may only bear the lion passant mark, sometimes even without the maker's mark.

In 1890 the duty on silver was no longer

payable and the monarch's head was dropped from the hallmark of all but special commemorative pieces such as coronation souvenirs.

Provincial assay offices used their own marks in place of the London Assay Office mark of the leopard's head. For quick reference there is a small booklet which can be bought from most silversmiths; larger books on the detailed hallmarking of silver are listed in the bibliography at the end of this section. The provincial, Scottish and Irish assay office marks most commonly found are:

Birmingham: an anchor
Chester: a shield with three half-lions and wheatsheaves until 1779; after that date three wheatsheaves and a sword
Dublin: a harp
Edinburgh: a triple-towered castle
Exeter: three towers
Glasgow: a tree and a salmon
Newcastle-upon-Tyne: three towers, two above and one below
Norwich: a castle above a lion, a crowned Tudor rose, both rare
Sheffield: a crown, sometimes combined with the date-letter
York: a cross incorporating five lions.

The date-letters for provincial assay offices did not run concurrently with those of the London Assay Office.

Cutlery was made in large quantities in the provinces, particularly Birmingham and Sheffield, the centres of steel and blade-making. Even if it was made with silver handles, in the 18th century it was often unmarked, having been made by a cutler rather than a silversmith.

Plate

The word 'plate' can be very misleading to the beginner. Plate is an old term used to denote objects made in silver and gold, and the trade continues to use the word in this sense, meaning articles made in ‹sterling silver. There are, however, at least three processes also described as 'plate', 'plating' or 'plated'.

Sheffield Plate

The first of these is 'Sheffield Plate', also known as 'Old Plate' or 'Old Sheffield'. Sheffield Plate was first made in the early 1740s and consists of a thin layer of silver which has been fused to a sheet of copper by heating the two metals and rolling them out to the required thickness. At first the metal was plated with silver on one side only and then silvered or tinned in the case of hollow ware: molten silver or tin was swirled around inside the vessel in order to protect the contents from coming into contact with the copper, which can be poisonous. By the 1770s Sheffield Plate was coated with silver on both sides for making a wide variety of objects. In this form it is often referred to as 'double plated', and the seams where the two coats meet are a good test of genuineness.

Sheffield Plate is a little cheaper than sterling silver, is much collected and has proved to be an excellent investment. It is still looked down on by some dealers and collectors, but that does not alter the fact that Sheffield Plate can be very desirable from all points of view. Incidentally, proper Sheffield Plate is not marked 'Sheffield Plated': that was a dodge resorted to by later electroplaters.

EPNS

The second use of 'plate' is to denote electroplated silver, a technique first used in 1840 and a timely invention for an age which gloried in ostentation and display. An alloy or base metal was thinly coated with a layer of silver by electrochemical action. Between 1840 and 1860 pieces were made using both processes: fused silver-plated copper for the main body of larger pieces, and detail and decoration in electroplated cast metal. Such silver is sometimes referred to as 'Transitional Plate'. Many alloys and metals were subjected to electroplating, the best-known being EPNS or Electro-Plated Nickel Silver, sometimes known as 'German Silver'.

Neither Old Sheffield Plate nor electroplated silver was subject to the same rigorous laws as sterling silver and there are many, many unmarked pieces. Some control was achieved between 1784 and 1836, when

The Britannia mark

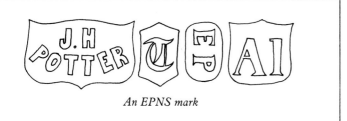

An EPNS mark

an Act required makers of articles resembling silver within a hundred miles of Sheffield, 'who desired to place a mark thereon', to register that mark at the Sheffield Assay Office, but this did not by any means cover all the makers or all the articles made between those two dates.

British Plate

Between 1836 and 1840 another version of Sheffield Plate, replacing the copper core with nickel alloy, was patented under the name of 'British Plate'. It often bore marks which at first sight seem to be silver hallmarks but which, on closer inspection, turn out to have a dog, for instance, instead of the genuine lion passant.

British Plate was soon replaced by electroplated nickel silver, cheap and easy to manufacture in enormous quantities, particularly for the growing hotel, restaurant and catering trade of the second half of the 19th century. An entire range of tea services, coffee services, tableware and flatware was actually called 'Queen Anne' by its Victorian manufacturers, who copied 18th-century silver lines openly and innocently at the time.

EPBM: Electroplated Britannia Metal, a form of silver plating despite the lavishness of its mark.

This electroplated 'Queen Anne' silver can be very misleading.

The fourth and perhaps most misleading development in 'plate' occurred after the end of World War II, when the price of nickel rose to such an extent that it was no longer economical to use for electroplating. Manufacturers of plated silver went back to using copper as the base metal now that it was cheaper than nickel. Electroplated copper can be worked in exactly the same way as Old Sheffield, unlike nickel which can only be cast. EPNS was used almost exclusively for tableware and flatware. A little knowledge is a dangerous thing: too many people assume, when they see the copper base showing where the silver deposit has begun to wear off, that they are looking at a genuine piece of 'Old Sheffield' and pay a high price for it. Disillusionment can be painful and expensive.

Although some genuine 18th-century Sheffield Plate is less expensive than heavily decorated 19th-century silver, the only advice must be to steer clear of the entire field until you have made a proper study of it and sought the advice of one of the very few specialists and experts in Old Sheffield.

Silver Gilt

Silver gilt is what it says: a silver piece coated in gold. Because it contains more silver (much more silver) than gold it counts (and is hallmarked) as the lesser of the two metals and is described here whenever it occurs frequently in a given period. An attractive variant on gilding silver all over was partial gilding, known as 'parcel gilt'.

Appreciation

The price of silver has risen by 600% in the last ten years, with one great leap in the late 1970s which was exceptional (and when, incidentally, quantities of heavy Victorian silver were melted down and sold at a profit by dealers as bullion). On average, the increase has been from 40–60% per annum. This does not, sadly, mean that your investment will show an immediate profit on this scale. The minimum profit margin of most dealers is in the region of 30% and is often higher. When you buy you pay the value of the piece plus the dealer's profit margin. When you sell, you sell at the dealer's buying-in price only. It will take several years for this gap to be wiped out before you even sell at the price you buy at, unless of course you have been very lucky – or clever.

Caution before buying silver

No one wants to make a bad buy but it is not difficult to make a mistake when buying silver. Hallmarks can be faked, or even cut out of one piece and transferred to another. Some fakes are very well done indeed, but many can be spotted by someone with sufficient knowledge. That is why it is best, until you have acquired a really sound working knowledge of silver, to go to a recognized silver dealer.

All this is not to say that you should never buy from other sources: the point is always to buy with knowledge, and if you haven't got it you want to be sure that the person you are buying from has. If you know what you are doing you can buy considerably more cheaply at auction. If you know what you are doing you can buy well or even get a bargain in ordinary mixed antique shops or from market stalls: the relative ignorance of more general dealers can work in your favour, and do not forget that the specialist silver dealers are buying some of their stock from the markets and the general shops.

Care and Restoration

Care

Silver is easy to care for as long as you do not mind polishing. Polish*ing*, not polish; elbow grease, not a patent product. Old, well cared for silver has a soft bloom that makes it both more attractive and more valuable. The only way to achieve a good patina is by polishing and use. There are no short cuts.

The way to care for silver is to wash it in hot, soapy water, dry it thoroughly on a soft cloth and then polish it either with a soft cloth or a chamois leather. Whatever you polish with must be absolutely free from grit, as silver scratches very easily. One important point about polishing: go easy on hallmarks, because they should remain as crisp as possible. It is enough to keep them clean.

All silver will tarnish if exposed to the air, and though washing and polishing is the kindest treatment, cleaning agents do need to be used from time to time to remove tarnish. Many of the silver cleaners on the market are abrasive and therefore harmful; they will succeed in bringing up brilliance but they will damage the patina. The cleaning agents favoured by the trade because they are effective and harmless are Goddard's Silver Dip for major work and Goddard's Long Term Silver Polish for occasional removal of tarnish. Don't use cleaning agents on plated articles. The old folk remedy for removing tarnish, incidentally, is to immerse the piece in skimmed milk, leave it for some minutes, remove, leave to dry and then polish with a cloth or leather.

Sterling silver that has been neglected for a very long time can occasionally become coated with verdigris. This is the natural result of the small amount of copper mixed with the silver oxidizing and can be cured quite readily by a silversmith.

Silver that is to be put away for a long time should be stored perfectly dry. The silver itself should be bone dry and it should be wrapped in bone dry cotton wool or fresh, acid-free tissue paper and then put in a sealed polythene bag. Never use newspaper, which attracts damp.

Always empty silver salt cellars and clean salt spoons after use. Salt corrodes silver.

Restoration

Whereas the care of silver is a relatively simple matter, the restoration of damage is not.

Many pieces you are likely to come across will have been repaired at some time. Feet break off, thin areas crack, arms or initials may be removed, tea and coffee pots are liable to part company with their handles. All these things should be looked for when examining a piece before buying. Repairs do lower the value if clumsily carried out (a visible line of solder round a cartouche, for example); they reduce its attractiveness too. On the other hand it would be silly to suggest that quality items should be melted down rather than repaired.

Some parts of pieces can be soldered back on without anything showing on the outside. Hollow pieces (teapots, for example) can often be repaired very effectively from the inside – a point you should always check before buying hollow ware. In this regard, be wary of pots that are so badly stained inside that you cannot see whether they have already been repaired. It is of course a straightforward matter to glue handles back on to cutlery and flatware.

Until, then, you have sufficient knowledge of your own, be guided by an expert dealer on what is worth repairing and do not attempt to do it yourself. By the same token, do not pay top prices for repaired pieces.

Periods and Styles

The periods into which the history and design of silver is divided are wider than those of furniture. Changes were not entirely based on the whim of fashion, and though silver shapes altered in detail from period to period, revolutionary changes in design occurred only when there was a major upheaval in the world of architecture, fashion, lifestyle or custom.

A particular feature of silver is that it has often been engraved with armorial bearings. The decoration surrounding the bearings varies from period to period and from style to style. The ensemble of bearings and surrounding decoration is known as a cartouche, and since it is such a prominent feature, is noted separately in the descriptions of period and style that follow.

The lists of Principal Products for each period are designed to help you see if an item is likely to be genuine. The lists cannot pretend to be all-inclusive, but you will find, on the whole, that if you are looking at an item whose kind is not listed in the appropriate period you are considering a piece that is unusual or rare (and therefore expensive) or a 'misunderstanding'.

Period: Up to 1700 and William and Mary

Influences: Dutch silver of the 17th century, which was ornate and fanciful; some oriental influence as well.

Decoration: Sheet silver, embossed and chased. Flowers – tulips in particular – and acanthus. Engraved Chinese motifs from 1680. Partial gilding of decoration and ornament.

Cartouches: Crossed plumes with rather coarse engraving – feathery plumes from 1680.

Principal products: Drinking beakers; apple corers; patch boxes; serving spoons; basting spoons; eating spoons; straight-sided spice and sugar casters; chocolate and coffee pots with ebony or fruitwood handles set opposite straight spouts; goblets; snuffers; two-pronged forks; box-shaped inkstandishes; pocket nutmeg graters; hammered, hand-embossed and chased candlesticks, usually 6-7ins high; ladles; monteiths; small tankards; one- and two-handled porringers, salts and footed trencher salts, meat skewers, apostle spoons; rat-tailed spoons; straight-sided lidded tankards; two-handled cups with covers.

Period: 1700–40 – Queen Anne, Early Georgian

Influences: Plain Dutch shapes and a simplified French style giving what was later called the 'Queen Anne' style. Later in the period silver became more ornate under the influence of rococo, but the plain shapes were continued as well. Famous silversmiths: Jean Berain, André-Charles Boulle, Paul de Lamerie, David Willaume.

Decoration: Elaborate ornament in the French manner, embossed and chased with cast-silver orament. Punched, fluted, with applied cast strapwork of shells, leaves, female heads, masks.

Cartouches: Baroque, architectural, scallop shells or masks with scrolled surrounds, symmetrical flowing shapes often incorporating animals unrelated to the coat of arms depicted on the shield proper.

Principal products: Lidded claret and other wine jugs, pear-shaped with silver scroll handles denoting their use for cold liquids; pocket apple corers; bread and cake baskets in pierced work; bells; snuff boxes; tobacco boxes; marrow scoops; spoons; pear-shaped low-footed sugar and spice casters; lidded chocolate and coffee pots with ivory, ebony or fruitwood handles at right angles to the body and curved spouts, sometimes with spout lids; creamers with moulded feet, rimmed and turned; pierced épergnes; three-pronged forks; inkstandishes; cast candlesticks; douters; small-sized round-bellied teapots; kettles on stands; silver-handled steel knives; straight-sided tankards; mustard pots; pap boats; punch bowls; punch ladles with ebonized whalebone handles; small-footed salts, pedestal-footed trays or salvers; double-lipped two-handled sauceboats; oval rim-footed sauceboats; matching sets of table, dessert and tea spoons; basting spoons and mustard spoons; covered sugar bowls; scroll-handled tankards; tea caddies; small pear-shaped teapots, two-handled soup tureens, porringers; wine-tasters (often called bleeding bowls).

Georgian crested silver sauce boat with hoof feet and C-scroll handle; one of a pair.

Period: 1740–60 – Georgian

Influences: French rococo, asymmetric forms derived from rocks *(rocaille),* seashells, ripples, waves. Famous silversmiths: Juste-Aurèle Meissonier, Paul de Lamerie, Nicholas Sprimont, Paul Crespin.

Decoration: Piecrust rims to trays and salvers coinciding with Chippendale period. Shell-bases, swirl-bases, oval feet and plinths; beading, gadrooning. Embossed chinoiserie decoration, pierced and punched work.

Cartouches: Asymmetric, rococo swirling shapes.

Principal products: Pierced swing-handled cake baskets, épergnes, snuff boxes, tobacco boxes; straight-spouted coffee and chocolate pots; creamers; sauceboats on cast scrolled legs; cruet sets on frames; four-pronged forks; candlesticks with removable drip pans; three-footed salts; three- and four-footed trays and salvers; three-footed boat-shaped sauceboats; sugar bowls; sugar tongs; baluster-shaped tankards; spherical 'bullet' teapots. Old Sheffield Plate makes its entrance, initially for smaller items, but gradually extending through the range.

Period: 1760–1800 – Late Georgian

Influences: Robert Adam and symmetrical, neo-classical motifs. Josiah Wedgwood's classical designs. Famous silversmiths: Hester Bateman, Bateman family, Matthew Boulton and John Fothergill.

Decoration: Severe, less flowing; leafed, palmate feet to sauceboats and creamers; festoons, ribbons, swags, anthemion, acanthus, symmetrical elegant elongated lines, teapots, jugs, sugar bowls and hollow ware raised on pedestal foot; embossing, gadrooning, reeding, fluting, 'bright cut' engraving, particularly from Birmingham; silver-gilt for important pieces.

Cartouches: Neo-classical with masks, swags, medallions, rams' heads, urns, acanthus, reed and ribbon until 1785; bright-cut, deeply engraved, simplified classical from 1785 to 1805.

Principal products: Asparagus tongs; cheese scoops; vinaigrettes; caddy spoons; cruet sets; pear-shaped and baluster coffee and chocolate pots with pedestal bases; helmet-shaped creamers; cow-creamers; jugs; branched standing candelabra; taller loaded candlesticks up to 12ins high; dish crosses; covered serving dishes; goblets; egg cups; fish slices; ice pails; hot water jugs; four-footed oval salts; oval trays, often with pierced galleries and handholds; covered sauce tureens; square-based or plinth sauceboats, creamers and jugs; barrel-shaped tankards; straight-sided, straight-spouted, oval, drum-shaped teapots; toast racks; tableware; flatware; plates and serving dishes; wine labels.

Period: 1800–20 – Regency

Influences: Classical to about 1810, then more massive styles deriving from Egyptian, baroque, rococo and French Empire patterns. Famous silversmiths: Bateman and Chawner families, Paul Storr, Benjamin Smith, Robert Garrard.

Decoration: Minimal, restrained decoration for classical revival: pure elegance of line with fine bands of delicate chasing and engraving, precise cast relief work. Sculptured forms for more elaborate work, chinoiserie and romanticism. The most prolific period for English silver, with new wealth and increased ability of rising middle classes to buy and display silver resulting in considerable quantities of poor workmanship, thin gauge and bad construction as well as the very best. Birmingham excelled in pierced, elaborate work. Victory for England at the end of the long Napoleonic wars in 1815 brought much commemorative work into fashion. Beginning of factory production, with simplified lines of average pieces. Excellence of handmade silversmithing rose to new and elaborate heights as a result of this competition. Vine leaves, scrolling, gadrooning and beading all prominent.

Cartouches: Sometimes absent altogether, with plain shield only engraved or bright cut. Otherwise flowery, leafy scrollwork, similar to but more delicately executed than that of the early 17th century.

Principal products: Massive table silver, matching entrée dishes, soup tureens, meat dishes; desk and dressing-table sets; toilet articles; tea trays; goblets; wine coolers; biscuit boxes; vinaigrettes; egg cruets; tea-kettles on stands; melon-shaped teapots; matching teasets comprising teapot, sugar bowl, milk jug; canteens of heavy table silver; wine labels; cast paw feet to sauceboats, salts; cruets; fine fluted candlesticks; standing branched candelabra with heavily decorated bases; table centre-pieces.

Period: 1830–50 – Late Regency, William IV and Early Victorian

Influences: Rococo revival, chinoiserie revival of Chippendale style, romantic, baroque and Gothic Revival.

Decoration: The exaggeration of all that was fine in the previous period into overblown, ostentatious designs in keeping with the taste of the time; much fine simple silver of previous periods given florid embossed ('late-embossed') decoration in pseudo-rococo designs, or fluted and reeded to emulate earlier Regency style; some good simple copies of Georgian and Dutch shapes; Adam designs in semi-mass-produced wares. Much silver of this period is engraved with flamboyant quasi-heraldic motifs. Old silver engraved, with consequent decrease in value. Monogramming and initialling very fashionable. Gothic Revival motifs.

Cartouches: Florid, romantic, gothic with curving central shield, flamboyant crests and supporters.

Principal products: Return of straight-sided drum-shaped and oval teapots; plain shapes for entrée dishes, serving dishes and for less expensive pieces to suit pockets of expanding market of buyers of silverware; heavy handles to cutlery, massive sets with much larger spoons, forks and knives than previous periods; soup spoons added to canteens of matching silver; wine coolers, ice buckets.

Period: 1850–1900 – Victorian, Late Victorian

Influences: French Empire, German Gothic, neo-classical, pseudo-Chippendale chinoiserie and rococo, Pre-Raphaelite romantic, Japan, William Morris and the Arts and Crafts movement.

Decoration: Heavy embossing, florid shapes, bulbous lines, many elaborate silver mounts to claret jugs, use of silver mounts for glass bowls, pierced silver much in evidence with new stamping techniques; much silver of this period considerably lighter in spite of heavy appearance, due to thinner metal with advent of machine-made spun silver. Proliferation of ornate, stamped, embossed lids to desk and toilet articles, silver mounts to most insignificant objects such as shoe-horns, button hooks. Card cases for engagement and visiting cards exceptionally well designed in a

Victorian silver-plated teapot of a 'half-reeded' design.

period not noted for its taste, even though die-stamped and not hand-embossed, and with shallow, acid-etched engraving; best made by Nathaniel Mills of Birmingham. Interesting square designs with clean lines and simple shapes (Japanese influence), especially for tea ware; domed lids identical with potteries' shapes for coffee pots, teapots, hot-water jugs.

Cartouches: Widespread engraving of armorial bearings on silver of this period may actually reduce value, even if contemporary. Only interesting, well-known armorials of famous people add to value.

Principal products: Anything and everything.

Period: 1900–20 Edwardian

Influences: The great age of machine copies. Only the English Arts and Crafts movement, similar to but not truly Art Nouveau, has any real design interest in this period, but many lower and middle range Art Nouveau pieces were produced in England, though the majority come from the Continent.

Principal products and Decoration: Shallow, acid-etched engraving, lightweight pieces, much electroplated cutlery, tableware, particularly for now well-established catering trade; coffee and teasets in plain, dull versions of early fine shapes. Good cutlery, tableware, flatware. Travelling cases, fitted toilet cases, writing table accessories, presentation sets of flatware in satin-lined boxes, christening spoons, fish slices, fish knives and forks, all glitter and little value at the time. In new designs, silver beakers, goblets, vases, baskets, bowls, rose bowls with swirling 'natural' designs similar to Art Nouveau shapes. Many copies of column candlesticks, varying sizes and quality. Curious mixture of lavish ostentation and rich simplicity.

Price Guide

The price of old silver is only governed by the world market price of bullion to a limited extent: during the great silver boom of recent years the price of all silver rose tremendously, but unless there is another similar surge, lesser fluctuations do not really affect the prices paid for antique or second-hand silver. Obviously though, the greater the weight of a piece the higher the price. Eighteenth-century teaspoons, for example, were often extremely thin and lightweight and consequently, unles made by a famous maker (Hester Bateman, for example) will be proportionately cheaper than heavy Georgian or early Victorian teaspoons, simply because of the weight of the silver.

Plain versus decorated

Articles in pure, simple plain silver are more expensive than those which are decorated with embossing or engraving for the simple reason that any blemish stands out. Decoration hides a multitude of sins. At the same time, fashion has pushed up the price of more ornate, elaborate ware against plain simple shapes, so it could be said that these two factors almost cancel each other out, except that plain silver is a better and safer investment than embossed. Sins of omission are meant to be covered by the Trades Descriptions Act, but there are dealers who neglect to add the vital information that a piece has been 'late-embossed' and often repaired in the process. Any large piece offered under £1,000 should be treated with suspicion. Remember too that much silver of the Regency period, though of good shape, was of poor quality and light gauge: prices are often unwarrantably high for actual value.

Note: Many people buying silver for weddings, christenings or anniversaries think it delightful to add a personal touch and have pieces engraved with initials or names.

DON'T. Your thoughtfulness will reduce the value of the item by 20% or more if it has any age at all. Better to hunt for old pieces engraved at the same period with appropriate initials.

Canteens of Cutlery and Flatware £750–6,500

For the purposes of this *Guide,* canteens are the most expensive items, but then to buy new would cost probably not less than £4,000 for a canteen with 12 place settings of an average of six pieces per place setting: two forks, two spoons, two knives per setting, plus two or more serving spoons.

Watch for wear on tines (prongs) of forks and on spoon bowls, for denting and for filing down of worn forks to an even length of prong. Old canteens of silver can be found in almost mint condition, having been put in the bank or only used on special occasions. Their excellent condition should encourage you to resist the blandishments of dealers offering less than top quality. For long-term antique investment value all pieces should bear the same hallmark – for bargain buys canteens which have had odd pieces replaced over the years cost less but will appreciate less.

Victorian canteens often have large place-settings, including teaspoons and coffee spoons as well as fish knives and forks and soup spoons. Edwardian canteens were most elaborate, often with seven or eight pieces for each place setting, plus four or more servers: they are sometimes still to be found in their original cabinets lined with green baize. Very often old knives have been replaced with new dishwasherproof ones with stainless steel blades, silver handles and modern cement-compound fillings. Old table knives had handles in ivory, green-stained bone or silver, with blade tails set in pitch or resin, steel or silver collars, and steel blades worn down with constant sharpening. Unless otherwise stated, prices are for matched canteens.

12 place settings:
Mid 19th-century King's pattern or Sand-

ringham, £3,600–5,000. Irish bright cut, £4,200–5,200. Beaded £4,000–6,500. Fiddle, £3,600–4,000.

Late 19th-century, just under 100 years old, £2,500–3,200.

Mixed hallmark canteens over 100 years old as low as £900, depending on the number of replacements and condition; they need searching out.

12 place settings hovering around 100 years old can be found from dealers specializing in flatware for around £2,500 and upwards.

Edwardian Old English 60-piece service, some replacements, just under £2,000.

1930s all matched, heavy reeded pattern, £2,800; beaded or feathered always more.

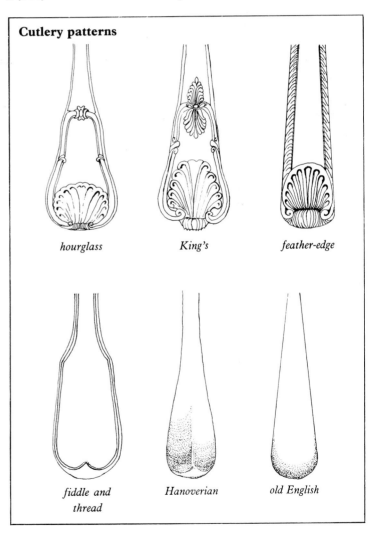

Cutlery patterns

hourglass *King's* *feather-edge*

fiddle and thread *Hanoverian* *old English*

If such a large outlay is out of the question, sets of six place settings are well worth considering, particularly if bought from a specialist dealer who can often make them up to sets of a dozen at a later date, providing you choose a date and pattern they advise. A 34-piece sterling silver canteen with six place settings all the same mark dated 1910 can be found for £750–1,000.

Additional items of tableware, such as large serving spoons and ladles, are almost half the price of brand new: soup ladles, sauce ladles, £40–75, whereas new ones are nudging £80.

Separate sets of teaspoons, coffee spoons, often in presentation boxes (particularly Edwardian) are good value –

Six matching:

London mark, 1760, £180–200.

1790, bright cut, thin gauge, around £50–60.

1800, heavier gauge, bright cut, £130–150.

1860, London mark, undecorated, £85–100.

1920–30, dozen boxed silver coffee spoons from £70.

1930, dozen boxed silver teaspoons, Sheffield mark, £55–75.

Fish Servers (£150–300)

Considered out of date and ostentatious to use, but very reasonable to buy and great fun to own.

Georgian, slice only, pierced, with silver handle, £150–300.

Victorian, ivory or bone handles, more ornate the better, £150–200 per pair, often still in presentation satin-lined boxes. Edwardian period, a little lower priced.

Water Jugs (£850–1,500)

1775, pear-shaped, lidded, silver handle, gadrooned rim and pedestal base, £850–1,400.

About 1785, more elongated shape, beaded pedestal and borders, £900–1,500.

Low demand for silver jugs with handles not insulated against heat with ivory or ebony collars. Water jugs more commonly made in china from the late 18th century onwards.

Coffee Pots (£200–1,250)

Seventeenth and 18th-century coffee pots of traditional shape are well outside the price range.

Teapot-shaped coffee pots, originally made in sets with tea services, not considered very collectable until recently, unless by named maker, now just under £1,200 *c.* 1790–1815. Victorian copies £600–1,000.

True coffee pot shape, ebonized handle, *c.* 1855, undecorated, just under £1,250.

Same date, semi-melon, some decoration, around £950.

1810–30, Adam-style, formal engraving, acorn finial, simple shape, £900 upwards.

Later, half-fluted, less attractive shapes, just under £1,000.

1830–50, heavier, more ornate, silver handles with ivory or bone insulating collars, originally parts of sets, £400–600. Pre-1830, £700 upwards. Same date embossed, £450–700. Engraved, appreciating recently, £375–600.

1870–90, wide variety of quality, weight, shape; better ones appreciating recently as 100-year band extends to this period; from £400.

Recent 'second-hand' coffee pots in good copies of mid-18th-century shapes are at once good value and a snare. Made in quantities in London, Birmingham and Sheffield between 1900 and the 1930s, at first glance they look like the real thing. Prices of between £200 and £500 should indicate what they really are.

Sets of coffee and hot water or milk jugs were rarely made in silver until very recently. Breakfast coffee sets were stoneware or bone china; after-dinner coffee pots had matching cream jugs and silver bowls for sugar, but only from the Edwardian period. Pre-1900.

OPPOSITE Pieces from a mixed fiddle and thread service. The full set, most of which is 1859, includes six each of tablespoons, dessert spoons, table forks and a pair of sauce ladles.

coffee pots matched four- or five-piece tea and coffee sets. Where sets are broken, usually the milk jug and sugar bowl are put together with teapots as three-piece sets, not with coffee pots.

Coffee Biggins (£650–900)

Biggins are cylindrical coffee pots on stands with spirit lamps (now frequently missing). Cover usually not hinged (check it has same hallmark). Bone, ebonized fruitwood or ivory handle, from £700–900 with stand. Even without stand, sturdy, well-proportioned, reasonably priced at around £650–750.

Chocolate Pots

Original chocolate pots, being 17th- or 18th-century, are way outside the price range. Early designs have not been extensively copied or revived, meaning that one rarely comes across them.

Teapots (£250–1,000)

The earliest teapots falling within the price range are: *c.* 1765–80, drum-shaped, straight-sided, straight low-set spouts, unhinged lids (check for same hallmark), flat tops, plain ebonized finial, elegantly engraved, often with swags or medallions, from £800–1,000.

1780–90, oval, straight-sided, straight-spouted, flat-topped, with engraved decoration, £350–500.

1790–1800, bright cut, tapered spout, slightly more curvaceous, hinged lids (check hallmarks all the same), around £450–1,000.

1800–10, embossed, less expensive, hinged, slightly domed lids, starting at around £450.

1804, embossed, boat-shaped, domed or curved hinged lids, curving spouts, also reeded, half-reeded, from around £250–450. More rectangular, sometimes with curved, fluted corners, often originally with stands, around same price. More with original stands, starting at £500.

About 1810, more boat-shaped, curving

spout, ball feet, around £500 and upwards, depending on weight.

About 1815, undecorated, squatter, curved spout, ball feet, much copied by Victorians, not much sought after at present, around £350 starting price. Same period, heavily decorated, if thick gauge with good modelling, up to £500.

1820–35, melon-shaped teapot, recent high appreciation mostly due to fashion trends, now starting at around £400–600 in good condition.

1830–50, Victorian version, thinner metal, cast scrolled feet, high-set spout, silver handle, around £300–450.

1835–60, more ornate half-melon with heavily embossed decoration, now much sought after for export; used to be around £80 not so long ago, now up to £400.

1850, rich rococo or Japanese decoration, heavy pieces from £350 to 500.

1870, good Victorian copies of plain Dutch shape, plain, round-bellied with curved spout, from £400–600.

1860, heavy-quality, round-bellied, with acorn or decorative finial, excellent Victorian copies of earlier shapes, from £400.

Tea Sets (£150–1,800)

About 1865, good quality Regency, Adam, classical shapes, originally four- and five-piece sets, now teapot, milk jug and sugar bowl from around £1,000–1,400.

1870–90, 'bachelor's' small-capacity three-piece sets, baluster and Japanese-influence shapes, suitable for early morning tea, £450–800.

Same period, more ornate, gothic, cast decoration often original and interesting design £1,500–1,800.

1880–1900, often wildly ornate embossing, at first sight rich and rare, but more likely to be spun low gauge silver, stretched paper-thin with embossing, which will wear and crack quickly. Prices should not be more than

Teapot shapes

bullet

Dutch style

drum

melon

late Victorian demi-melon

£550. Good copies of Georgian sets, same date, from £500.

Just under 100 years old, Edwardian copies of traditional patterns made as three-piece tea sets: bullet-shaped, half-reeded, boat-shaped, but the silver looks more metallic and has less sheen than earlier models, around £150–350.

Candlesticks (£45–1,000)

From the end of the 18th century, candlesticks were made in large quantities in Birmingham and Sheffield as well as in London, with techniques that required very little hand-finishing. Thin sheet silver was die-stamped, then soldered together and filled with pitch or resin, often with an iron bar up the centre to add strength. This method continued to be used right through the 19th century, but as demand for silver increased, makers became less fastidious and continued to use die-stamps which were blurred and blunted, resulting in poor modelling and detail. These candlesticks are known as 'loaded' or 'filled' and are the most common. Seventeenth- and 18th-century candlesticks are now very expensive.

1820–30, late Georgian styles, taller than any other period, usually 11–12ins, Adam shapes or versions of Greek columns, less ornate designs, just over £1,000 a pair, with sets of four more than double the price.

First in reasonable range are Victorian copies, made in Sheffield or Birmingham, copies of Corinthian column type, 5–6ins, around £400 for pairs.

About 1830, Sheffield Plate, singles to £45.

About 1895, variety of classical shapes: square-based Georgian, oval-based Adam, round-based with gadrooning or beading, £350–600.

Some good copies of 18th-century shapes made around 1890–1910, just under 100 years old, around £200–350 a pair and better long-term investment than copies from previous two decades. Watch always for wear at corners, bruising, frilled bottom edges due to wear. Sheet silver is very susceptible to

damage which can only be repaired by 'unloading' and is costly. Where very thin gauge silver has been used, it is often stretched by die-stamping to the point of wearing through completely. If it is already very thin it will deteriorate quickly with consequent drop in value. Occasionally odd little chambersticks, Birmingham made, copies of 18th-century rococo styles, turn up at around £350–500.

Edwardian, well-made copies of Adam shapes but slightly taller, around 7–8ins £200–350 depending on condition.
Warning: It is not unknown for a pair to be made up by casting a second candlestick from the first one, marks and all. If the placing of marks and minute imperfections seem suspiciously twinned, this is certainly the case and the pair is not worth investing in unless offered very cheaply for what it is.

Caddy Spoons

These charming little objects have been made since the days of Queen Anne. Their purpose was to take tea from the tea caddy and put it into the teapot, and they were originally shell-shaped in imitation of the shells that

---

OPPOSITE (a) *Silver plated double struck King's pattern soup ladle, 19th century.*
(b) *Silver plated fiddle and shell pattern basting or stuffing spoon.*
(c) *One of a pair of Georgian bright cut engraved dessert spoons, c. 1783.*
(d) *Embossed Dutch commemorative spoon with cherub on the stem, late 19th century.*
(e) *Georgian silver embossed spoon.*
(f) *Small Georgian mustard spoon.*
(g) *Silver plated jam spoon with mother-of-pearl handle, 19th century.*
(h) *French sifter spoon, 19th century.*
(i) *Dutch parcel gilt spoon (19th century copy of a 17th century style).*
(j) *Victorian silver christening spoon with engraved initial.*
(k) *Georgian silver egg spoon with characteristically shaped bowl gilded to prevent tarnishing on contact with egg yolk.*
(l) *Silver salt spoon, 1908.*
(m) *Silver caddy spoon, 1834.*

came as scoops in teachests. Prices start at £20, but there is a very wide variation in price to match the wide variation in styles and decoration that developed. Early examples can be very expensive. Collecting caddy spoons demands detailed knowledge.

Cream or Milk Jugs (£120–300)

Originally part of matching tea and coffee sets, considerable numbers to choose from of all qualities and designs.

Unlidded, 1770s, similar shape to pear-shaped pedestal coffee pots, £175–300.

1775–1806, helmet-shaped cream jugs, often very fine gauge silver, but nevertheless most desirable, now fetching from £150 to £300 and more in fine, unrepaired condition; handles in particular have often been completely replaced with consequent drop in real value: approach them with care.

1795–1810, more practical, flat-bottomed, often with punched decoration, £150–275.

1815–55, half-reeded, squatter, typical teaware patterns, £120–180.

1855–80, embossed, engraved, often with Chinese, Japanese motifs, £150–200: danger area for 'late-embossed' and thin Victorian spun silver.

Cruet Sets, Salts, Mustard Pots

Given the size of the objects prices of these items are very high – often little less than very adequate pairs of candlesticks. Commonplace items less than 100 years old can be found from about £50 upwards (in these cases taste and pocket are the best guides) but serious collecting in this area is so specialized that it is desirable to study detailed books before starting.

Tankards

The weight of silver required to make a good tankard of any date puts the large pint-sized tankards at around £500. Lidded tankards and good quality heavy gauge tankards of any age are therefore effectively outside the price range. Prices start at £700; nearer £1,000 for lidded.

Left: *salt pot with gadrooned rim and lion's paw feet. Edinburgh, 1816.* Centre: *Pepper pot by Robert Hennell, 1809.* Right: *Mustard pot by T. Jenkinson, 1814.*

Christening Mugs (£125–450)

Half-pint and child-sized drinking mugs are a happy hunting ground for people wanting to invest a little money for the future. Single initials, monograms and names tend to lower prices; with a bit of searching the appropriate one can sometimes be found at a very reasonable price.

1790–1800, turned barrel-shaped small tankard, around £150–200. George IV, similar shape, heavier gauge, £175–250.

About 1840, children's mugs embossed with nursery or children's scenes, from £250–450.

About 1870, plainer embossing, small shields, swags, flowers, £150–300.

About 1890, Gothic mugs with animal handles, though often light gauge, can cost more at £175–250 because of today's fashion.

Good bet: plain tankard shapes first made by Garrard c. 1860; around £125–175 (but they still make identical ones today).

Goblets (£100–300)

1790–1810, plain, good shapes, round foot, used to be around £150 a pair, now not less than £300 a single. With square, beaded plinth base, classical Georgian shape, singles around the same price.

1850–70, thinner gauge, embossed, around £140–200 each. Some excellent plain shapes with engraved bands, glass shapes at around £100–120. Better, more decorative Victorian Tudor and Romantic more and can reach £300. Compare the price of modern manufacture and the prices will seem extremely reasonable.

Napkin Rings and Miscellanea (£10–170)

Napkin rings are largely a Victorian/Edwardian addition to the table, fun to collect and give. Set of six matching, over 100 years old, from £170. Singles of all sorts of dates and prices: plain band with milled edge, £16; engine-turned, £17; reeded edge, £16.

Good quality heavy silver spoons from £10–30, sugar tongs from £20, wine labels with maker's mark from £45, often very decorative: pierced, vine-leaves, rococo designs.

Silver boxes are no longer pretty little nothings: if considering any of these, brace yourself for a starting price of £150 for an undistinguished, unmarked piece. If serious, study books on the subject before proceeding further. It is amazing what can be made from remnants of larger pieces with early hallmarks.

Silver Terms

Acanthus Elegantly scrolled leaves originally used as decoration in classical architecture, later by 17th- and 18th-century woodcarvers and metalworkers. See illustration page 47.

Acid-etched Adaptation of copperplate engraving techniques where acid bites into unprotected parts of metal to form shallow patterns; used to decorate late 19th-century silver; recognizable by shallowness and lack of crispness of line.

Anthemion Stylized form of honeysuckle flower originally used in Greek decoration. See illustration page 47.

Apostle spoon Spoon with a figure of an apostle as the end of the handle; in sets of 12 or 13 (Christ and the twelve).

Assay Analysis of gold and silver to assure that it has no more than the legally permitted proportion of alloy, before being hallmarked by an assay office.

Baluster Characteristic shape in late 17th and early 18th centuries for candlesticks, glass stems, silver, with slender form swelling out to a pear shape below. See illustration page 47.

Beading Edging of small raised domes like beads.

Beaker Straight-sided, slightly tapering drinking vessel without stem or handle; slimmer, taller than a tumbler.

Blade tail Metal shank of knife blade running down centre of knife handle, secured by pitch or resin.

Bleeding bowl See **Wine taster**

Bright cut Method of engraving silver and

Cartouche types

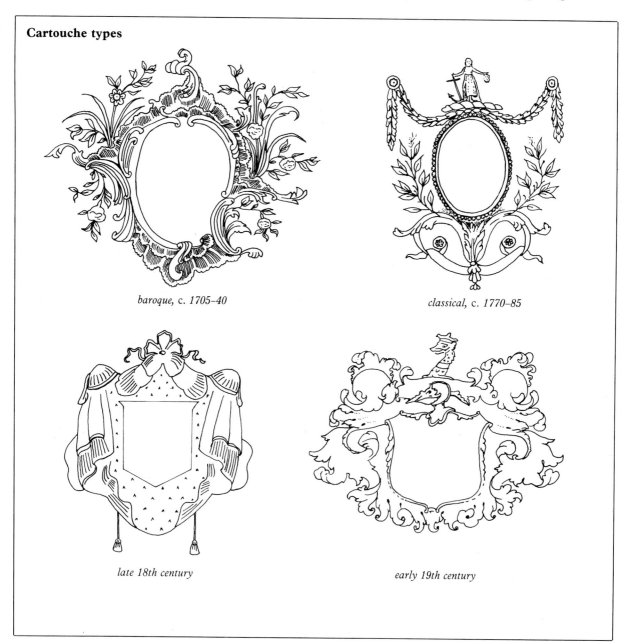

baroque, c. 1705–40

classical, c. 1770–85

late 18th century

early 19th century

brass, with V-shaped or bevelled cut giving extra brilliance.

Britannia standard Higher silver content (95.8%; sterling is 92.5%) required by law from 1697–1720; still in occasional use.

British plate Version of Old Sheffield using nickel instead of copper as core; very short period of manufacture, from 1836.

Bullet Spherical-bodied; a teapot shape.

Caddy spoon Spoon with (usually shell-shaped) bowl and short stubby handle for measuring tea from tea caddy.

Cartouche Scrolled decoration forming part of armorial engraving. See opposite.

Caudle cup Usually two-handled cup with lid and (maybe) saucer, often in presentation sets of two for mother and child for warm drinks; also known as caundle cups, porringers and posset cups.

Chamberstick Low-stemmed candlestick with integral wide dish base, sometimes fitted with conical snuffer.

Chased Sheet metal decorated with punches, chisels, hammers for fine raised designs; often combined with embossing in 18th century to sharpen detail; flat chasing in low relief was popular in the 18th century combined with engraving.

Chocolate pot Distinguished from coffee pot (sometimes) by small hole in lid for the 'moliquet' or whisk. Usually early 18th-century with straight side-handle.

Close plating Sheet, cast metal, usually steel, plated with thin sheets of silver by means of solder; used from around 1805 mostly in association with flatware, table knives and domestic tableware likely to rust, e.g. meat skewers.

Demi-melon See **Melon**

Die-stamping Method of embossing metals and coins mechanically with an engraved metal stamp.

Dish cross X-shaped frame, sometimes with small burner in centre, to hold dishes and plates and keep them warm.

Douter Candle snuffer shaped like a dunce's hat; also scissor-shaped snuffers with coin-shaped ends.

Electroplate Nickel or copper thinly coated with layer of silver by electrochemical action; patented in 1840, largely ousting Sheffield Plate.

Embossed Decoration beaten out from the back of the metal with punches or, by the end of the 19th century, semi-mechanically.

Epergne Elaborate table centrepiece dating from 18th century with central bowl and arms for candles, sweetmeat dishes; a great showpiece for silversmiths.

EPNS Electroplated nickel silver.

Filled see **Loaded**

Finial Knob as terminal decoration for lids of teapots, coffee pots etc.

Flatware Forks and spoons; knives are cutlery.

Fluting Parallel concave grooves; the opposite of reeding.

Gadrooning Similar decoration to beading, consisting of raised domes but on a slant; originally deriving from knuckles of a clenched fist. See illustration page 47.

Gallery Raised border in pierced silver to trays etc.

German silver Also known as Argentan and Argentine: a form of electroplated nickel silver.

Part of a set of Old English flatware of various dates between 1783–1819. All are marked with the same family crest. The set consists of 12 each of tablespoons, table forks, dessert spoons and dessert forks.

Hollow ware Vessels, jugs, pots, etc. as distinct from flat tableware.

Inkstandish Ink stand dish: tray for ink, sealing wax etc.

Late-embossed Prevalent particularly in early 19th century, the practice of embossing plain shapes from the previous century, often of relatively thin gauge, with lavish decoration.

Loaded Sheet silver embossed, stamped with decoration and filled with pitch or resin, particularly for candlesticks and candelabra; also known as 'filled'.

Marrow scoop Long, narrow-bowled implement for scooping marrow from bones.

Melon Shaped like a canteloupe melon; also demi-melon or half-melon, with the segment shapes on the lower half only.

Milled Ground fluted edges as on coins.

Monteith Large silver vessel, usually of heavy oval shape, with scalloped rim for cooling wine glasses; said to have derived its name from the Earl of Monteith's scalloped-edged cloak.

Mount, mounted Bases, rims and handles of silver added to wood, ceramics and glass (claret jugs, coconut cups etc.) to cover raw edges and add decoration; in cast silver from 1780s, stamped, often with alloy fillings, from 1790s, and with elaborate decoration from 1815; on Sheffield Plate to hide the copper core of the sheet metal on exposed cut edges.

Old Sheffield see **Sheffield Plate**

Palmate Design originally based on the shape of the palm of a hand.

Pap boat Small lipped or spouted vessel shaped like an invalid's feeding cup; often elaborately engraved with commemorative designs for an infant.

Parcel-gilt Partially gilded silverware.

Patch box Small shallow box with polished underside to lid serving as a mirror, used for keeping 'beauty spots' worn by fashionable 18th-century ladies to hide spots or skin blemishes.

Pedestal foot Originally of columns, the raised base of a vessel, usually in stepped or classical shapes.

Pierced Decorative patterns cut with punches to the end of the 18th century, stamped from 19th century.

Pitch Thick tarry resin, originally used to caulk ships, used for loading and filling knife-handles.

'Plate' Trade term for English objects made in silver and gold; not to be confused with 'plated' or 'plating' which describe electroplate and silver-plate.

Porringer see **Caudle cup**

Posset cup see **Caudle cup**

Punched Decorative strengthening rows of raised beads formed by using a punch on undersurface.

'Queen Anne' Usually meaning Queen Anne style, not Queen Anne period; of late 19th-century manufacture.

Reeding Parallel lines of convex decorating, as in classical pillars; the opposite of fluting.

Repoussé Relief decoration to sheet metal made with punches and hammers on the reverse side, using a block of pitch as an anvil; often finished by chasing to sharpen detail.

Semi-melon See **Melon**

Sheffield Plate Also known as Old Sheffield, a method of plating copper with thin sheets of silver, invented by Thomas Bolsover of Sheffield about 1742 and used by him for small objects such as snuff boxes and buttons; first made into candlesticks by Hoyland of Sheffield shortly after. The recognizably warmer colouring of Sheffield Plate compared with electroplate is due to a minute alloying of the two surfaces of copper and silver. The highly skilled techniques of Sheffield Plate were gradually superseded by the advent of electroplating in the 1840s, though for a time the bodies of large pieces continued to be Sheffield Plate with the smaller parts electroplated.

Silver gilt An object made in silver and then gilded.

Silver plate Technical term properly meaning articles made of silver; see **Plate**

Spun silver Mechanically shaped hollow ware in thin silver made by pressing a disc of metal against a shaped block revolving on a lathe.

Sterling Silver of the standard British value of purity (92.5%), assayed as such and then hallmarked.

Strapwork Strictly, ribbon-type applied ornament, but the term is used to describe any applied ornament.

Swag Looping curve of flowers, foliage, fruit or drapery used on silver during Neo-classical period, particularly Adam in latter half of 18th century.

Tine Prong of a fork or tooth of a comb.

Trencher salt Small low bowl on three or four feet or low pedestal for holding individual salt, as opposed to the grand, standing table salts.

Turned Silverware made, decorated or finished on a lathe.

Vinaigrette Small double-lidded box to hold sliver of scented sponge, originally soaked in aromatic vinegar; inner lid always pierced, exquisitely decorated; the whole of the interior should be gilded; forerunner of the smelling bottle, popular and fashionable 1770s–1880s, often in shapes of miniature fruit, nuts, books etc.

Wine taster Small dish with (usually) one looped or flat handle, often mistakenly called bleeding bowl.

Further Reading

Frederick Bradbury, *Book of Hallmarks,* Sheffield, 1975

Michael Clayton, *The Collector's Dictionary of the Silver and Gold of Great Britain and North America,* London, 1971

Elizabeth de Castres, *The Observer's Book of Silver,* London, 1980

Ian Harris, *The Price Guide to Antique Silver,* Woodbridge, Suffolk, 1969 (price revision lists are published periodically)

John Culme, *Nineteenth-Century Silver,* London, 1977

Frederick Bradbury, *A History of Old Sheffield Plate,* Sheffield, 1912, reprinted 1968

Index

This index is designed to help you reach the main subjects of this *Guide*. Many points of detail and many definitions are given in the lists of terms appended to each chapter: Furniture, pages 43–52; Glass, pages 66–72; Pottery & Porcelain, pages 77–86; Rugs, pages 126–130; English Silver, pages 149–154.

Photographic Acknowledgements

The publishers gratefully acknowledge permission to reproduce photographs as follows: The National Magazine Co. Ltd and, for the frontispiece, Jean Sewell (Antiques) Ltd; p. 13 Sotheby's Belgravia: p. 29 National Magazine and Whytock Reid, Edinburgh; p. 30 National Magazine; pp. 33-34 National Magazine and Suffolk Fine Arts, Bury St Edmunds; p. 36 Ann Lingard, Rope Walk Antiques, Rye; p. 38 National Magazine; p. 40 Ann Lingard, Rope Walk Antiques, Rye; p. 41 National Magazine and Farmhouse Antiques, Stoke Ferry, Norfolk; p. 46 Ann Lingard, Rope Walk Antiques, Rye; for photographs appearing between pages 55 and 98 National Magazine in conjunction with: for p. 53 Delomosne & Son Ltd, London: p. 58 A. & J. Stuart Mobey, Oxford; p. 60 Maureen Thompson, London; p. 62 Delomosne & Son Ltd, London; p. 63 Lacquer Chest, London; p. 73 Joanna Warrand, London; p. 76 Hemingway Antiques, London; p. 78 Lacquer Chest, London; p. 79 Torstore, Glastonbury; p. 80 Lynn's Antiques, Sheffield; p. 89 Sue Norman, London; p. 90 Delomosne & Son Ltd, London; p. 91 Belinda Coote, Hartley Wintney, Hants; p. 92 Libra Antiques, London; p. 93 Jean Sewell Ltd, London; p. 96 Joanna Warrand, London; p. 98 Libra Antiques, London; pp. 101, 110, 115 Sotheby Parke Bernet; p. 116 National Magazine and Smith-Woolley and Perry, Folkstone; p. 119 Sotheby's; for photographs appearing between pages 124 and 152 National Magazine in conjunction with: p. 124 Alaadin Ozutemiz Halici, Ankara; p. 131 D. & B. Dickinson, Bath; p. 137 Manchester Auction Mart; p. 139 John Roe Antiques, Finedon, Northants; p. 140 Shrubsole Ltd, London; p. 147 Knightsbridge Silver Co., R. S. & S. Negus, Robin & Valerie Lloyd, John & Janet Simpson; p. 148 Hennell Ltd, London; p. 152 Kate Green, Bath.